FLOOD TIDE

JOHN RIDGWAY
FLOOD TIDE

Hodder & Stoughton
LONDON SYDNEY AUCKLAND TORONTO

PHOTOGRAPHIC CREDITS
Aberdeen Journals Ltd: facing p 49, below; Stuart Brook: endpaper (from a colour transparency); facing p 65, below; facing p 81, below; *Daily Mail*: facing p 177, above left; facing p 193, below right; George Konig: facing p 193, above; Glyn Satterley: facing p 112, above left and right; facing p 128, above and below right; facing p 129, above; Scotsman Publications: facing p 32, below; facing p 192, above; *Sunday Mirror*: facing p 177, above right; Blair Urquhart: facing p 177, below.

British Library Cataloguing in Publication Data
Ridgway, John, *1938–*
    Flood tide.
    1. Ardmore (Sutherland) – History
    I. Title
    941.1'65   DA890.A56

    ISBN 0 340 32027 3

For Marie Christine

The love that I have,
Of the life that I have,
And the life that I have is yours.
And the rest of my days,
In the long green grass,
Shall be yours and yours and yours.

There is a tide in the affairs of men,
Which, taken at the flood, leads on to fortune;
Omitted, all the voyage of their life
Is bound in shallows and in miseries.
On such a full sea are we now afloat,
And we must take the current when it serves,
Or lose our ventures.

William Shakespeare

N
↑

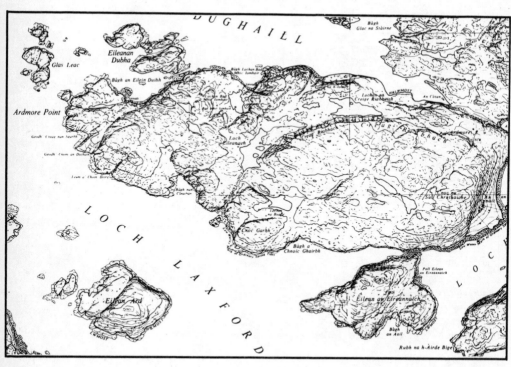

2.75 ins to mile

The Ardmore Peninsula

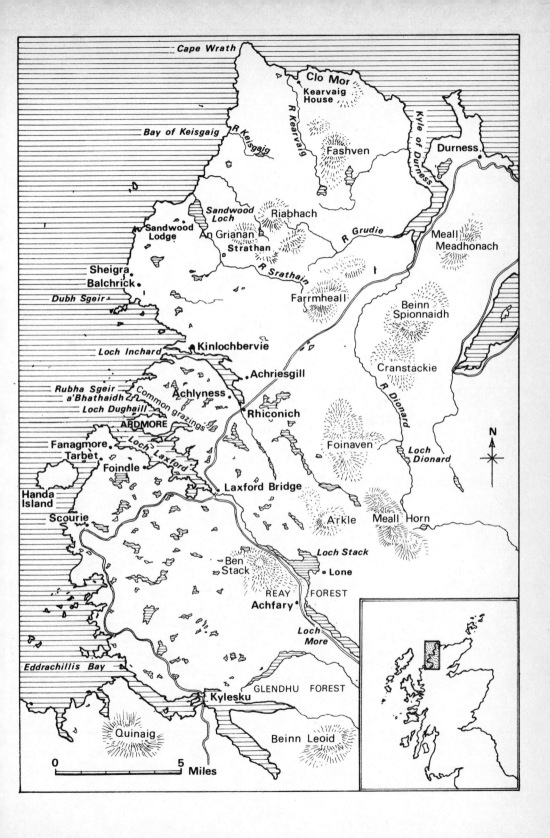

Cape Wrath

Clo Mor

Kearvaig House

R Keisgaig

R Kearvaig

Bay of Keisgaig

Kyle of Durness

Fashven

Durness

Sandwood Loch

Riabhach

R Grudie

Meall Meadhonach

Sandwood Lodge

An Grianan

Strathan

R Srathain

Sheigra

Balchrick

Farrmheall

Beinn Spionnaidh

Dubh Sgeir

Loch Inchard

Kinlochbervie

Cranstackie

Achriesgill

R Dionard

Rubha Sgeir a'Bhathaidh

Achlyness

Common grazings

Rhiconich

Loch Dughaill

ARDMORE

Foinaven

Loch Dionard

Fanagmore

Tarbet

Loch Laxford

Foindle

N

Handa Island

Laxford Bridge

Scourie

Arkle

Meall Horn

Loch Stack

Ben Stack

Lone

REAY   FOREST

Achfary

Loch More

Eddrachillis Bay

GLENDHU   FOREST

Kylesku

Quinaig

Beinn Leoid

0   5

Miles

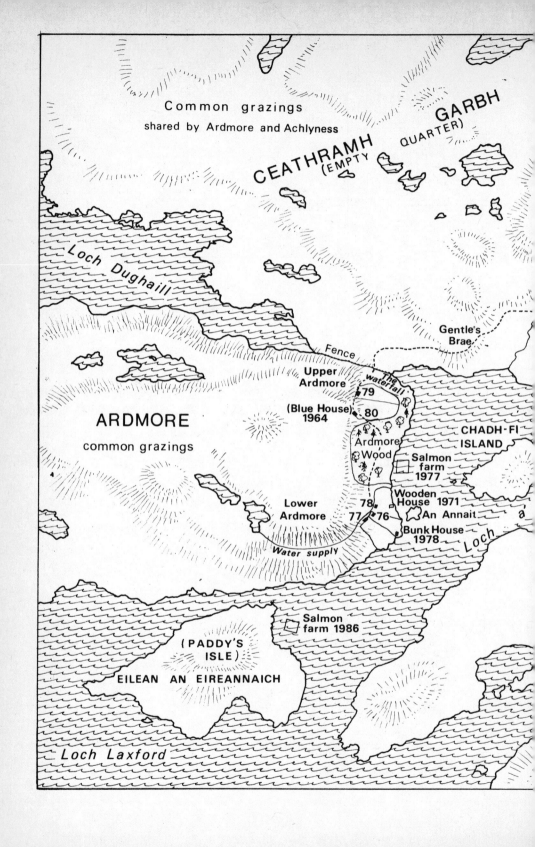

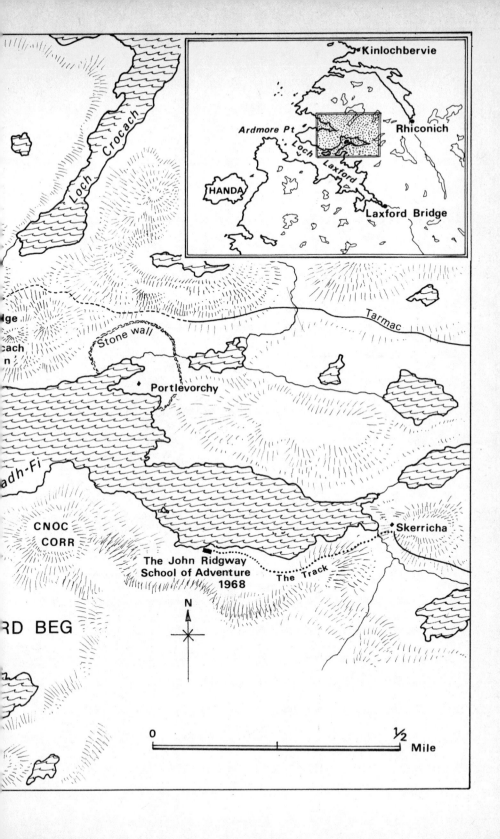

Kinlochbervie

Ardmore Pt

Rhiconich

HANDA

Loch Laxford

Laxford Bridge

Loch Crocach

Tarmac

Stone wall

cach n

Portlevorchy

adh-Fi

CNOC
CORR

The John Ridgway
School of Adventure
1968

Skerricha

The Track

RD BEG

N

0   ½
                                      Mile

THANKS

This story has been made possible by the goodwill and encouragement of very many people. Inevitably, people get bruised in the heat, or cold, of dramatic events, but with hindsight I am astonished at the great kindness so many people have shown me in the rough and tumble of it all.

My Father, Reginald Ridgway; my Mother-in-law, Sybil D'Albiac.

Lance and Ada Bell of No. 80 Ardmore.

The Chief Instructors: Richard Shuff, Krister Nylund, Jim Marland, Murdo McEwan, Jamie and Mary Young, Tony Dallimore, Peter Aldred, Giles Butler, Roy Davies, Keith Longney, David Hubbard, Edward Ley-Wilson, Justin Matterson.

The Skippers of the Yacht: Colin Ladd, Bob Duncan, Peter Aldred, Andy Briggs, Alistair Arnold, Sue King, Justin Matterson.

The Instructors and the Cooks – inhabitants of the *Rising Sun*. The Ladies, The Businessmen, The Young People, The Cruisers. The Doctors of Scourie. The Wardens of Handa. Michael the bus. The Posties: Willie, Donald-Hugh, Charlie, Marion and George.

Anne, Duchess of Westminster. The Mackintoshes of Laxford. Jack Elliot of Balnakiel. The Osbornes of Oldshoremore. The Mackenzies of Elsrickle. The Sandals of Oldshoremore. The Rosses of No. 77. Hughie Ross of No. 77. Gordon and Barbara Monshall of No. 79. The Corbetts of Portlevorchy. Donald-Hugh (the Gaffer) Ross of Skerricha. The Macdonalds of Mariveg. Dick and Helen Donaldson of Foindle. Reg and Marion Rookes of Kinlochbervie. Rhoda Mackay of Badcall. Donald Davidson of Findhorn. Ian Smith of Inverness. Gordon Stewart, Bill Henderson and Nigel Hunter-Gordon of Inverness. The Liddons of Skye. Huey Nedd and Old Murd. Danny and Morag Mackenzie of Foindle. Norman Mcleod of Achlyness. The Mitchells of Bryn-y-Cadno. Jim Archer-Burton. Kay Price. Margaret Body. John McConnell. Jim and Cathy Ross of Rhiconich. Billy Calder of Achriesgill. John and Rachel Mackay of Badcall. Iain MacAulay of Drumbeg. Marshall Halliday and John Lawrie of Badcall Scourie.

And many others.

JOHN RIDGWAY

AUTHOR'S NOTE

Twenty years ago I wrote a book called *Journey to Ardmore*. It told of my life from adoption when a few weeks old, through school, Nautical College, Merchant Navy, Sandhurst, and on into the Parachute Regiment; and also of rowing across the Atlantic and my ill-fated entry in the race to become the first man to sail non-stop alone round the world. It ended as Marie Christine and I finally managed to lodge a permanent toe-hold on Ardmore: on Saturday 5 July 1969, the day the John Ridgway School of Adventure opened. We were, we hoped, about to realise our dream. *Flood Tide* takes the story on, and shows how we survived and consolidated. Ardmore is the centre of our lives: a still centre in the winter; organised, perpetual motion from Easter to October.

The core of this book is how we have become part of a dwindling coastal crofting community in the remote north-west Highlands of Scotland.

In 1968, during the fifty days it took me to sail alone across the Atlantic to Brazil, I made up my mind to continue an adventurous life on the land as well as the sea. So most winters I have been travelling to recharge the batteries for the season to come. I have already written books about several of these trips. *Amazon Journey* (1972) described a journey from the source to the sea; *Cockleshell Journey* (1974) told of exploration on Patagonian icecaps; *Storm Passage* (1975) was a winter journey to the Spanish Sahara; *Round the World with Ridgway* (1978) followed our entry in the Whitbread yacht race; *Round the World Non-stop* (1985) recorded the non-stop circumnavigation made by Andy Briggs and me; *Road to Elizabeth* (1986) tells of another journey to Peru, in search of a murdered friend.

Because these books exist the expeditions in them receive only brief mention this time. *Flood Tide* is a celebration of Ardmore and the twenty years we have been running the school here.

In March 1964, a few days before Marie Christine and I were married, a Tilley lamp arrived in the post; it was from Don Holland, who'd been my Housemaster at Pangbourne eight years before. Sadly, he died only a couple of years later, but I often read his letter which accompanied the wedding present:

> The great thing in life is to do what you are fitted for, and what you are called for. As Borrow wrote in *Lavengro*: "Follow your calling, for however various your talents may be, ye can have but one calling . . . Bound along if you can; if not, on hands and knees follow it, perish in it, if needful. But ye need not fear that. . . ."

Ardmore has certainly been that calling.

1

I am a crofter, and I have lived now at Ardmore for nearly twenty-five years with my wife Marie Christine and our daughter Rebecca. Ardmore (the Big Hill) is as remote a place as you can get to live on the British mainland. There is no access by road, and main electricity only reached us in 1981. It lies at the outermost end of Loch a'Chadh-fi, a crooked elbow off the northern shore of Loch Laxford. Loch a'Chadh-fi is the sea loch on which we travel when we visit the outside world, whether the next anchorage be Laxford pier or Capetown. The name means Loch of the Spindrift, and that seemed peculiarly appropriate to my restless condition when I first arrived on this beautiful but fearsome coast of north-west Scotland, determined to make a life of my own.

I had discovered and fallen in love with the beauty and freedom of this wild world while flying over it with the Parachute Regiment. However, trying to find a way of living there presented as many survival problems as contemplating one's second parachute jump. But in 1964 when we got married and I resigned my commission, Marie Christine and I were young and optimistic. We had no ties, no mortgage, and no fixed ideas about the future. With hindsight I can see that what I was really looking for was a lasting challenge, something worth spending a lifetime at.

For I am one of those trying people who think nothing is worth having unless it's been hard won. In my platoon in 3 Para in the early sixties I found two kindred spirits. Chay Blyth was platoon sergeant. I remember him fighting a straggler on the morning run, a man much bigger than Chay and already notorious for trying to kill a sleeping colleague with a trenching shovel. And there was Private Tom "Moby" McClean, who had spent his childhood in a Barnardo's home near Dublin. Short, powerful and impulsive in speech and action, Moby was a loner. I recall haranguing the platoon about their poor performance on an escape and evasion exercise, telling them the time would surely come when Moby's dash and commitment would count above all else. But looking round the room, I could see only Chay, Moby and I believed it.

Chay Blyth, Moby McClean and I all left the regiment at a fairly early age. We tried to find adventure in civilian life. Chay and I rowed the North Atlantic from America to Ireland in 1966. Moby rowed it alone in a smaller boat a couple of years later, and then started his own adventure school for the Army, beside Loch Nevis. In 1982 and '83 he broke the record for the smallest boat to sail across the Atlantic. Then again in 1985 he captured public attention by colonising remote Rockall to confirm British seabed rights far out into the Atlantic. Most recently, in 1987, at the age of forty-five, he has broken the record for rowing the North Atlantic alone. Chay became the first and only person to sail alone non-stop round the world against the prevailing winds. After that he became a successful professional yachtsman, racing across oceans with his own huge boats. I sometimes wonder how we might have got on as a three-man patrol behind enemy lines.

In 1964, while Marie Christine and I were looking for somewhere to live in the north-west Highlands, we got jobs at the little fishing village of Kinlochbervie. Marie Christine was secretary to the fish auctioneer, and I helped set out the bag nets along the coast for salmon. But once the season got under way the crew was reduced and my work cut to mending fish boxes by day and loading the lorries by night. We had every weekend for our obsessional interest: finding a croft of our own.

On the first day of May, Marie Christine was in London at her brother's wedding, and I was driving our green mini-van as far as I could along a rough track in search of a remote spot mentioned by the salmon crew. "Footpath to Ardmore 3 miles" the fingerpost had said at the turning off the coast road. A couple of miles along the switchback moorland track the gravel gave way to mud and the van sank to its axles as the rain slashed down. To the west, across the sea loch, I could see two white croft houses and a ruin clinging to the steep green hillside of Lower Ardmore. Then to the right lay a wood and beyond that the two houses of Upper Ardmore.

By the time I had the vehicle out and turned round, the afternoon was gone. But I was still full of curiosity, and looked round to see if there was anywhere I might ask about the place. Leaving the van, I made my way down through heather and loose rocks, through a small gate in a stone wall, running the last hundred yards or so in the rain, across short-cropped grass to a solitary croft down on the north shore of Loch a'Chadh-fi. This was Portlevorchy. My wet clothes were soon steaming as I stood in front of a glowing peat fire listening to the old brothers Donald and Angie Corbett telling me about Ardmore. Retired bachelor shepherds, who kept a supply of warm socks for the hill in the upper left oven of their kitchen range, they knew the district like the back of their hands.

"It's a bonny place in the summer, right enough, but it's kinda cut off in the winter." Donald's eyes twinkled behind thick horn-rimmed glasses, while I gulped down hot tea and cakes, brought in by his niece Ruby. She was full of crack too, and I quickly realised I was going to like the Corbetts.

"Would you know if any of the crofts are vacant over there?" I asked, holding my breath.

"There's no many folk'd want to live over there these days. No road and no electricity on Ardmore," Angie grunted, sucking noisily to get his pipe alight. All three of them shook their heads doubtfully, and my heart sank. The rain pattered against the window.

Donald leaned forward in his chair, as if coming to a decision about me. "Well but, Johnny Macpherson's had a heart attack – he's staying over in Strathnaver just now. I doubt we'll see him back here again, and I think he's wanting to give up the croft."

Within a week old John Macpherson had agreed to assign his croft to me for £180. Assigning a croft, that is transferring it to someone who is not a member of your family, involves the consent of the Crofters Commission and the proprietor of the estate on which the croft stands. In spite of the forward-looking attitude taken by both these parties, the bureaucracy of it all took some time, long enough for Marie Christine and me to discover that unless we gave the matter some more realistic thought than we'd done so far, there was no way we could earn our livings from a base at Ardmore. But it would take more than that to shake me loose of the place.

"If there is a place on this earth which nobody wants, that's the place I'm hunting for." This is what Brigham Young is supposed to have said as he led his harried Mormons on foot across North America. When he came down on the forbidding land surrounding the Great Salt Lake in Utah, he said, "This is the place."

A grim start indeed. But this is exactly how I felt about Ardmore when I first saw it that rainy afternoon in May 1964. Born in 1938,

I was fortunate enough to be adopted at the age of three months, and, like so many others, my adoptive parents were always on the move during the tumult of the war years. Of course, I didn't know then just how lucky I was not to have been part of one of those mass children evacuations of those times. I joined the merchant navy after boarding school and then the Army kept me on the move right up until I saw those crofts on Ardmore. I'm not an overly religious man, but I knew I'd found my own Salt Lake.

By the time our assignation came through, we were already retreating, temporarily defeated absentee crofters, back to the south of England. I was fortunate enough to be accepted back into the Parachute Regiment, but we kept closely in touch with Ardmore and always spent my leave there. So when the Atlantic rowing project got under way two years later, it was to Hughie Ross of Lower Ardmore I turned for advice on the best type of boat to survive the Atlantic. And it was Hughie's advice that saved our lives. Without it I would have chosen the same sort of boat as the one that failed. Ever since rowing the North Atlantic with Chay in the summer of 1966 I have hated talking or even thinking about the past. But there is one factor I never allow myself to forget. Two other men, Johnston and Hoare, set out to row from America about the same time as we did. They were never seen again, but their upturned boat was recovered by a Canadian warship in mid-Atlantic months later. This knowledge is what forces me to regard everything since 1966 as a bonus, and to justify this bonus, life must be lived to the full. No coasting by. It could so easily have been Chay and I who died in the small dory *English Rose III*.

We rowed from Cape Cod in Massachusetts to the Aran Isles off the west coast of Ireland in ninety-two days and the experience changed us both for ever. A whole new world opened up for us, beyond the Army. Within two years we were racing one another to become the first man to sail non-stop single-handed round the world. This time we both failed. I was forced to land in Brazil and Chay in South Africa. During those fifty days alone on the ocean, I thought a lot about the future. I'd talked so much about Ardmore while we were rowing that Chay had even called his house Foinaven. I knew I must return and take up where I had failed in 1964. I decided to try and build a place where people could come and experience the same direct confrontation with the natural

16

world and the elements, which I had found so stimulating and satisfying myself.

Before the single-handed race I had spent six months on the selection course for the Special Air Service Regiment, together with Rod Liddon, a good friend from my 3 Para days. We both passed, and while I went on unpaid leave for the race, Rod soldiered on with our new regiment. On my return to England, Marie Christine and I got together with Rod and his wife Jeannie. The four of us shared a flat in Hereford, and the Liddons had also stayed with us at Ardmore. After much discussion we decided to leave the Army and build a School of Adventure at Ardmore. I well knew that by resigning my commission a second time, I was forfeiting my chance of ever returning to the security of the Regiment, which apart from being my livelihood had, as importantly, been my family, with comradeship like nowhere in civilian life. But I did so long to stand free, to make my own mistakes, and expend all my energy on an idea of my own. By mid-September 1968 we were all four at Ardmore, with a brochure already printed for our first season in 1969.

In 1934 there were five crofts on Ardmore, numbered in the order they were built and recorded in the Register for the Parish of Eddrachilles. The first house you come to as you scramble up the track into Upper Ardmore is No.79. It's a stone house built in the middle of the last century at the top of the waterfall, as we call that part of the footpath which winds up a hundred-foot cliff from a gate in the fence. The fence joins Loch Dughaill on the Atlantic coast to Loch a'Chadh-fi at the neck of the Ardmore peninsula, some three miles from the coast road. At No.79 lived John and Kate Mackenzie with their daughters, Winnie and Mary.

Just beyond them at No.80 were John and Christine-Anne Macpherson and their children, Jimmy, Alexina, Geordie, Barbara, Joey, Jessie and Christina. Five minutes' brisk walk through the most northerly wood on the west coast of Britain and you emerge on to the three crofts of Lower Ardmore, standing side by side exactly one hundred feet above the sea. Whitened with lime, they cluster together, sheltered by Ardmore, the "Big Hill", from the storms which come booming in from the Atlantic. At No.78 lived John and Lexy Macdonald, with their daughters, Winnie, Angusina, and Katie. The middle house is No.76, where the widower Angus Mcleod lived with his sister Shona and his

17

children Frank and Nelly. Next door, on the southern side in No.77, lived Hector and Robina Ross with their children, Jeannie, Heckie, Ina, Robert, Bessy, Molly, Jim-Angus, Hughie and Minnie.

Thirty years later, in 1964, when we first arrived, five members of the Ross family in No.77 were the only remaining residents of Ardmore.

Our first home, at No.80 Ardmore, had black corrugated iron walls badly streaked with rust, and several sheets on the roof clanked ominously in every gust of wind. Old Johnny Macpherson had been over eighty, and the wild weather had gradually over-powered him. Corrugated iron sheeting had been the wonder building material in the early 1900s. It's known as "zinc" locally, from the coating which is galvanised on to the thin corrugated steel sheeting to prevent rust. In isolated places without timber, and where stone is hard to come by, a wooden frame clad with corrugated iron and lined with matchboard proved the answer to so many housing problems that corrugated iron has become almost traditional. At No.80 only a central part of each gable end is made of stone.

One afternoon, soon after our 1968 return to build the Adven-ture School, Rod and I walked along the southern shore of Loch a'Chadh-fi with "Old Bill" Ross from Skerricha, and his son Donald-Hugh. After looking at several sites, we all agreed on a place where a small burn flowed into the sea by the ruins of an old stone wool store. The Adventure School's main building would have to be set into the side of a gently sloping hill. We already had our eye on what the Dingwall auctions rooms were calling a "Ninety by twenty-four foot superior wooden building" and intended bidding for it at the forthcoming sale.

Near our chosen site, a few stones showed where a croft house had once stood. "Old Bill", a wiry figure in his late seventies, was the crofter of Skerricha, at the inland end of the loch. Long before, he'd carried a machine-gun tripod at the battle of the Somme, where 60,000 allied soldiers were mown down like so much corn before breakfast on the first day. Erect, slightly built, and pretty deaf, he still suffered from trench foot, but his peppery sense of humour was as sharp as ever. He generously agreed to renounce an acre of his outgrazing beside the sea loch, if the proprietor of the estate would agree to feu the site to us to build the School.

18

"Be gone now – and be getting on with your work," he'd bark, with a broad, toothless grin.

After the others had left, I remained, sitting on the stones of the ruined wool store, looking out over the loch. A pale autumn sun warmed my back. It had been one of the driest summers in living memory. There was that vast reassuring silence, which reminded me of the ocean and shut out the problems of the outside world. I was home.

There had been a particular day, during the rowing, in a storm in the Atlantic, when I'd silently bargained with God for my life. It was my turn to bail with bucket and pump, while Chay lay asleep in the stern. I was very much afraid. The storm had lasted for five days, soaking clothes felt like sandpaper on our skin. *English Rose III* had been swamped several times, and the seas were running so high it looked as if we might soon be capsized. I was leaning over the thwart, resting between pumping sessions, when I suggested to God that I'd live the rest of my life with a broken back – if only he'd let me live.

Well, we'd been spared. Now it was time to make proper use of that bonus of life.

I thought of those who'd lived on this now ruined croft. They had known hardships too. Victims of the notorious Highland Clearances of the last century, sold out by their clan chief, and driven from the fertile inland straths by the English landlord who sought to put sheep on the land in place of people. They had arrived on the barren, rocky coast with little else besides what they stood up in. They'd built the house from the rocks about them, and wrested this tiny patch of green inbye land from the heather and peat with their own sweat, laying dry-stone drains and spreading tons of seaweed. But they'd given up the unequal struggle, emigrating to Canada like wretched cattle aboard the chartered sailing ships from Bristol which had moored to those iron rings, still hanging from the rocks in a sheltered part of nearby Loch Laxford.

No, we had not chosen an easy place to live, as that first winter was to make clear.

Rod Liddon hired a JCB earthmover and the fine weather held good. He soon cleared a track half a mile from the road-end at Skerricha and along the southern shore to the site of the School. It was rough, but at least it was a means of moving building materials by land, and saved us all the double-handling involved with boats. Before winter set in, we had cleared the foundations for the ninety-foot building bought at auction for only £340. There had been one other bidder, but he wasn't too convinced it could be dismantled and removed from its original site near Bonar Bridge, sixty miles away on the east coast, within the one month stipulated as a condition of sale. This presented no problem to Rod and Hughie Ross.

On the Ardmore side of the loch we managed another purchase, croft No.76, which was no longer in crofting tenure and had been empty for fifteen years. With the white stone house went two acres of land running down to the shore on the south side of the wood. In mid-October the Liddons moved in. No.76 was the middle house. No.78 was now a ruined shell, with rowan trees growing inside its broken walls, but the Ross family had been in No.77 since they couldn't remember when. One by one they had seen the other families leave. Hector and Robina were both in their seventies. Robina, always known to us as Granny Ross, was a great friend and support, and we came to love her dearly. She was especially fond of our one-year-old daughter Rebecca, who in later years often delighted her by taking in posies of flowers. Granny Ross was born in No.76, she married the boy next door in No.77, and had nine children, but only three now lived at home.

Heckie was the eldest son, in his early fifties. He was tall with dark, brooding good looks. Unmarried and very shy, Heckie said little in the normal course of things, but with a dram inside him after the lamb sales or at the turn of the year, he became quite eloquent. Heckie lived in the past. His stories and the poetry he remembered were to liven many a winter's evening for us. The hills of Ardmore belong to Heckie; I never walk there but I expect to come upon him still, in his long dark coat with sheep dog Mona at his heel, leaning on his stick and gazing silently at the land spread out below him – and beyond to the snow-capped mountains inland. As the eldest son, Heckie was heir to the croft, and when we arrived at Ardmore he was already looking after the family's sheep on the eighteen hundred acres of Ardmore common grazing. His father, Hector, loved the sheep and he spent much of his time tending them, or slowly wending his way up from the shore with a sack of peat on his back, even when he was eighty. Old Hector was one of the most courteous men I've ever met. His eyes were bright blue and they shone with sincere friendship. We let him have the run of our crofts for his sheep as all our time was taken up with the school, but he always wrote formally each year, offering to pay the croft rent of three or four pounds for us in return. His spidery writing began "Dear Friend" – what a good friend he was.

His two daughters, Molly and Bessy, were in their early forties. They were dark and attractive but like Heckie they had both remained unmarried. Instead they took it in turns to stay out at Ardmore and look after the family as is the Highland custom, each working away on the east coast for a year or two, before changing round. The family was Free Presbyterian by religion, and we were apprehensive at its reputation for severity. The "Wee Frees" as they are known, evolved during the Highland Clearances. When the traditional Church of Scotland sided with the landlords, many parishioners decided to break away and form their own Church. It was a time of great bitterness. After living at Ardmore for twenty years, I can see now what a shock we must have been to the quietly ordered way of life the Ross family had known. They had every reason to feel outraged, yet they never showed us anything but courtesy. I cannot recall one single occasion when they disagreed with any suggestion I made. All the same they must have smiled at our early blunders.

Hughie was the youngest son and so the nearest in age to ourselves, but at thirty-eight, still ten years my elder. Sandy-haired and always good for a cheery smile, Hughie was of average build but unusually strong and seemingly impervious to the weather. He was the very best sort of companion for any job involving hard going. His usual work was as a painter and decorator with his elder brother Robert, who had his own croft at Foindle over on the south shore of Loch Laxford, some two and a half miles directly across the water from Ardmore. Hughie made the trip across in all weathers, winter and summer alike, in an antique twelve-foot yawlie, powered by his trusty Seagull outboard motor. It was black nights in that boat which had given him the experience to advise us on the dory for the Atlantic row. His yawlie had iron fastenings, but seemed held together more by copious layers of pitch. Inside, the edges of the clinker planks were worn smooth by the bailer on many a desperate crossing of Laxford. Juggling with the throttle, Hughie could make that boat do everything but talk, and I often wondered if he wasn't listening to it do just that.

21

Throughout the summer when Chay and I were rowing the Atlantic, Hughie had worked away at the redecorating and plumbing of No.80, our first house on Ardmore. He painted the black corrugated iron walls blue and soon No.80 became known to all as the Blue House. Often he'd climb the hill behind and look westward into the ocean, anxiously willing the long weeks of easterly wind to veer west and help bring us home. Now he made himself available for most of the winter to help with the building of the School, just at a time when we desperately needed support. There's no doubt that without the tireless efforts of Hughie Ross, there never would have been a John Ridgway School of Adventure.

By the time winter gripped the Highlands, both crofts were well stocked with driftwood from the beaches on the Atlantic coast and drums of paraffin to light the lamps. Marie Christine sent letters to every conceivable corner which might help fill the courses in the following year. There were no distractions from the work: weekends, television and such like no longer existed for us. Jeannie Liddon also helped with the typing between painting sessions in No.76. It was my task to travel to exhibitions and give lectures, as well as write a lot of letters. I'm afraid I found it all very worrying. I was investing everything and painfully aware, that with "Willie the Post" bringing us only six bookings by the New Year, we still had 194 places to fill. In darker moments I kept asking myself the same question over and over again: "Aren't we just building a big bonfire on the other side of the loch?" There would be few buyers for a third-hand ninety-foot building in that remote spot.

The real burden of the construction of the School building fell on the shoulders of Rod Liddon. Once the rains set in, the first hill on his makeshift track became impassable to the Land-rover for the rest of the winter. There was no time to spend repairing the track: we had a building deadline to meet. Living somewhere as remote as Ardmore has undeniable romantic appeal if you are cosily established and all you have to do is batten down the hatches every time the weather turns bad. Actually building something in the winter is quite another business. The counter-attraction of that magical quality estate agents call "access" was borne in on us time and time again that winter.

We managed to move the main sections of the big building from Laxford pier four miles away on a raft hired from the County

Council, using an old diesel-powered launch we bought for the purpose. But the engine blew up as we tried to start it one cold Sunday morning. The elder Rosses, no doubt, considered the con-rod bursting through the crank case a direct proof of the displeasure of the Almighty at our violating the Sabbath, but they were far too courteous to mention it, or perhaps they just thought it would be stating the obvious. The loss of the launch left us with limited access to the site. We could either hump materials half a mile along the track, or move everything from Skerricha road-end in the fourteen-foot blue yawlie, towing an eight-man rubber dinghy. We chose the latter. The sand for the foundations came from the edge of a freshwater loch ten miles away. The forty-pound blocks of concrete were carried 200 yards down to the boat on our backs, loaded, motored across the loch, then off-loaded and lugged up to a stockpile on the site. By this means we moved all the timber, plumbing and electrical materials, bunks, tables, chairs and equipment for sixty people, as well as the half-ton generator we'd carted up on a trailer from Hereford.

There were some narrow escapes when physical and mental tiredness brought mistakes. A 650-gallon water tank tipped over on the steep bank down to the boat. I was lucky to jump inside it before it caught me. We laughed. Rod and Hughie capsized the boat with an overload of timber one evening, just as a thin skin of ice was forming on the water. This heralded several more days of walking the three miles round to the school until the tides and the next gale together drove the ice away once more. Granny Ross was furious with Hughie for ruining a twelve-pound bag of dried milk in that accident. Confined to her chair with arthritis, she thought the whole story was rigged to cover the loss of the precious milk.

When the south-easterly winds come in March, crofters on the coast fire the heather to encourage a fresh new growth for the sheep later in the year and vast clouds of grey smoke swirl out to sea as if signalling the end of a Viking raid. The wind is funnelled by the hills surrounding Loch a'Chadh-fi into storm force gusts. We learned to heed the Gaelic names on the map. The wind races down the length of the loch, streaking the slate-coloured waters with lines of white foam and lifting curtains of spray up the hillside to blanket our windows with salt, fully a hundred feet above. Loch of the Spindrift indeed.

The white, mist-filled air is exhilarating at first, but soon the noise and the buffeting on the house make sleep difficult at night and give us headaches from the tension. Of course, this was all new to us in the early spring of 1969, and over on the other side of the loch, where the school was being built, the wind was gleefully bent on destroying all we had achieved. At the height of the storm we had a small party of boys from Dunrobin School on the east coast staying with us for a weekend. We put them up in the hut we had built to house *English Rose III*. They had enjoyed whirling downwind along the footpath from the road, but once at Ardmore there was little for them to do in the high wind so we had a party and Marie Christine made a huge meal of spaghetti.

Next morning the boys had to return to school, and we decided to cross the loch in the blue yawlie at the narrows to the south of Chadh-fi Island where it was comparatively sheltered behind Cnoc Corr (Odd-shaped Hill). But as soon as we straggled over the top of the hill and pushed ourselves into the gusts, racing down through the heather, we could see something was very wrong. We now had an Odd-shaped School under an Odd-shaped Hill: two of the heavy roof sections were gone, sucked off the empty ninety-foot box which was our pride and joy. And it wasn't box-shaped anymore either. The whole structure was leaning drunkenly towards the loch, in an imminent state of collapse. Those roof sections were an eight-man lift: one was afloat in the bay; another spread in splinters across two hundred yards of rocky beach. It had come to rest in a prayer-like attitude against the ruined croft. "Another half hour and we'd have lost the lot," Rod shouted above the boom of the wind as we frantically hammered struts of timber into the angle between the walls and the floor, while the boys heaved together to push the walls something like upright.

It was one of those jobs which just could not be done by two people. The extra arms and legs of the boys saved more than the day. Within three hours there were so many props the floor looked like a forest. We'd managed to fasten the five doors which had burst, but of the empty generator shed there was no trace – the wind direction indicated it must be down the other end of the loch somewhere.

We had survived. A few days later the new track was opened to the Land-rover, thanks to the sterling effort of Donald-Hugh and his uncle Hughie Nedd, who used to work for the County

Roads Squad. Using the vehicle, Rod was now able to tow the building into its final upright position. Mustering everyone we knew, we lifted the roof section back into place, repaired and strengthened. No lasting damage had been done, and the project rolled on towards the arrival of the first course.

In May we started to run boat trips from Skerricha to see the colonies of nesting sea birds on Handa Island five miles down the coast. *English Rose III* was something to see along the way. A newly fitted, reconditioned 60 hp diesel engine in the launch did all that was asked of it, and Billy Calder from Achriesgill ran the boat for us. His cheery "turned out nice again", always helped things along if it was raining.

All the while we were filled with a dread that things were not going to work out and that the bookings wouldn't come in to see us through the first season. One might suppose that in a remote place such as Ardmore, life could be a simple matter of hard work and a clear mind. Perhaps that is what draws people from the pressured life of the city; maybe the reality drives them back again. Pressures are similar in both places. Learning to cope with them seems to be a trick. I haven't learnt it yet. All the same we planted a good supply of potatoes in the hope that we'd still be around to eat them in the autumn.

We laid an alkathene pipe to bring drinking water to Lower Ardmore from a lochan half a mile away up in the hills which rise a further 150 feet behind Nos.77, 76 and 78. We had some fun trying to get the syphon to work, as the pipe had to be almost a mile long to get round the hill. Even though Granny Ross still insisted on drinking water from the spring a couple of hundred yards from her house, she was pleased to have a tap from our supply for cooking and washing.

Rod and Jeannie moved across the loch to their caravan to be close to the School in early May, and Marie Christine, Rebecca and I moved from No. 80 into our new home at No.76 Lower Ardmore, next door to the Rosses.

The telephone was shifted from the lonely red kiosk at Upper Ardmore through the wood to our house, on condition that anyone resident on Ardmore could use it. The kiosk itself had to be broken up on site by the telephone engineers, since it couldn't easily be taken away and it wasn't allowed to be sold intact. However, it lives on as cold frames, and I sometimes meet parts of it when I dive to check the dinghy moorings in the summer –

25

the concave top filled with concrete makes an excellent mushroom anchor.

As our School opening day drew nearer, across the loch two thousand polystyrene tiles were stuck to the ceiling, curtains went up, and floors were polished to a glaze which we hoped would be maintained through the season. Marie Christine brought Rebecca over to the school in a basket each day.

"Here it comes at last!" It was opening day and the special bus was an hour late after a breakdown on the 100-mile drive from Inverness station. The owner was driving it himself, and he wanted payment before he left. The food hadn't come on the regular mail bus, and it was raining stair-rods. Leading the thirty young people down the narrow winding footpath to the John Ridgway School of Adventure on the loch shore at Skerricha, I thought what an adventure it had been just building the place, and I wondered what adventures lay ahead, down the track.

2

It was a small and rather weary team which greeted the arrival of the first course. Over hot soup and rolls I called out the names. Most people came from Britain but some were from Europe, America and even West Africa. By the time lunch was over Rod and I managed to split the course into three age groups, twelve to fifteen, fifteen to eighteen and eighteen to twenty-five, and give them the outline of the programme for the coming fourteen days.

Most of them had only just finished their school term, and they were wary that we might turn out to be school all over again. I was determined to avoid this. It was a help that the course was made up of individuals, and not a single group from one school. How much better for a boy or girl to come down that path from the bus unknown to the others – it didn't matter how good or bad they were at school, the two weeks with us were a fresh start. Their position in the group depended only on their performance at the canoeing, rock climbing, sailing and expeditions.

"To get the most from this course, you'll need to put a lot into it – and we'd like to try and follow three principles, which I hope will make each group a success." In the upturned faces I could see the whole range of expressions you might expect from an age range of twelve to twenty-five about to get some sort of message from a fellow who had rowed across the Atlantic: enthusiastic, earnest, sullen, bored, sceptical, apprehensive, excited, amused. Some of the foreigners looked as if they couldn't understand a word. The roundabout of other people's expectations never stops.

"Self-reliance is the first. Some of you will never have been away from home before; here you will learn to do everything for yourself. Once you are self-reliant, then you can start to look after others in the group."

"Positive thinking is the second. When the group is discussing the problems of the course, if it looks at them in a positive way, then it is likely to succeed. You will probably have rain, wind and cold as well as sun. None of these will last for long. Every storm comes to an end – try and see that, and you will be thinking positively, and that will help the whole group to do the same. Think negatively, and in hard going you will not succeed. Instead you'll be swallowed up in your own self-pity."

"Leave people and things better than you found them, that's the third. If you're feeling cold and wet on the mountain look around you, identify someone worse off than yourself, and concentrate on cheering him up. It's the beginning of leadership; and you'll forget your own feelings. You will be relying on the clothing and boots which you have brought with you, and the equipment you are issued with here. Your comfort and safety depend on it. Try and think of each thing you have with you as having to last for ever – in the middle of the ocean, or any survival situation, your length of life will depend on how you make things last."

Some of them were keen to practise these principles immediately, and those dismissing them as the platitudes of an overgrown Boy Scout would have plenty of opportunity to see the value of putting them into action in the next fourteen days.

The first event was the swimming test, and it helped to get people talking to each other. They also learnt that when their canoe turned over they would not be trapped inside, and that the life jacket did indeed keep them afloat. Finally, each person proved swimming proficiency on the free swim into the shore. After a shower the three different age groups set off for a short introductory walk with their group leaders. From the top of one of the hills near the School they could orientate themselves with the surrounding mountains and lochs.

The main factors which make up Ardmore are the sea, the mountains and the isolation. All three are apparent from the top of Cnoc Corr just behind the main School building; the land is a mass of little hills, each barely a couple of hundred feet high, but rising sharply as if to emphasise their own individuality. The common grazings of Ardmore run to close on 2,000 acres, but the ratio of sheep per acre, or souming as the Scots call it, is only 200 sheep, which shows just how much of the ground is bare rock. No matter how Hughie may enthuse about the quality of the grass in the sheltered valleys, many of these are under water. The parish of Eddrachilles is reputed to have more freshwater lochs than any other in Britain. Looking down from the Foinaven Ridge this is easy to believe. These bright lochans are filled with wild brown

trout. Old Donald Corbett from Portlevorchy has taken many a
fish of more than four pounds from these waters over the years.
Patient, and stooped as any grey heron, he waits silently with his
twenty-foot bamboo pole, and on the end of his line wriggles a
tempting worm.

Inland the ground rises rapidly in a series of foothills to the
flanks of Beinn Spionnaidh, Cranstackie, Foinaven, Arkle and
Ben Stack. These bastions of the North-west, such prominent
landmarks for our homeward crossings of the Minch in the yacht,
are part of the Moine thrust plane which has been forced up from
the south-east to overlay the ancient Lewisian gneiss. Standing
on top of Cnoc Corr it is easy to explain why course students
should pay attention to the correct way to put up a tent: storms
in the mountains are frequent and they exploit any weakness,
especially at three o'clock in the morning. Eight or nine feet of
rain falls up there each year, twice as much as on the coast. As if
by magic, shifting tones of light and cloud sometimes appear to
draw the mountains closer to Ardmore, sometimes push them
further away; they are plum black on occasions – gloomy and
threatening, but this will change through shades of grey into
green in early summer. Sunsets often pick out the red in the rock
so it looks to be glowing with fire. But I like it best in mid-winter,
looking out from the warmth of the croft on a still, dark night
with the loch frozen and the land covered with snow – the
mountains then look bright as day in the light of the full moon.

How can I describe the sea? It has played such a part in my life.
I wouldn't be happy unless I could see it from my window. The
tide comes in and goes out, set to the movement of the moon
through space; the big spring tides occurring every sixteen days
are at their peak two days after the new and full moon. Our lives
at Ardmore are ordered by the tides. Only a fool would move
stores on anything but a high tide, and unless we are careful the
Land-rover gets stranded at the School when the tide submerges
the track to Skerricha. From the mooring under the wood I have
twice set off to sail round the world.

It is principally the sea which provides Ardmore with its isolation. If it were possible to drive right to the door, the place
would be changed completely for me. I feel just as proud of the
isolation of Ardmore as Ratty felt about his home in the river bank
in *Wind in the Willows*. Looking out across the loch from the croft
at night, there is just the faint glimmer of the Tilley lamp from the

Portlevorchy window against the blackness of the mountains beyond. The Corbetts tell me they feel just the same comfort from our light, which is the only one visible to them. Isolation, privacy, independence, a secure base from which to venture – I love these things.

Rod and I planned to do most of the instructing ourselves, and we'd found five instructors to help us with the general running of things. We recruited young men with a pretty firm idea of what they were going on to do later, but who wanted an opportunity for a change and a challenge between school and university, or before entering the services. For the first season we simply selected from those who volunteered by means of a two-week trial, but in subsequent years we ran a month-long Instructors' Course before each season. On the catering side, Jeannie and Rod's sister Sally would be doing the breakfasts and organising the packed lunches at the School, while Marie Christine prepared the main evening meals and ran the office over at Ardmore.

Next morning began with a short run or swim to wake everyone up for breakfast, then we went through the practical business of packing rucksacks, erecting tents, basic map-work, first aid and camp hygiene. These were not so much lectures as a chance for the course to practise skills which they would soon need up on the Foinaven Ridge. In the afternoon there was some introduction to rope and boat work, as well as map-reading and use of a compass. Early the following day the three groups set out for the start of the circuit of activities which would keep them apart for the remainder of the course: one group went off on the two-day expedition to Foinaven with Neil McNair. Neil came to like the mountain so much that he took every one of the fifteen expeditions, spending thirty of the seventy days of that first season on Foinaven. Meanwhile, the other two groups were either on rock climbing, canoeing, sailing, orienteering or survival training. The whole circuit took nine days, with a choice day at the end. The final three days of the course were spent on the main expedition which took each group to a separate beach on the lonely area known locally as "Cape-side".

Cape-side, the extreme north-west corner of Britain, ends in Cape Wrath. It's aptly named, too, some visitors might say. But the name Wrath is actually derived from the Scandinavian word for "a turning point", for it was round Cape Wrath the Vikings came on their way to the Southland, now known as the county

30

of Sutherland. A narrow winding road, with passing places, leads nine miles out to the west coast, along the northern shores of Loch Inchard from Rhiconich which is a shop, a hotel and a police station with one constable whose beat covers 120 miles of coastline. Another similar road stretches thirteen miles up to the village of Durness on the north coast. The Cape-side lies to the north-west of these two roads, going on for a hundred square miles of wilderness, inaccessible to road vehicles. True, there is a road from the Kyle of Durness out to the Cape Wrath lighthouse, but this is linked to the main road only by a little wooden boat which carries people but not cars. The lighthouse is treated as a rock station and keepers' families live away on the east coast. The area is ideally suited to the various skills taught on our courses, and individuals need to be self-reliant, positive thinking and able to look after one another, as well as their food and equipment.

The beach at Sandwood on the Cape-side is a truly stunning place, especially after the long moorland walk which is the only way to reach it. The track, winding through rolling hill country dotted with lochans, was built to serve the peat cuttings of the crofts scattered along the coast road as far as Sheigra, which is the most northerly community on the west coast of Britain. The shifting white sands of the bay are the best part of three-quarters of a mile long and stretch some three hundred yards inland at their widest. The overspill from the freshwater loch threads its way across the sands at the northern end in an ever-varying skein, scarcely a foot deep in dry weather. Each summer, big salmon wriggle across this obstacle on their way into Sandwood loch, and on up to the spawning redds of the Shinary river beyond. But after a spate, a night-crossing of this torrent on the beach can be quite a test. At the southern end of the beach the sandstone stack of Am Buchaille pokes like a crooked finger from the sea, and there are several other stacks scattered just off the coast in the half-dozen miles north of Cape Wrath. The sandstone cliffs have their finest monument on the north coast at Clo Mor, four miles east of the Cape, where they rise to 920 feet and reign as the highest sea-cliffs on the British mainland.

One of my early dreams while working on the pier at Kinloch-bervie, was to own a 30' double-ended timber boat and fish great-lines in the channel between the stack at Am Buchaille and an off-lying island called Am Balg. How I envied the fishermen their way of life on those fine June mornings in 1964. I'd pause from the endless task of nailing broken fish boxes to watch them haul their catch of halibut, some up to twelve stone in weight, with their cranky derrick from the decks of the battered black lineboat up on to the pier. The rest of the day was their own, for they fished in the early hours in the half-light of mid-summer. If they had no luck with the halibut they'd switch on the sounder and rip handlines for "greens" as they called the handsome cod. It seemed a delightful life of freedom.

Old Donald Morrison of Kinloch used to shepherd at the lonely bothy of Strathan three miles inland from Sandwood up in the Shinary valley. In the middle of the last war, he remembers a couple of Spitfires patrolling the skies above Cape Wrath. Suddenly the engine of one of the planes began stuttering, and then cut out altogether. Donald knew fine the only possible landing place could be Sandwood beach, so he made his way to the top of a dune and waited. Sure enough the Spitfire glided down and crash-landed right before him. The pilot scrambled out with his inflated Mae West and Donald hastened down to meet him. The other plane made a pass along the beach, waggling its wings to signal it had seen the pilot was OK, before flying back to base. The Spitfire was not seriously damaged, but of course in those days there was no way to remove it from such a remote spot. The objective for our first expedition that day was to search for remains of the plane, which still appear out of the sand now and then, though on this occasion we found nothing but a few fragments of aluminium.

We had split the course into two halves. The slow walkers and younger people were lifted part of the way by Land-rover to Balchrick, some ten miles from the School where the north shore of Loch Inchard opens out to the Atlantic.

The course spent the first night in the ruins of Sandwood Lodge, in company with the ghost of an old sea captain who appears sometimes in full uniform with polished brass buttons and cap. Next morning they walked up the Shinary River to Strathan, which looms out of the valley mist like Shangri-la at the end of a long day. In later years we were to carry out materials to re-roof the bothy but even in the early days it was a welcome shelter, for the valley has a great atmosphere of isolation and the house lies deep in the strath close under the 1,500 foot bulk of An Grianan.

From Strathan the group made their way south, using map and compass, and spending the third night in the hills before they

The anti-tank platoon, 3 PARA, 1964. Author centre front row, with Chay Blyth on his right and Tom 'Moby' McClean back row, end right.

Inset: I sold the MG for the engagement ring.

Still propping me up twenty years later, Marie Christine greets *English Rose VI* with a welcoming salvo as we pick up the mooring again at the end of a record-breaking non-stop voyage round the world.

Molly Ross, Marie Christine, Granny Ross with Rebecca, and her husband Hector outside No.77 Lower Ardmore in 1968.

No.77, No.76 and the ruins of No.78 Lower Ardmore, from an RAF Buccaneer, 1973.

reached the road. Once there, thoughts of sweets and milk in the little Rhiconich shop gave them renewed strength for the last couple of miles along Loch Skerricha and so back to the hot showers of the School.

Another expedition was designed to be more demanding. Leaving the small suspension bridge which crosses the Dionard River at the southern end of the Kyle of Durness at nine o'clock in the evening, fifteen of the course, with myself and two instructors shadowing them, set out to make the cross-country night walk to the Cape Wrath lighthouse. This involved eleven miles of map and compass work, moving through the hills and between lochs.

In early July there are almost twenty-four hours of daylight on the north coast of Scotland. However, on this particular night a heavy mist rolled in from the sea, and it was a fairly dispirited party which first picked up the booming of the lighthouse foghorn around midnight. By the time the tents were up in the lee of the massive stone outbuildings around the lighthouse itself, it was early morning and the team wanted nothing but to collapse into their sleeping bags.

Breakfast was a meagre affair. The course had been searched for extra supplies before they left, and they'd consumed much of what we had brought with us during their wanderings in the night. But at least the mist lifted for their ragged walk down the coast to the Bay of Keisgaig, and I was able to see more clearly how the teamwork was coming along. We were now beginning the survival stage of the expedition, and on the coast walk each individual was briefed to gather anything useful for the building of his or her survival shelter once we reached the Keisgaig River. Most people picked up pieces of bleached wood to build a fire, but as we were always some hundreds of yards inland from the cliffs there appeared to be nothing available to eat. There were one or two small burns which might hold fingerling brown trout, but the group decided to keep on going, to build their shelter while the weather held fine, so there was no fishing.

The four French boys had not distinguished themselves on the teamwork side of things. Their main interest lay in sailing, and the other activities were seen only as something to stop them from sailing. Long walks and wet boots did not appeal at all, and their patience with *les Anglais* had worn thin long before this particular morning. The other eleven members of the party were mostly British, and they had lapsed into the unfortunate habit of calling the tight little French group "the Frogs". The French boys responded with determined isolationism. They decided to speak only French, and among the Brits nobody seemed fluent in that language, or if they were, were equally determined not to show it. Discomfort had neatly polarised the group. The pack of dates and part of a can of sardines, eaten at the lighthouse before we set out, soon lost effect and hunger set in. Now and then gulls would circle above, mewing derisively while eyeing the party as a possible source of food. Tiny sundew plants were busy digesting the small insects which they trap on their sticky red rosettes, and in the distance we caught a glimpse of three stags grazing peacefully on the flat ground over towards the Kearvaig River. They lifted their antlered heads for a while, but seeing we were so far away and going in another direction, they soon resumed feeding.

It was getting on for midday, and we were nearing the steep descent to the mouth of the Keisgaig River, when one of the French boys let out a whoop of excitement. We all stopped – the group was halting for any excuse by this time. The boy scooped something up from the ground and his friends all gathered round chattering and laughing wildly. It was a frog, and to the French the chances of survival suddenly looked much better than average. By the time we reached Keisgaig Bay a dozen frogs were safely tucked away in a side compartment of one of their rucksacks and they were singing French songs to annoy the empty-handed Brits, who had no intention of eating frogs at this stage.

I split the group into pairs along the banks of the river for the survival phase, and they set about building shelters using a black plastic sheet and the bits of wood they'd found on the rocky beach and along the river. The French foursome insisted vehemently that as they had brought a tent, they were going to use it.

With Gallic pouts and a bit of shoulder shrugging to show their contempt for the others, they soon disappeared inside their tent with the frogs. Once the shelters were well under way, the rest of the group gathered plentiful supplies of mussels and winkles from the beach in their mess-tins, and a few of them decided to stew up some seaweed as well. I showed them where to find earthworms under the stones in the well-drained soil on the edge of the river, and soon the first six-inch trout was pulled from one of the pools on the length of nylon and single hook they'd each been issued with. One of the girls found some wild thyme, and

34

a piece of silver foil appeared from somewhere to wrap the fish before they were buried in the embers of a fire to bake.

Everything seemed to be going all right. The French boys had cooked and eaten their frogs and were now asleep in their tent. Here and there figures were curled up in their sleeping bags. So I decided to go fishing.

I always carry my Hardy "Traveller's" rod with me in the hills; its five pieces of "Palakona" split cane and reversible handle make four different types of rod and it fits easily into my rucksack. There was a gentle, easterly breeze and the sun was just off the water by the time I arrived at a sandy beach at the windward end of the loch. In the powerful silence, I felt I might have been the only person ever to have visited the place, but the atmosphere was warm and friendly. I sat on a peat hag where a small burn trickles across the beach to feed the loch, and I could see cruising trout dimpling the surface thirty yards out from the edge of the sand. I felt the familiar tremble of excitement as I put up the rod into its maximum 8'3" fly-rod length, clipped on my old 3 1/8" "Perfect" reel and threaded the ivory floating line through the rings. My half-blood knots were rushed as I tied on the Invicta and Soldier Palmer. A Black Pennel went on the bob, and I just hoped I wouldn't regret those hurried knots. The fish browsed unconcerned as I waded quietly out until the water was up to my knees. This was no time to worry about wet feet. The noise of the reel check seemed much too loud as I stripped off the line and began the air casts to lengthen my final shoot to the edge of a small patch of weed. A fish came with a rush as soon as the flies landed on the water, but I snatched in my excitement and I never felt him. However, within half an hour I had four plump rainbows on the beach, all between one and two pounds. Expeditions were going to be a highlight of the course for me!

The fish were greeted with great enthusiasm as they came out of the tin foil, and there was a sudden rush of interest in learning how to cast a fly, but it was late and we all went to bed.

Next morning I woke to hear the rain pattering down once more, and with only the food they had caught the previous day for breakfast, there wasn't a lot of spark for the day's walk south to Strathan.

Outside the French tent lay a pool of vomit. Perhaps these weren't the same frogs they were used to eating in France. The team made slow progress up the six-hundred-foot haul from the river to the top of the first hill to the south, and when we gained the top I called a halt. At the rate we were going it would take a very long time to reach Strathan, where we had pre-positioned a supply of food to cover an emergency. I reminded them that while "survival" seems an attractive thing to learn about, in practical terms they must expect it to be an unpleasant experience. They might be finding it hard going, but that morning in Biafra and Vietnam a great many people were doing more work on less food.

The rest of the expedition went well. The practice of looking round to encourage someone feeling worse than yourself helped individuals to forget their own discomfort. They reached Strathan in good time, and with the food they found there inside them, the party had little difficulty in covering the rest of the distance back to the School on the following day.

I felt the expedition had been successful up to a point, but I was keen to increase the mental activity – even if this meant cutting down the distance covered. Too much plodding along watching the heels of the man in front could easily discourage people from taking up walking as a pastime, and this was the reverse of our intention. While sustained physical effort is necessary to achieve a realistic survival environment, mental problems would help maintain the course interest. We made a point of having a de-briefing session at the end of each expedition to reinforce learning and to encourage constructive criticism.

While the courses were running we continued launch trips down to Handa Island from the mooring at the Skerricha end of the loch. Most people who came on the boat were families on holiday in the area who'd seen our sign up at the mail box. The scheme wasn't tremendously successful as our minds were more on the School than anything else, so each trip was more of an exception than the rule. Either Rod, Billy Calder or I would drive the boat, towing an eight-man rubber dinghy for landing purposes.

One day, when Rod was doing the job, a family of six came down the path, and at the last minute the grandmother decided the rocks looked too slippery for her to get down to the shore to board the dinghy. However, when it was pointed out that the trip took three hours or more, she eventually allowed herself to be persuaded, rather than have the rest of the family worry about her sitting back in the car. She was a large lady in her late fifties, and when the launch arrived at the foot of the crofts on Ardmore she sensibly agreed to stay in the boat while the others went off to see the Atlantic dory in its shed.

Rod was explaining how the cooking had been done in the stern of the dory when he heard a thin scream. He ran across the tidal path, up on to the Annait (the green knoll at the far end) and saw the empty launch below. Floating nearby was a brown hat with flowers round the brim, just like Gran's hat in a Giles cartoon. Granny herself was in the water, holding on to a rock under the bows of the launch and looking for all the world like one of the seals in the loch. The horrified family came running up behind Rod, and together they hauled the sodden old lady out on to the rocks and led her shakily into the dory hut. Marie Christine ran down the hill with towels and spare clothes, but nothing would possibly fit Granny, who was showing some signs of spiritual decline by this stage. Rod felt thoroughly embarrassed by the whole thing. The hill was too steep for Granny to get up to the house, so cups of tea and an old green tracksuit of mine were brought down while Rod found a huge khaki greatcoat in one of his trunks. Shortly afterwards the party was shepherded carefully back into the launch and taken back to the far end of the loch where we had built a small wooden garage to keep our car out of the salt spray. While Granny changed into dry clothes brought from their car, Rod told her this was our usual changing room, for at the back of the garage hung my own suit, ready for the next trip to London. Shortly after this experience we abandoned the boat trips to Handa and concentrated on running the School.

Just when we were beginning to worry about how we would fill the courses in the following year, the British Travel Authority decided to bring a party of journalists up from London. It was an inspired plan from our point of view, but what surprised me about the visit was the visible shock those experienced writers had when they saw our house. Men and women who made their living travelling the world couldn't believe people still lived so primitively in Britain and still less could they relate it to their idea of a "celebrity" lifestyle. Perhaps this shock helped them, because they certainly wrote most successfully for us, and soon Marie Christine was flooded by up to sixty enquiries a day.

As our first season drew to a close, we felt confident from the response of the students that we had a good programme and that logistically the School could be maintained, even though things like groceries were coming from more than 200 miles away. With reasonable planning we had no doubt we could hold a month-long Instructors' Course before a season running from Easter to the end of September, if people were willing to come to us. The end-of-the-season dinner was quite a festive occasion, although we were sad to say goodbye to the instructors.

We stored the canoes and sailing dinghies in the dining room, and tents and sleeping bags were hung with the climbing gear from the dormitory ceilings of the main building. *English Rose IV*, the thirty-foot sloop I'd sailed to Brazil the previous year, was brought up the beach on a high spring tide. She sat happily on her bilge keels at the foot of the croft neatly shielded from the easterly winds by the wreck of an old fishing boat called the *Argo* which was ten foot longer than the sloop. Quite suddenly the hubbub subsided, and in its place there came absolute silence; it was as if the courses had been just in our imagination.

3

The last sheep sale ever to be held at Rhiconich, at the head of Loch Inchard, took place on Saturday 13 September 1969. I leaned on the rails on that clear autumn day and watched the white-coated auctioneer rattle through the programme well before mid-day. It was a pretty small sale, even though one or two crofters had taken this opportunity to sell up. In future all sales would be held fifty miles inland, over in Lairg. This was another nail in the coffin for the crofting way of life. The dealers buying the sheep well knew that once in Lairg the cost of transport ensured the sheep must be sold, whatever the price. And no amount of drinking in the Rhiconich bar could hide the sadness of the occasion.

In the afternoon sun, on that same day, we carried old Hector Ross from No.77 gently down the hill on a stretcher. I looked once, quickly, into his bright blue eyes. He looked pale and drawn but his face was as serene as ever, and I wondered sadly what he must be thinking as he left Ardmore after eighty-two years. Hector was the last of the Ardmore patriarchs. The father of nine children, he had done all that could be asked of him to give the place life, like the other crofters of his generation on the peninsula. But times had changed at last, children were now taught to expect a higher standard of living and they went away. Would they live to eighty-two? Would they find the same serenity? Would I?

A month later I stood head bowed, as his coffin was lowered into the sandy soil beside Scourie Bay. No one I've met was more of a gentleman.

Heckie, as eldest son, was now the crofter of No.77, but his heart was not in it. He told me he wished he'd emigrated to Canada when he left the Royal Navy at the end of the Second World War. For Heckie nothing ever quite matched that moment in a Norwegian fiord long ago, when his frigate closed up to "battle stations" and headed towards the German warships lying pinned against the mountains at the head of the fiord. Like most

39

Scots he was a Nationalist at heart, but for him the only real flag was the White Ensign. Heckie loved the sea, and his dog would stand in the bows of his little yellow boat as they headed out into Loch Laxford to haul the lobster creels. Painfully shy he would speak only in monosyllables, and not even that if he could avoid a conversation altogether. Marie Christine said she thought he looked like Gregory Peck, and that would have brought a wry smile to his lips. But after a few drams Heckie loved talking of the past. His boyhood hero was Simon Mackenzie who lived with his sister in No.78. Simon was a great storyteller and Heckie hung on his every word about ghosts and magic powers – he firmly believed Simon to be the illegitimate son of a duke who had moved him to Ardmore from Ullapool to avoid a scandal.

Heckie was already fifty and unmarried when he took over the croft. He had his own chair under the window by the stove in No.77. His back was still bad from a wound received that day in Norway, and he lay almost at forty-five degrees to the ground, with the dog curled up under the table at his side. Heckie smoked heavily and he was already suffering from high blood pressure; and though none of us knew it, this was the cause of the painfully slow way he moved about the hill.

Much of the time when he was out of the house he could be found halfway down to the shore in a ramshackle green corrugated iron hut, surrounded by ropes and lobster creels in disrepair. On Fridays, he and the dog would set off in the boat to pick up the week's supplies from the travelling van which always came to the road-end above Portlevorchy in the late afternoon. Heckie had a rough mooring near where the Portlevorchy wall ran down into the loch. At the van he'd meet up with Donald and Angie Corbett and they'd have a bit of a yarn about sheep, the weather, and such like, and Irwin the van driver would give them the local news. This was all the social contact Heckie had with the outside world. Perhaps this is what made him such a good friend. He never said much and was very much his own man, yet he was very conscious of being part of Ardmore. Sometimes as I climbed the hill to the house, I'd see Heckie high up behind the houses leaning on his stick and looking down at all the activity spread out at his feet. He'd wave back with his stick and then turn wearily upward to make his way out to Ardmore Point, checking his flock, leaving me to wonder what he might have been thinking.

40

After a few drams at the turn of the year, he'd usually come round to saying his thoughts were always of the old days, when over thirty people lived on Ardmore, and the great thing was racing the lobster boats with their dipping lugsail rig out to the creels. Sometimes he'd say the coming of the School had all been foreseen years before by those with second sight. An old lady had seen lines of figures in red and blue on the hillside, and at the time it was said these were British and French soldiers, but Heckie thought they were really the red and blue anoraks of people on the courses at the School in years to come. This sort of thing is easily imagined at a place like Ardmore, where a trick of moonlight in mid-winter can make someone walking along the track swear blind that lights are on in the main School building half a mile away across the loch.

We feared the onset of winter as soon as the courses finished in early September, but this is not really the case. The end of summer is signalled by the first nip of frost, and the hillsides change overnight from light and dark shades of green as the patches of bracken turn red. Foinaven, Ben Stack, and Arkle just inland to our east, and Cranstackie and Beinn Spionnaidh further north, all get their first dusting of snow, but it doesn't last. September and October are the time of heavy gales, mostly from the southwest, which roar over the top of the hill behind the crofts and make it difficult to stand, down on the shore. At this time the houses are nicely in the wind shadow; only the spindrift on the loch below shows the true wind strength. Just occasionally a down-blast will breathe peat smoke from the fireplaces to serve warning of the storm.

But there are many beautiful still days in the autumn too, when the sun, now lower in the southern sky, makes a paler and more delicate light and precise stillness is the order of things. Running alone along the stretch of coast road to the south of Rhiconich on such a still day, the spiky shadows of the rushes invade the rain-whitened tarmac on the coast road, and only the distant coughing roar of a stag in rut disturbs the silence. Nearer home the thunder of the Crocach burn, bursting with brown spate water, is a reminder that the next gale is only hours away.

For me, running has always been the source of original thought. The rhythm of an hour or more alone on the track and empty road from Ardmore to the School, seems to calm troubled nerves and stimulate fresh thinking. My dreaming – that vital ingredient –

41

returns and hope flares up again. The future is an elusive spiritual fourth dimension, part dream and part realism – running imparts the enthusiasm which stops me from giving up on the dreams. Rather childishly, I've always felt that the man who can't cry in the movies never lives.

That first autumn, funds were low, and we tried to add to the larder with things we could catch for ourselves. A seven pound salmon came from the Dionard River on the last day of the season. Then Rod and I were given a few days' stalking on the near end of Foinaven. We were very excited about this, for we needed the meat and we believed we could do the whole job ourselves. Not for us the luxury of stalkers and ponies. We looked on it more as a test of self-reliance.

The western end of Foinaven is only a shade under three thousand feet above the sea, and the walk in from the road starts at two hundred and fifty feet. Two and a half hours of fast going across boggy ground at first, followed by stiff climbing, takes you into the tumble of rocks at the western summit. It's a windy place at the best of times, the home of the eagle and the heavy black raven. Snowy ptarmigan lie low until the last moment, before bursting out like rattling white clouds to startle and confuse the predator. Sheep prefer the grass well below the ridge, but a fox will scramble through the rocks in search of unwary prey. On a clear day the view is unforgettable: seventy miles away off the north coast stand the Orkney Islands; the same distance to the south you can see the northern end of Skye; while half that distance away across the Minch, the Butt of Lewis, that northern tip of the Hebrides, juts into the Northern Atlantic. On the mainland, majestic peaks of the north-west Highlands sprawl to the southern horizon, while at your feet lies a moonscape of hill and loch, silver and grey and brown in all the shades. Far below, at the edge of the sea, the green crofts and white houses of Ardmore look tiny and secure.

It's usually cold on the tops, for the wind is seldom still, and so it's a quick bite at the "piece", and a gulp of hot coffee from the flask, and it's time to move on. A breeze from the south-west is best for stalking on Foinaven. The deer descend into the valleys at night and graze slowly up the sides of the mountain in the morning. From the ridge you're downwind of the beasts as they come steadily up towards you on the southern slopes. Although they are wary animals, they expect danger to come from below rather than above. On top of all this you have the comforting thought that for once in your life you're ahead of the game! The heavy work is done and all you have to do is gather yourself and "get it right first time".

Rod and I had a cut-down sporting version of the old Lee-Enfield Mark IV rifle, the one used by the British in the Second World War. We'd zeroed it carefully at Ardmore on the previous day, and for the shot at the deer we had some soft-nose .303 rounds in our jackets. The mountain slopes south-west in a series of rough steps with small corries gashed into them here and there; each step presents a new skyline to the deer below, so each skyline has to be approached with extreme care. If the deer are frightened off, they may clear the whole mountainside as they go. The area open to us was very small in stalking terms, and one mistake would mean the end of our chances for the day. That was one of the exciting challenges. We had an old Ross telescope with us, and before crossing the skyline we spied out the ground from a sitting position, using a knee as an arm rest, making vertical rather than horizontal sweeps of the ground.

"I've got 'em!" whispered Rod after we'd been moving desperately slowly for almost an hour. I felt a prickle of excitement return, for in spite of the pullover I'd put on at the top I was beginning to feel the cold.

"What like?" I replied, tossing a few blades of grass in the air to check the wind.

"Looks like an old six pointer, standing up – there are a few others lying down, but they're nothing much."

I was already busy looking through the little handbook we'd brought, under the heading "What deer to shoot".

"Well, that seems to be the one to go for: the six pointer standing up," I confirmed.

"OK, let's get back and go down through the corrie on the left – that should get us to within about seventy-five yards from it – I reckon I can get a heart shot from there." Rod couldn't hide his excitement now.

Ten minutes later we crawled up to the skyline from the corrie floor. The stag had moved. Luckily it had come up a bit and was if anything even nearer than seventy-five yards – also it had its head up, and was gazing intently right at us.

"Just keep still. It won't see us if we don't move," Rod hissed.

In our excitement we'd moved a bit too carelessly coming down

43

the corrie. The staring match seemed to go on for ever but in the end the stag lowered its head and began feeding again.

Rod wriggled silently into a prone position, slowly eased his arm through the rifle sling, and inched the weapon back into his shoulder. The stag grazed unconcerned. I watched Rod's left hand tighten its grip and pull the rifle back and down into the shoulder. I thought of the long cold days we'd both spent on firing ranges teaching Parachute Regiment recruits weapon training. There was a quiet sigh as he breathed in and then exhaled. His trigger finger took up first pressure. A giant CRACK shattered the silence – Rod still had the rifle in his shoulder, retaining the aim picture, just as we'd been taught.

The stag dashed forward for a few paces and I thought for a moment that it hadn't been hit. But it staggered, and slowly folded at the knees. Hitting the ground, its neck went slack and the great head rolled over on to its side.

"Well done, Cap," I said quietly. Rod cleared the rifle and we both stood up. The other deer were already clattering away in a line through the rocks below.

We reached the beast about three minutes after it had gone down. It was quite dead, shot neatly through the heart. We turned it so its head was down hill. Then, with his I-XL knife, Rod cut a hole in the lower part of the neck just above the breastbone. The blood ran quickly for about half a minute. Pulling the gullet tube out through the hole in the neck he tied a knot before cutting it; this was to prevent any food from being spilt into the deer during removal of the stomach. He swiftly slit open the abdomen and the whole of the stomach and intestines slid on to the grass, leaving the heart and kidneys in the cavity. Luckily the bullet had not hit a bone and there was little or no damage to the carcass.

The beast was not in prime condition; it had gone back a bit with age and we guessed it weighed around eleven stone all up. The challenge was for us to butcher it on the hill, pack all the venison into plastic bags inside the two Bergen rucksacks, and manpack it down to the Land-rover. It was already three o'clock, darkness would come about five – the situation could be a lot worse. Rod was skilled at skinning and butchering with knife and machete. By four we were on our way, leaving the remains of the animal neatly rolled up in its skin under a rock, where the foxes and hoodie-crows would soon take care of it, just as they did with sheep which died on the hill.

The prospect of winter was not as grim as it had been the previous year. At least the main School was built, and therefore much of the work would be internal decoration, out of the weather.

We were lucky enough to have two real stalwarts helping with the track building from Skerricha down to the School. Donald-Hugh's uncle, Hugh Mackay, was well into his seventies and known throughout the district as Hughie Nedd after his home village away on the other side of the Kylesku ferry. It was as good as being foreign. Hughie had helped build the track to the School the previous year. Before his retirement, he'd been foreman of the County Roads Squad or "Easy Six" as they were known. This nickname came from the popular belief that they were always either going to or coming from somewhere, but never actually doing anything; but I doubt if many of the critics had done much digging themselves. In a sparsely populated area like the north-west, unemployment is high and a place on the "Easy Six" is much sought after. Certainly the nickname owed nothing to Hughie Nedd, who for years had been the foreman of the gang.

"What I want today, boys, is production!" was his daily roadside address, and in some quarters he was still known simply as "Production".

On the School track, Old Murd was Hughie Nedd's sidekick. Murd left all the talking to Hughie. Age and bitter winter weather limited their work schedule somewhat, as did Hughie's other job: the seventy-five mile each way Red Cross Run, ferrying patients by car to and from the cottage hospital over at Golspie on the east coast.

Old Bill of Skerricha was becoming increasingly deaf, and his burly son Donald-Hugh, known as the Gaffer for his powers of direction, assumed responsibility for most of the running of the place. Old Bill's herd of athletic black Galloway cattle spent much of the time decorating the track, or eating the wires of our ex-Army telephone. When they'd had enough "winding slowly o'er the lea" they usually paused for a while to chew the cud, and they found our bright blue running-mooring ropes, out to the boats, quite irresistible. There were also some two hundred sheep which ebbed and flowed along the track at the whim of a pack of keen collie dogs.

The Gaffer was understandably getting pretty sore with strangers knocking on his door at all hours asking if he was John

Ridgway. The only solution was to dig out a gravel car park at the top of the hill above his croft, and put a sign there to direct people to the School via a footpath which would skirt round the hillside, keeping a couple of hundred yards away from the house down at the loch end. This new high path was built by Hughie Nedd and Old Murd, and a grand job they made of it too; as well as clearing the drains and improving the main track along the lochside to the School.

Even on his worst days the Gaffer was a bit careful about throwing his weight around too much with his uncle, Hughie Nedd. But wobblers were his speciality and sometimes I'd walk over after a stormy scene to hear what it had all been about.

"The Gaffer's playing hell again," Hughie would grin, leaning on his huge shovel at the gravel pit in the hillside, and Old Murd would cackle with laughter at the fun of it all. Then they'd spit on their hands and get on as if nothing had happened.

While the Gaffer could be pretty wild after a hard night at the Rhiconich Bar, his generosity matched his huge shaggy frame. "He'd give you the shirt off his back," people said. And we should never forget, it was the Gaffer who'd offered us the site on the edge of the loch in the first place; we never had to ask.

In November Rod and I embarked on another new experience. Lance and Ada Bell were coming to see about a job for Lance. Rod and I were used to dealing with men, mostly in their twenties in the Parachute Regiment, but neither of us had much idea about interviewing a real live adult person for a job. I was thirty-one and Lance Bell forty-nine. I could see he rapidly summed me up as the type who has never had to do a day's work in his life, and nothing would ever change that. Lance had done a day's work all right, every day since leaving school at the height of the Depression in the north-east of England at fourteen. But because he'd never been out of work, he didn't have much idea about what he was looking for either.

The onus was on Rod and me. After a pleasant meal in the kitchen of No. 76 Rod explained a bit about the School and how we'd come to build it, while Lance and Ada sat and listened without saying a lot. I wondered if there was much point in going into any great detail. No fifty-year-old couple would want to come and live in this sort of remote and primitive situation. I just thought they weren't suited. How could they cope with everyone being so much younger than themselves? Surely Ada wouldn't

46

live at Ardmore, after a lifetime spent quite happily in a neat semi-detached with all main services in Thornaby-on-Tees. What about all her friends?

Round the fire after supper, Lance began to explain how he had come to write to me in the first place. A lean, wiry sort of fellow of medium height with a wry grin, his grey hair was fast turning white, and this made him appear older than he actually was. For a man used always to hard manual labour, I thought his hands unusual; they showed the signs of hard usage all right but their shape was more like those of a pianist. When he relaxed, he smiled rather more than he would have wished, for he wasn't really what you would call an enthusiastic sort of man, much more used to pointing out the pitfalls than rushing into things headlong – so why on earth was he at Ardmore on a miserable November night?

Lance had always been around iron foundries, apart from two self-employed years before the war, when he'd made bicycles and sold them under the "Lance Bell" brand name. When war came he found himself in a "reserved occupation", and only with great difficulty did he manage to become an engineer aboard an oil tanker. His one and only trip abroad with the ship took him to Cuba, where he wasn't very impressed with their attitude to life. He'd never been abroad again and never been in an aeroplane. In the foundry he was a moulder, a highly skilled job, and latterly he had been the foreman of some forty-five men in the general engineering department of a Stockton foundry. In his younger days he had been a rebellious sort of fellow with political views pretty far to the left, but gradually he'd found himself swinging further and further to the right. In Lance's view, a man's work was a monument to himself, the thing he should be judged on. At the foundry he'd found himself increasingly at odds with the management. They wanted work done in a time span which prohibited Lance from achieving the standard he needed to find satisfaction in his job. One morning Ada was shocked to find Lance coming back in the door at nine o'clock in the morning – he'd told the manager that if he wanted to get the job done his way, he would have to look for someone else to do it, and with that he'd turned and walked away, after nineteen years, never to return.

By chance he read an article on the School in the *Daily Telegraph*. He'd often brought the family up to Drumbeg for their summer holidays on the other side of Eddrachilles Bay. There was no mention of any employment in the article but he just felt he might be useful. He sat down there and then to enquire if there might be a job. I'd written a short reply and was surprised when I heard back that they would indeed like to come and meet us.

He made it clear that although he could do woodwork and ironwork, he didn't want anything to do with the instructing, neither did he want anyone working under him. He suggested a job building things if the School seemed to be capable of paying for some expansion of facilities, and otherwise maintaining the buildings it already had. The job was to be more or less voluntary for the first season. We'd supply the Blue House for them to live in and all food and fuel. Lance and Ada decided to sleep on the offer, and went off to bed in our spare bedroom over the kitchen, where it was at least warmer than our bedroom at the other end of the house. Before we went to sleep, Marie Christine and I were agreed: they just wouldn't like the place.

Next morning the ground was covered with snow as Marie Christine and I took them up to our pride and joy – No. 80, the Blue House. Compared to our own house, this was luxury. For one thing it had a bath. Lance turned on the hot tap. "It's not very hot," he said, in his blunt way.

I couldn't believe my ears – "Not very hot?" I thought of how long it had taken to carry the cast iron bath up through the wood from the shore. "No, I suppose it isn't," I heard myself reply weakly. But I was thinking if Lance and Ada decided to come to Ardmore, I wouldn't be able to have a nice hot bath at the Blue House anymore, on my way home from the run.

That afternoon we showed them the School, rather as if we had built the Pyramids. Lance wasn't particularly effusive about our achievement; he seemed to see the faults mostly. Ada, neat, particular, and white haired, continued to say very little. They stayed with us for another night, and I could see quite clearly how much we needed them, but not how they needed us.

When Rod came to collect them in the boat next morning they said goodbye, and I wrote in my diary: "They shook hands as if they mean to return!"

The plan was, unless they came to their senses in the interim, they would move into the Blue House in January.

This brought to a head the subject of where Rod and Jeannie should build their house. They had chosen to spend the winter

The only lights around the loch in winter come from Skerricha and Portlevorchy.
Top left, Donald-Hugh Ross of Skerricha, the Gaffer; Angie (top right), Donald and Rubie Corbett of Portlevorchy.

No.80 Upper Ardmore as we found it in 1964, now the Blue House.

Ada and Lance who made it into a home.

in the cabin over at the School to save Rod the daily boat trips across the loch, but the cabin was originally designed as a garage and for three months of the winter the sun never climbed over the hills behind, so it was a cold place of permanent shadow.

At first they were keen to build a timber house on Paddy's Isle at the mouth of Loch a'Chadh-fi, where it enters Loch Laxford. Paddy's Isle, or as the Gaelic has it on the map, Eilean an Eireannaich (Island of the Irishman), is separated from Ardmore by a narrow sound which dries out at low spring tides. The island is half a mile long by a quarter wide, with steep cliffs plunging a couple of hundred feet into the sea on the north side. A once-cultivated valley lies across the eastern end, and the choked drains and overgrown lazy-beds always make me feel it should be brought back to life. High above us as we hauled the lobster creels, wild goats scrambled dangerously along the ledges on the cliffs where the Peregrine falcons nest.

Legend has it that two Irish smugglers stayed at Ardmore one winter at the end of the last century. They dodged the Revenue cutter by slipping out through the sound and hiding among the islands in Laxford until the government men were gone. But the tale ended unhappily: one of the Irishmen fell through the ice on a loch on Ardmore, and his companion fell in while trying to rescue him. They both drowned and were buried in unmarked graves on the island, which was ever after called Paddy's Isle.

Eventually the Liddons decided it was impractical to build a house on the island, so the hunt was on for a better site on Ardmore itself. Level ground, easy access for materials from the sea and shelter from the south-westerly gales: these were three vital factors. We found the third, but had to compromise rather on the first two. The foot of croft No.78 curves around the margin of Bagh an Annait (Bay of the Green Knoll), the shore is well sheltered but access is steep and rocky. The only practical site was on a hillside ledge some thirty feet above high tide. Unfortunately this ledge wasn't really large enough to take a complete house, so some digging would be necessary. While the back of the house would sit on the ground the front would have to be supported by a wall a dozen feet high. It was one of those things which would look nice when it was done but would take a bit of doing – at least forty tons of materials would have to be brought in the little wooden boats from Laxford pier four miles distant. We all gave the project a good bit of thought. The house would have to be built.

In the middle of January 1970 Hughie Ross installed our bath at No.76, as the Blue House's mod cons were about to be handed over to Lance and Ada Bell. When they arrived on 30 January we had a fire going, the beds made, and a fish pie in the oven for them and after a bit of a struggle we got all their luggage up the hill and through the wood. They were keeping their house on Teesside, and their daughter Anne was living in it, so Lance's ancient blue van had brought only essential gear to start with, mostly his proudest possessions – his tools, and these could be left over at the School.

Shortly after they arrived the weather grew colder, and we found a second reason to be glad we had recently manhandled a new bath up the hill to No.76. We were frozen up for fourteen days and we kept the bath topped up with buckets of water from the Rosses' spring. We saw nothing of the Liddons at the School because the loch was frozen, and they were three miles from the nearest phone. Snowdrifts piled up to the top of the fence at the foot of the waterfall and so walking round the loch was only for emergencies. The phone worked intermittently and Mrs Fraser rang to say Willie the Post wouldn't be out. Marie Christine and Rebecca really loved the snow. We had a red plastic toboggan like a tray, and Rebecca squealed with pleasure riding in front of her mother or me. Marie Christine got her skis out. She'd spent a winter at school in Switzerland, so she had little difficulty in mastering the hundred-foot drop to the sea. It wasn't quite the same for me. I became rather tired of hearing "Are you all right?" from my wife. Granny Ross chuckled with excitement watching the skiing, though she thought it would all end in disaster, with one of us in the sea.

The frozen loch cracked round the edges with the changing of the tides, so there was no chance of crossing to the School side, but it did give us a good sight of the otters when they took fish up on to the edge of the ice to play with, like cat and mouse. Darting about on the rocks they look rather like dachsunds at a distance, but they'll run right past a standing gull without causing it to move at all. There is no shortage of otters around Ardmore. They are more evident in the quiet of winter, but sometimes they're surprised among the seaweed by silent canoeists in summer. But I think the best way to see otters is from the cliffs on the south side of Loch Dughaill, where they play on their backs in the pale greeny blue water over the sand.

The only human threat to our otters appears to be from synthetic netting on lobster creels. They are unable to bite their way out when they go in after the bait. But we don't find many drown this way. There are several green patches beside lochan and burn where the otter sits to eat his fish in peace and quiet before sliding down under the water for more fun. These patches, made green by the droppings and fish bones, are often linked by a network of narrow paths through the heather, some shared with the sheep.

After the ice was broken up on the loch by a warmer south-westerly gale in the middle of February, we began to think summer was coming, but it was still a long way off. On the next still clear night, after a day of rain, the ice formed again in the layer of fresh water from the burns which stayed unmixed on top of the salt water from the ocean. The salt water rolls in along the bottom and makes a complete change of all the water in the loch every three days. With the ice went several of our dinghy moorings, for when the wind takes hold of a piece of ice the area of several football pitches none of our moorings can stop it. Too late we found the solution: have sufficient weight on the buoy so that it is just over half submerged when the ice forms. Then when the ice moves, the buoy will harmlessly slide under the surface and reappear when the ice has gone. The snag is that with a good mussel growth the buoy could sink for ever, so the ropes have to be cleaned regularly. Luckily buoys are in plentiful supply along the shores: plastic, metal, iron and even glass floats are always being washed up, along with all manner of plastic containers. Unsightly though plastic is, I always try and calm myself with the thought that it isn't poisonous.

The coming of spring-like weather in March brought the instal-lation of diesel fuel-tanks up at the new car park above Skerricha: red diesel for the boats and generator, and clear derv for the Land-rover. The tanks were a step towards self-sufficiency, for we could now hold a year's supply of diesel. We'd already found that at the first sign of trouble in the oil industry, the road tankers stop coming to Rhiconich with petrol and people's cars are quickly immobilised in the district. We didn't want to be caught out in the coming season.

4

When the parachutes opened over the Dropping Zone in the late afternoon of Friday 13 March 1970, we wanted nothing to go wrong. 216 Signals Squadron of the 16th Parachute Brigade were our first course of the year. Rod and I had trained a team of fit young instructors for a month and we were well prepared. Our luck held.

Pied wagtails and eider ducks signalled the beginning of our first course for twelve to fifteen-year-old children over the Easter holidays. Jim Archer-Burton arrived with a large party from Westerleigh School down on the south coast near Hastings and this was the beginning of an association which was to last for the next decade. The other courses were filling up too, and the instructors were coming together pretty well.

I felt this struggle was the key to my happiness; I had everything I'd ever wanted in life. But what I failed to notice was that the Liddons were beginning to flag. They'd put in a terrific effort, particularly Rod, on the construction of the main building during the winter of 1968 to '69. But the recent winter in the cabin over at the School, with an active young child, had not been easy for them. And their interest in a long-term involvement at Ardmore was beginning to wane. For me there was no question of considering some other job in another place. I'd made as big a commitment as I was ever going to make in my life. I pinned my hopes on them changing their minds.

We were well supported by the County Planning Department who were keen to see some employment breathed back into the dying community, and they did everything possible to speed outline planning permission. Within a few days of it being granted we had the first hundred of the 800 concrete blocks brought over by boat from Laxford pier. The manufacturers of the timber house Rod had chosen were keen to see one of their buildings at Ardmore, as they were confident it would stand up to the weather. Rod's choice appeared perfect: it came as some eighteen tons of individual Canadian red cedar planks and beams – every item could be manhandled by two men working together. The house would be warm, with a good layer of fibre glass wool between two walls of inter-locking vertical planks. Another benefit was the natural fire resistance of the cedar, enhanced with a special varnish; this was especially important as we were on the west coast and the fire engine on the east. For his part, Lance was confident that if the materials were brought to the site, he could build the foundation with a wall of timber-clad concrete blocks rising ten feet at the front and diminishing to one foot against the hill at the back. The supporting concrete block pillars would be linked with shelving to increase our storage.

But first there was the Easter course to run. One morning I took a party of children up the west shoulder of Foinaven. The cloud was low, and snow didn't look far away. It was already lying down to below 1,000 feet. Lance and Ada came with us as we made our way along the route Rod and I had followed to go stalking the previous autumn. The children were not too happy with the wet moorland to begin with, but as soon as we reached the first snow they cheered up and began throwing snowballs at one another. We moved at a steady pace, each encouraging the other to avoid dwelling on his own discomfort. Flasks of tea and sandwiches enlivened the breaks; and hoods, gloves and scarves kept the warmth inside waterproofs, as feet stamped and warm breath rose like mist. But as I'd feared the cloud began to lower rather than rise, and what had been light rain at sea level when we set out was falling now as snow higher up. I looked around at the faces, particularly of the slower ones, and decided regretfully that we must make our way down to the Land-rover. This party just wouldn't make it to the top of the ridge that day.

There was some grumbling as we started our descent, but I could see the weaker ones were secretly rather pleased not to be put to the test. The snow was swirling wetly round us, and we had to be careful not to skid. The passing hours of hard walking and snowfights had now cut the chatter to just the occasional murmur. Everyone knew how far we had to go before we reached the vehicle. New snow had covered our up-coming tracks, but we didn't follow quite the same line on the descent anyway; more important were the ledges which made for easier going. Gradually the cloud became thinner, and we began to catch glimpses of brown moorland, and beyond that the thin ribbon of road, far away across the valley.

We rounded the end of a buttress of rock, and suddenly the air was filled with a clattering crash as a golden eagle took off from a ledge not ten feet from the leading child. We stopped in our tracks, astonished and not a little frightened by the surprise. Then, just as suddenly, it was gone, somehow making the silence even more complete. I asked the children to hold back while I made my way down to where the eagle had been sitting. He'd been eating a late lunch when we surprised him. The whole story was written there in the snow for us: the scrape across the surface as his outstretched talons sliced down on the unfortunate ptarmigan, whose snow-white feathers had not disguised him well enough. The eagle must have swung round the corner of the buttress just as we had done, and his prey never got off the ground. Marks of the impact and the short struggle which followed, were imprinted in the snow; once the ptarmigan was dead the eagle took his time to eat the meal properly. The remains lay neatly plucked and gutted on the ledge, where the eagle had been dining at his leisure as he surveyed his domain below – but not above.

There was a break of a couple of weeks after the Easter course before we began our first efforts at one-week courses for business-men aged between thirty and seventy. We planned to have twenty men on each course and give them something to take their minds right away from their normal lives. Any adult male was welcome, but we called them Businessmen's Courses to avoid giving an impression that anything too physically demanding was involved. It was a new idea, and one on which our reputation was largely to be based in the years ahead. Beginning each Saturday through April, May, June and September, we planned seven-day courses for people who lead fairly high-pressure lives and find it difficult to unwind in a deckchair. Seven days is as long as many people can spend on a holiday without their family, but for that week they could come to Ardmore and spend a week enjoying a whole range of physical activities it would be difficult to pursue with the whole family. We included hill walking, rock climbing, dinghy sailing, canoeing, sailing over to the Hebrides in the yacht, clay-pigeon shooting and fishing. The aim was to make the change as good as a rest, to keep busy from before breakfast until last thing at night, to keep the mind occupied and away from worries about work and the family. Though the programme has varied and the

54

accommodation and equipment improved since those early days the aims have remained the same for the past nineteen years.

Ten men arrived at Laxford Pier for the first of the Businessmen's Courses. The accommodation was simple – two 160 lb. Army tents set up on the sheltered side of Paddy's Isle. A cold water stand-pipe on the island was served by a branch pipe we'd run down the hill and under the sea from the Ardmore supply. This runs right round the hill above the sound on its way from the lochan. Marie Christine and I served breakfast and supper half a mile away in the spare bedroom of our home at No.76.

After everyone had sorted themselves out and had tea, I took the course for a walk out to Ardmore Point before supper. Mostly the men were doctors, solicitors, accountants, that sort of thing, but every so often we had someone quite different – like the man from Colombia. Max was a Rumanian Jew, and he'd spent the War in Russian and German concentration camps. He claimed he kept alive only through bribing the guards with jewelry hidden in his belongings. Years of cutting stone blocks on slender rations nearly finished him off, but the end of the war found him still alive. Immediately, he applied for a visa to the first country which would accept him: Colombia was the only one. At first he got himself into import–export, but the government closed him down, so he decided to concentrate on manufacturing only one thing, household taps, or faucets as he called them. He got the designs from America.

By the time he reached Ardmore, he claimed to be the biggest faucet maker in Colombia. "When you are ze only faucet maker in Colombia – zen you are ze biggest!" he explained. "When someone else starts up – I cut my price by half – and pfff – they are out of ze business."

Max was fifty-two and balding, with a sort of long desperate stride, but the ten cubic feet of stone he'd cut each day in temperatures down to thirty degrees below zero had left him with a wiry resilience. On the introductory walk out to Ardmore Point the weather was warm. The Englishmen were in that relaxed affluent and philosophical frame of mind which was common in the late sixties and early seventies – before the oil crisis came along and reminded us all that life really wasn't going to go on getting better for ever. Max suddenly stopped, and without a word, removed his trousers. The Englishmen looked mildly astonished and sheepishly amused. "Too hot," says Max. "I'll pick zem up on ze way

55

back." By the time we reached the Point, Max had had enough of cosy philosophy. He startled his fellows with his own view of life. "Life is like a baby's nightgown," he insisted, "short and shitty!" We walked on in silence for a bit after that.

The morning lobster fishing with Lance and me was always eventful, even if the lobsters were sometimes scarce. We set off at six thirty. Rain or shine I'd be at the door of the tent to collect the party, and then Lance would take us round the fleet of fifteen creels in the *Ada Bell*. We'd bought this ancient black wooden lobster boat down at Kylesku. It was powered by a trusty Kelvin petrol-paraffin engine of great age, and Lance had put a lot of work into getting it ready for the season. We kept some of the creels off Paddy's Isle. Under the cliffs among the rock falls was a favourite spot, though it could be chilly there, out of the early morning sun. Sometimes we split the fleet, half off Paddy's Isle and half in the small bays out towards Ardmore Point, like Leum a'Choin Deirg (Leap of the Red Fox) and Geodh Creag nan Sgarbh (Cormorant Rock Bay).

Each creel was shot individually: a large flat stone lashed inside its wooden base of slats sank it fast and kept it the right way up. Hoops of hazel from the wood at Ardmore made the frame, and old fishing net covered it. There were two "eyes" for the lobster to enter through, and these projected four inches into the trap, making it difficult to find the way out again. The bait of smelly fish from the brine barrel was held in place between two vertical tightening lines in the centre. The whole apparatus was supposed to have a fatal fascination for the lobster, which had to measure at least nine inches from nose to tail on Lance's board, or be thrown back. Waiting for the creel as you haul it up, seeing its faint outline and straining your eyes for a first glimpse of its contents, is a fresh thrill every time you do it.

Sometimes an extra large lobster is unable to squeeze through the "eyes" to get in at the bait, and as the creel comes up through the water you can see his dark blue shape sitting on top of the netting as he tries to reach the tempting food. The trick then is to slow the rate of hauling and take hold of the creature before it breaks the surface. Once clear of the water, he'll abandon his hold on the net, and shoot down through the sea, rapidly curling and uncurling his tail to propel himself backwards at high speed. However, a firm grip across the back and you have him. No amount of waving his massive claws can raise them along the top

56

of his back to reach your hand. Once in the boat, the claws can be secured with stout rubber bands or line, or immobilised with the point of a screw driver through the muscle, before putting him in a cool damp box in the shade under the bows. If the claws aren't immobilised lobsters try to kill each other in the box.

Until we had enough to sell, we kept our lobsters in a storage box on a sheltered line in mid-water with a depth of some thirty feet. If the box was too near the surface, the layer of fresh water would kill them, and if it was on the bottom crabs would get in and attack them or they could drown in the mud.

The smelly pieces of bait attract more than just lobsters. Usually there are a number of crabs, sometimes the large edible brown kind, but more often the greenish shore crabs, swarming around the inside as the creel is lifted from the water. Spiny stone crabs and hermits in old whelk shells are common too, along with whelks in their own shells, starfish, and sea-squirts, and even sea urchins will fasten themselves to the outside of the netting. But the most unpleasant fellow-occupant of a creel as far as the lobster is concerned, is an octopus. It has the ability to overpower the comparatively clumsy lobster, and then suck all the meat from inside the shell. Lance was never keen on octopuses either; he draped them over the heat-exchanger on the engine to kill them.

Conger eels are frequent visitors, but their size is luckily limited by the creel. A three foot conger is a difficult customer to get out of the small lace-up baiting aperture when it's snapping at everything around it; and once on the floor of the boat it needs a quick club in the stomach to slow it down, for its head seems impervious to blows or thrusts with a knife. Conger steaks made good eating, but we've not had much success with them as bait. Small flat fish squeeze themselves through the "eyes" of the creel sometimes, but they usually fall prey to the crabs once they do get in.

After breakfast if I took half the course sailing, Rod would take the others out to spend the night in yet another 160 lb. Army tent, this time on a spectacular corrie high on the north side of the Foinaven Ridge. The snow still lay in deep cornices around the northern side of the ridge itself, and with the warmer spring weather there were frequent avalanches which often brought debris down the slopes. The first time we tried this excursion, we left the tent erected and well tied down for a week. When the next party arrived they found only wreckage: stout wooden poles splintered, ropes shredded, and the heavy green canvas badly torn. They had a poor night.

One of the advantages of being so far north is that by mid-June it never gets really dark at all, but I found that with the lobster fishing in the early mornings and activities all day, I was pretty tired by evening. Luckily we weren't involved with the lambing as well. Heckie was up at all hours, visiting the ewes all the way out to Ardmore Point. The womenfolk nursed lambs abandoned by their mothers, and these became pets. Heckie's sister, Molly, fed them with a baby's bottle and kept them in the byre. Rebecca thought the whole thing quite wonderful.

For me, the real snag came after supper. The instructors might be tired, but some of the course would still be full of go, and keen to make the most of their week away from the office. Off we would go to some remote inland loch, and sometimes it would be nearly midnight by the time we began to fish. Often it would be almost three in the morning when I finally tumbled into bed. But I love the fishing so. The fellows in the course tent sometimes complained they couldn't sleep for the noise of the oystercatchers, but Marie Christine and I slept like the dead. By mid-June I was becoming so tired that on the expeditions to the Capeside my eyes began to play up in a way I'd never experienced before: towards evening as the light faded I noticed the sky would seem to flicker, particularly if I was on the coast and looking out to sea. On top of this there were the usual financial worries connected with buying new equipment and improving the buildings. All the while, I was hearing a distant call urging me back to the wide open skies I'd known on the long days on the ocean – to a place where everything would be simplified and the job was just to get through each day as it came, where nobody could reach me, for they wouldn't know where I was.

We had agreed to another diversion that summer. The Shelter Charity for housing the homeless was organising a sponsored walk right round the coast of Britain, and we agreed to walk across the top of Scotland for them. The most practical route lay from Golspie on the east coast, seventy-five miles across to Ardmore; and the boys of Dunrobin School agreed to provide the team if we would guide them through the mountains. It was in the preparations for this, at Dunrobin, that I first met Sinclair Mackintosh, the factor of the Westminster estate, just inland of Ardmore.

Sinclair was to become a great friend of ours in the years ahead. The walk was unforgettable: three days in the hills, crossing only one narrow road with a fit party of twenty-seven boys who all made it to Ardmore, where Marie Christine's splendid celebration supper awaited them. My left ankle was hurting badly as we came down from the saddle between Foinaven and Arkle, and next day I was confined to bed with back-ache for the first time in my life – it was not to be the last.

Looking back now, I can see we were all doing just too much in our eagerness to make the School succeed. Perhaps Marie Christine was setting an example we could hardly live up to. For me the cure seemed to be a winter expedition. For Rod, the cure was to quit. He and Jeannie felt they wanted a more sensible life with weekends and holidays to look forward to – something like returning to the security of Army life.

Why I resisted Rod's wish to leave so hard, I'm not sure, but with hindsight I think it was my old insecurity reasserting itself. I was doubtful if I could manage the School on my own. But in the usual way with these things, nothing definite was settled straightaway, and Lance and Hughie built the foundation for the Liddons' house just as soon as the blocks and sand were on the site. By the end of July the eighteen tons of timber were brought over in two separate loads on our four little boats. Two men from the firm who'd supplied the building managed to erect it on the prepared site in just under three weeks, but by that time the Liddons had decided to leave the School and sell the house to me – and in my gloomier moments I feared it was doomed to become just another future bonfire to add to our collection in this remote situation.

The last part of the season at Ardmore was the most taxing. When the main summer courses came to an end on 12 September, we ran the hardest course the School had tried so far. The students were thirty high-potential management executives aged from twenty-one to twenty-eight, and they came from six international companies, under the watchful eye of a training officer from each company. They carried out an exacting mental and physical programme lasting fourteen days, devised largely by the companies between them, but based on elements of the selection process for the Special Air Services which I had experienced myself. My friend, Peter Mitchell, co-ordinated the course with tremendous flair, and to back this up, there was my own staff of eight instructors and a signal network provided by a detachment of fifteen soldiers from the 14th Light Regiment, Royal Artillery.

With Rod now away, I felt I was going through one of the last stages of growing up. Feelings of insecurity and a lack of confidence, useful spurs in some circumstances, finally had to be confronted. Unfortunately, parting with the Liddons seemed to harden my resolve to stand independent of anyone else but Marie Christine, and regrettably I began what was to become a long separation from my adoptive parents. The Scots have a word for it – thrawn.

I was thirty-two and the future of the School depended entirely upon the direction I gave it – but how lucky I was to have Marie Christine's support. We were both well aware that any mistakes would be our own personal responsibility. As these mistakes involved many other people's safety, I felt the weight of responsibility keenly. The burden of it is not easy to express in words, but with the passing years and the mathematical narrowing of the odds against an accident, it took an ever-increasing toll of my energy. Attention to detail is of paramount importance, and the meticulous checking of people, machinery, and programmes were to cause much loss of sleep in the early hours of many a day. "Have some faith," people would say optimistically, but experience had taught me to try and cover every eventuality – many of my more optimistic friends in the Parachute Regiment were already dead.

There were, however, a couple of bright spots to relieve the considerable gloom. The first was that Lance and Ada had agreed to stay on for the next season. Lance had worked like a Trojan ever since his arrival and made himself indispensable. And Ada had become such firm friends with Rebecca that our daughter now seemed to spend more time up at the Blue House than at home. The second gleam of optimism was that my dream of a winter expedition was becoming a reality.

5

During my fifty days alone on the sailing voyage which had ended two years earlier in Brazil, I had dreamed up the idea of trying to live two separate lives, spending half the year in each. The attractions were obvious. One would complement the other. The summer would be for Ardmore. But winters should provide a contrast. I must avoid falling into a rut and wasting my life, that bonus of time Chay and I had been given when we survived the Atlantic row. Each winter, I planned to make a "Journey", either mentally or physically, to broaden my experience of life.

Landing in South America had been entrancing after fifty days alone in the thirty-foot sailing boat, and after two ocean trips I now wanted to try a different element. So crossing South America seemed a good start.

The plan was to be the first expedition to trace the course of the Amazon from its furthest source in the Peruvian Andes for some 4,000 miles to its mouth at Pará Belém on the eastern seaboard of Brazil, a mouth so wide that if you translated it into European distances, one shore would be in London and the other in Paris. The Amazon lends itself to extravagant statistics. The sights and sounds, and above all the savage rawness of the vast areas away from the main thoroughfare of the river itself, these are the things which fulfilled the yearnings I had had at Ardmore for some experience to parallel the wide open skies I'd known on the Atlantic Ocean.

There were four of us on the trip. John Cowie, whose phone call had jerked the notion into reality, I had known very slightly when we were both subalterns in 3 Para. He wanted to take a camera down the Amazon in order to compile a professional portfolio and then to set up as a photo-journalist. Being London based, he was also ideally placed to bear the brunt of most of the organisation while I was fully committed at Ardmore. John recruited another ex-Para, Sergeant Sean Macdermot, now with the Royal Army Medical Corps. From what little background reading I was finding time to do at Ardmore, I could immediately see the advantages of taking along a trained medic. Snakes, insects, fish, disease, Indians, the river itself, all seemed to be queuing up to finish us off. Mac was a heavy smoker who had swum for the Army. He always insisted he did his best times at both breast stroke and butterfly if he could nip away for a quick fag before the event. But his obsession with water purification and the range of equipment he insisted we carry in place of extra rations certainly paid off, as not one of us suffered from any form of stomach upset in a country where dysentery is endemic.

The fourth and final member of the team was also found by John at the Berlitz language school where he was painfully trying to acquire some Spanish. Anna Asheshov, a British champion skier, was also a fluent Spanish speaker whose brother, Nick, happened to be editor of the *Peruvian Times*. He would be able to provide us with a most useful starting point in Lima. The advantages of including Anna were obvious to John and me, less immediately so to Marie Christine who would be staying at home with Rebecca. The fact that Anna was twenty-nine, slim, long legged and fair haired may have had something to do with it, and the enthusiastic response of the newspaper we were sending reports back to didn't help much either. They were quick to see possibilities along the lines of "Three married men and an unmarried girl find themselves together in the high Andes and the steaming jungle of the Amazon – all four complete strangers to each other. Follow next week's gripping episode . . ."

I had only met John Cowie on three brief occasions, I hadn't met Mac the medic, and Anna flew off to Peru before I reached London at the end of the season.

However, this was part of my plan. As an extension of what I had learned about myself in the Army, on the rowing and sailing alone, I wanted to try and develop my own particular style of leadership. Although still childish (hopefully for ever), I knew well enough that I wanted more than to be just an observer/writer. I wanted the action itself.

In planning this expedition, I had decided the less the four individuals knew about each other the more interesting it would be, like being the only survivors of a plane crash. I was pretty confident of my ability to manage a team of four strangers. But on our arrival in Lima it soon became clear that John, Mac and Anna were three strong personalities who were used to working individually. They were all achievers. They expected success and were impatient for it.

We were to be tested soon enough. The tributary of the Amazon we were going to follow out of the Andes was the Apurímac, which is Inca for Great Speaker. The name served early warning of the power and frequency of its rapids. In the first tumbling 600 miles the river falls 16,000 feet. We were soon all suffering from altitude sickness, and the pressure of keeping ahead of the rains, when the river would be impossible for us, made for ragged personal relations. The mountains were desolate places, the haunt of the condor with its twelve-foot wingspan. We saw herds of alpaca and flocks of pink flamingoes. The Quechua Indians complained of mountain lions attacking their llamas. Bandits were always a threat, and we carried Chinese firecrackers to sound like rifles if we should be attacked, as we could not afford the weight of the real thing and ammunition.

Two 15,000 foot mountain ranges and five days' walk from the nearest track, we descended into an area where the maps showed only empty spaces. They made no mention of human habitation, and as we could carry only limited supplies on our backs, we constantly worried about running out of food.

We were now in what the Quechuan Indians call the Eyebrow of the Jungle, where the green tentacles of the jungle reach up towards the startling white of the mountain glaciers. The Indians warned us that in another two days we should arrive at "the home of the German", a very private man who discouraged visitors with fearsome little Campa Indian guards from the deepest jungle. Laughingly, we imagined meeting Hitler, and the size of the barriers placed across the narrow forest path and the snarl of the huge dogs as we approached Hacienda Osambre, certainly encouraged the illusion.

Señor Berg was no Hitler, but a lightly built figure in his mid-sixties, clad in faded brown denims, who seemed somehow to be expecting us. Grizzled fair hair gave the clue to his Norwegian father. Berg's mother had been a Quechua Indian, as was his wife, who had borne him five sons and a daughter with no medical assistance besides Berg's own care. Around 1945, he had abandoned civilisation to carve himself a farm from the jungle, where he struggled to become totally self-sufficient. The concept seemed curiously similar to my own dreams for Ardmore, and I felt strangely drawn to Berg from the start, but when I entered his idyllic jungle stronghold above the Apurímac River, that day in late 1970, I had no idea of the extraordinary link our families would form fifteen years later.

The red mud huts formed a square, almost fortress-like compound against the jungle. But inside, the white-washed walls bore neat little notices extolling the need for greater agricultural efficiency. As well as abundant fruit, Berg produced coffee, yucca, sugar cane, soya and maize. His yard swarmed with fowl, pigs, and cattle. The jungle teemed with game, and the river was full of fish, easily dried for storage.

Berg's adversaries were the jaguars which preyed on his cattle, and to tend the herd, he employed a Campa Indian family. Short, lithe and coal-black, the Campas are wary of the outside world. Dressed in one-piece black sack-like garments which they spin from wild jungle cotton, they live a nomadic existence, burning a patch of jungle to plant soya, and then moving on after the harvest.

The Campa family greeted Señor Berg with childlike enthusiasm, and we sat drinking yucca beer, which the wife had made by chewing the root and spitting it into an empty gourd (it was her saliva which caused it to ferment), while the husband showed his bow and the different types of arrow he used for fish, birds, and small and large animals.

"This is the fellow who warned me of your approach yesterday," smiled Berg, as the Campa fingered an arrow with a flame-hardened head, over a foot long. "They always aim at a man's back, and usually the blade sticks out of the chest."

Señor Berg used the Spanish word *tranquilo* to describe his life-long search for peace of mind. Campas from the deepest jungle had come nearest to it, he felt, and sophisticated Europeans were most distant. Thinking back to the purity of life on the rowing boat, the simplicity of the early days at Ardmore, I felt most strongly that the Campa "is", whereas the modern European only "has".

But it was Berg's eldest son, Elvin, whom I came to know better. Elvin was twenty-two then, a fine upstanding young fellow with plenty of spark. Never without his battered pith helmet and precious hunting rifle, he'd already killed fifteen of the marauding jaguars. When at last we had to leave Osambre, it was Elvin who offered to come on down the river as our guide. He led us through dense jungle, warning against stinging plants and vicious insects

Mrs Bell's Academy for Young Ladies – school days at the Blue House for Rebecca and Ada.

Lance working on the rudder of *English Rose VI* off the pier at the foot of our croft, No.78 Lower Ardmore.

Rebecca on the way home from school through the wood.

True grit – one of the Ladies.

Elan – Krister Nylund aboard *English Rose V*.

The Foinaven Ridge.

by day, and vampire bats, which would suck our blood and leave us with rabies, by night. He knew everyone along the way, and helped our Para medic Mac with the dispensing of medicines to sick children.

When eventually we arrived at the first navigable point on the river, Elvin impulsively agreed to come still further with us, acting as look-out in the bow of the forty-foot canoe as we hurtled down through the rock-bound torrent. He joined us on the chain, when we strained to control the fragile craft, lowering it through the edge of the rapids. These were dangerous days, filled with action, and by the time we reached the Benedictine Mission at Granja Sivia, Elvin had long since become a close personal friend. When he had to turn upriver for home, I gave him my watch, and promised to return one day. I wrote in my diary: "At the end of my life, there will still be Bergs at Osambre – just as there will be Ridgways at Ardmore."

Fifteen years later I was to return to the Apurímac, to search for Elvin in a guerrilla war, and though I had learned from the rowing that things seldom turn out as you expect, I could never have imagined the outcome of the search.

The only way downstream from the Mission was on a balsa log raft we had to build for ourselves. At night we slept on islands because we feared what might come on us on the banks. Forty-foot anacondas had been recorded, and the Indians were full of stories of their hypnotic luminous eyes and foetid breath, while lonely Franciscan missionaries vouched for the vampire bat's preference for the hairline and the exposed big toe, when they attacked the sleeping traveller by night.

Our raft provided comparative silence, a rapid floating island twenty-four by ten foot long. We built a leaf-thatched roof for shelter from the burning sun, as we were by now only twelve degrees south of the equator. For fear of rapids, we kept close in to the bank. Insect, bird and animal sounds throbbed in tune with the drumming heat. Once we passed another Campa family, painfully poling a dugout canoe upstream through the shallows. They had a gaudy macaw parrot in a crude twig and vine cage, which they were taking to sell in a village upstream – the first stage perhaps of the poor creature's long journey to a caged life in somewhere like Surbiton on the banks of the Thames.

We whirled on, sometimes through narrow black gorges with cliffs rising a thousand feet or so from the water's edge, never quite certain if we should come to a waterfall or not. As a child, a recurring nightmare of mine had been that of canoeing on a river and finding falls round the next bend. In adult reality, the first warning of rapids was a distant rumbling and a sound like breaking bones as millions of pebbles rolled over one another under the raft. And there really was always a hint of fear as we approached the next bend in the river, for without a motor, we could only guide the raft in a general direction. We couldn't stop, except by running aground.

But we managed to negotiate the rapids, and with time we became over-confident. We even took on board a crippled Campa child and his father, offering to take the boy 150 miles downriver for treatment at Atalaya, the next mission village.

Our undoing came the day after we'd celebrated being only one day from Atalaya, where we planned to board a river-boat, since there were no rapids below the village. Up ahead we heard the sound of water thundering over a reef, and in clearing that, we misjudged the situation completely. The real threat was making no sound at all – an ugly bulge marking a rock just under the surface. We ran right on to it. The front of the balsa raft rose high into the air, and as the back swung round in the current, the left-hand side was pinned under the surface. A wall of creamy brown water overwhelmed the raft. The shelter went for good. Anna went over the side with a wail of horror, but Mac grabbed her left ankle and pulled her back inch by inch. Practically all our kit was gone, Anna's expensive cameras drifted rapidly out of sight, floating high on the water in their elegant aluminium case. Patricio, the Campa boy, looked terrified. The raft was at an angle of thirty-five degrees and seven of the ten balsa logs were held under water by the flood.

I felt that fleeting moment of relief which always ends the tension of waiting for something to go wrong. Now all we had to do was find a way out of our predicament. We had six hours to nightfall and the river was some 300 yards wide. The current roared like a runaway express. The nearest bank was only thirty yards away and our best swimmer, Mac, eventually swam ashore to seek help, clad only in his Army Dracula-green underpants. On the raft we just waited. The coal-black face of the crippled Campa boy's father was square and primitive, his eyes, ears and nose reacted to every subtle sound or movement. Suddenly he uttered a grunt, "Campa." Then we all saw them, three dugouts poling up against the current, with Mac waving from one of them.

We spent that night in a Campa village. Too nervous to do anything but please the unpredictable Indians, we ate the dish of fish they offered us whole, in the Campa style: heads, tails, insides and everything. And we washed it down with grubby-looking beer, which we knew had been fermented from roots chewed by the heavily pregnant female who was watching us so intently.

Next day the Campas paddled us all the way to the jungle village of Atalaya in their simple dugout canoes. Once through the last of the rapids between us and the far-distant sea, I was filled with a wonderful calm sense of peace and love for the world. We had emerged from the mountains of the "Eyebrow of the jungle", and the river could slumber and slide undisturbed on its way to the ocean. Banks of gleaming white shingle changed to bright green grass backed by the bottle green of the jungle. As we neared Atalaya in the early evening, the Campas suddenly seemed shy and out of place, as if sensing they were coming into the "gringos'" own special type of jungle and they wanted to be gone – back behind the safety of their rapids.

For me the expedition really ended there at the barrier rapids above Atalaya. The thousands of miles which followed, travelling in big boats and small, was an interesting experience; Marie Christine flew out and joined us in Iquitos for the remainder of the trip down to Belém, and this made it all much more fun. But I was impatient to get back to Ardmore – my time with the wide open skies had come to an end.

6

Soon after arriving home at Ardmore we went next door to have tea with Granny Ross. She was in good spirits, but the arthritis in her hip was keeping her in the big brown armchair by the stove for most of the time. She and Molly were delighted to see Becca who had been staying with her grandmother in the South, and even Heckie managed a few shy smiles of pleasure. I looked fondly round the room. The clock was ticking away on the sideboard, just as I'd remembered it far away in Peru, and no, the Westminster chimes weren't working any better now. The white paint on the grooved pine matchboard wall lining was yellowed by the peat smoke. In the centre hung a framed cutting from the *Daily Express* of 1937. It was an artist's impression of "The liner *Queen Elizabeth* – as she will look when she is launched." This was the only change in the room. When we'd left in the autumn, it had been the turn of the other favourite to take pride of place, a colour print of Turner's "Last voyage of the Fighting Temeraire". The familiarity of the room, the ticking of the clock, and the taste of the tea from the pot on the stove. It all meant so much to me.

Our friend, Old Bill Ross of Skerricha, had died while we were away, and so now his son Donald-Hugh really was the Gaffer on the croft at the inland end of the loch. And while we weren't so desperately sad to hear that he had decided to sell the rope-chewing black Galloway cattle, we'd sorely miss the cheery crack from Old Bill on the bad days. On a grey winter's day with the loch dark as slate and the mountains hidden in cloud, realising that everyone around the loch was either old or dead, this sometimes weighed like a heavy load on my back.

At least Hughie from next door was doing well at the lobsters. He was catching eight to twelve a day from his black twelve-foot yawlie out on the open coast around Ardmore Point. For easier access to his fleet of creels, he was now keeping the boat at the inner end of Loch Dughaill, where the winter swell rolls straight in from Greenland 1,500 miles away to the north-west – Hughie was pinning a lot of faith on his trusty Seagull outboard motor.

Ada had been dealing with the mail in our absence, but now a postal strike had paralysed everything just at the time when we should be getting our greatest number of bookings for the next season. The Amazon and carefree days in the high Andes now seemed far away, and economic pressures bore down again. The Inland Revenue had written with some routine enquiries during our absence, and in the rush I'd forgotten to ask Ada to send all financial correspondence to our helpful accountant Gordon Stewart in Inverness. The suspicions of the Revenue were first aroused when Ada replied telling them I had "gone to South America"; they persisted, wanting to know how to reach Mrs Ridgway. Ada sent their letter down to Marie Christine in Brighton, where she was staying with her mother, but by the time it arrived there, she had left to join me on the Amazon. The Revenue weren't at all happy to hear from Ada that Mrs Ridgway had now also "gone to South America"; and they wasted no time in sending a third letter demanding to be put in touch with whoever was dealing with our financial matters immediately. Ada was more than a little concerned by this stage, and she straight away sent the unpleasant letter down to Gordon Stewart; but now the postal strike had swallowed the whole affair, and I could only wonder what the Revenue men must be thinking about "Captain" Ridgway as they persisted in calling me.

Inevitably there was a feeling of anti-climax after we returned from the Amazon, just as there had been after the rowing and the attempt to sail round the world. Huddled in front of the kitchen stove after supper one night at the end of January, we discussed the idea of making another winter trip to the southern hemisphere summer the following year. This time we would both go, to Patagonia, at the southern tip of South America, where the Andes run into the Southern Ocean.

Life at Ardmore had certainly altered the expectations of the secretary from the Arts Council whom I'd married seven years before. At least it was a healthy kind of seven-year itch. Again it confirmed my feeling that people are able to adapt to changes in their situation much more readily than they fear. So much is not achieved because of people's lack of self-confidence. Marie Christine could have quite happily settled down with someone with a job in London, and Surrey would have suited her fine. At Ardmore, her high-speed typing is a tremendous asset with the office work, but cooking had barely entered her idea of things when she had her flat in London. Before the cooking can begin at Ardmore, stores have to be ordered over the phone from the wholesaler 200 miles away; there is only one delivery a fortnight, and mistakes are costly if it comes to buying for eighty people from the village shop at Rhiconich, which gets its own supplies from the same wholesaler. Mistakes could work the other way, though, like the time when Marie Christine ordered six-dozen doughnut rings from the baker in Inverness. They left six gross instead: in, around, and on top of the mailbox. But we did manage to eat 864 doughnut rings all the same, though some were perhaps a little disguised.

The actual cooking is another matter. Marie Christine put two normal household Calor gas cookers side by side and just got on with it. I've always tried to tell her I only married her in the first place on the strength of an inexpensive fish pie she cooked one night in London. But now, with the best of fresh fish from the pier at Kinlochbervie she soon showed everyone that cooking for eighty people wasn't going to prevent her from producing dishes an awful lot more fancy than just more fish pies. During the first season we had the course over to our croft for the evening meal. There were always two sittings of forty in a tiny candlelit room only thirteen feet square. The two silver-plate candelabra had been given me by the Parachute Regiment after the rowing, and I'm rather proud of them; luckily the flames from the candles didn't burn too high the night a girl fainted in the far corner of the room and had to be passed from hand to hand to the outside door for a bit of fresh air.

Marie Christine and I had always agreed that we didn't want to become the 134,383rd largest corporation in the world, but we could only find satisfaction if we were genuinely striving to build the School into the best of its kind. In Lance and Ada we had found two skilled perfectionists. Although he'd hardly ever admit it, Lance really did rather like Ardmore, with all its need for self-reliance; like most people he felt it important to be needed, and he'd certainly come to the right place for that. He lost two stone during his first season, and among a host of other things that winter he fought a war against the ever-bursting plumbing, dug wiring from under the snow, persuaded the ancient generator to work at the School, and installed lighting in the main building. Facing the inside of the septic with cement after it had been

70

in use for a season was one of his more memorable projects.
"Retirement, you say? I'd call it more like a very cold Burma
railway!"

Ada helped Lance at Ardmore and the School by painting
everything in sight. She kept the Blue House like a new pin. It
was she who made the cupboards-full of home-brew in the old
screw-top bottles from Middlesbrough, which everyone thought
Lance made. But there was never any doubt she made the Yorkshire puddings we'd have before the main meat course for our
supper, when we walked over the top of the hill at the back of
the houses and down to the Blue House. Coming back through
the wood in the dark with a failing torch, we more than once
tumbled down into the trees – but that was the home-brew not
the Yorkshire puddings.

At last there was a bit of a thaw, and we got the first running
water in the croft since returning from the Amazon. Soon after
that, at the end of February, Richard Shuff arrived to take up his
new post as chief instructor. I'd met him a few years previously,
while he was active in the TA Special Air Service. He'd done well
as an instructor the previous season, had a good knowledge of
the local area and plenty of experience at all the activities we
taught, but his main asset was his personality. Richard was the
sort of fellow the young and homesick always took to be their
friend. Perhaps he was at his best as a teacher, when his obvious
sincerity and patience and his self-deprecating smile beneath a
shock of brown hair won over even the most sullen teenage rebel.
Richard settled straight into the business of preparing the set of
lectures we planned for the first week of the month-long Instructors' Course which we always run in the cold days of March.
The potential instructors arrived and the new season was under
way.

One stormy evening, when a cold north-west wind was blowing
flurries of snow round the crofts, there was a rough knocking on
the door – we were just getting the supper ready and couldn't
believe anyone would be coming out along the path on such a
night. I went out into the porch, and the light from the Tilley
lamp in my hand showed two wild-looking fellows on the other
side of the glass. I recognised one of them as a fisherman from
Kinlochbervie, and as soon as they came through the door, I could
see they were soaked to the skin. "We kinda had an accident,"
one of them laughed gruffly. "The rudder broke. We came into

Loch Dughaill with the wind – steering with a floorboard – then we beached her down there on the bay on the north side. There's a little black boat in there too," he added.

"Yes, that'll be Hughie – next door's," I replied. "Come on in – we'll run you a bath, and you'd better ring home and let them know you're safe."

John and George Morrison were lucky to be alive. Their lobster boat was very small, with a tiny wheelhouse – more like a sentry box – perched right on the stern. With darkness drawing on, the weather had suddenly worsened, and they'd been caught out as they were hauling the last of their creels out among the Black Rocks – a good place for lobsters, but a bad place for boats. The rudder had gone just at the worst moment for them. There was nothing for it but to run before the wind, away from home and without a radio. Loch Dughaill lay ahead. If it had been a straight stretch of exposed coast who knows what might have happened. Not long before, a father and son from Tarbet, the little village beside Handa Island, had heard a gale warning on the radio and gone out to take in their creels before the storm. Their engine failed and before they knew it they were on the rocks. Like most local fishermen they couldn't swim, preferring a quick death by drowning to a lingering death in the icy water.

The coast has seen plenty of wrecks, but not much in the way of salvage. Vessels going ashore are quickly smashed by the seas, rough weather and strong tides. More than one of the sturdy sixty-foot timber seine netters has shouldered its way through the steep winter seas, only to have the diesel engine suddenly go clean through the bottom, with the boat following it down within seconds. For a lobster fisherman, who must always be near the rocks, a rope round the propeller is the greatest fear, but losing the rudder is enough to send shivers up my spine. The Morrison brothers had been blown helplessly past Rubha Sgeir a' Bhathaidh (the point of the Skerry of Drowning), out on the northern side of the entrance to Loch Dughaill. It was there that a family of crofters from Kinlochbervie had died when their boat, full of seaweed for the croft, had foundered on the way back from Ardmore. The brothers looked shaken at supper, but they wolfed down a hearty meal and went off to bed fairly early, leaving Marie Christine and me in the kitchen to reflect on what it would be like to rush up Loch Dughaill in the cold darkness before a gale, with no rudder save an old piece of floorboard. I could see it all too clearly.

The Instructors' Course went well. Lectures are reinforced with much practical work at a time of year when every mistake meets with discomfort; capsizing a dinghy is something which encourages skill at keeping from overturning. Night compass marches, alone, bring home the importance of getting things right first time. Trips along the Foinaven Ridge before the snows have cleared transport the would-be instructor into an Arctic world for a day, consolidating "Theory of hill walking and mountain safety" with some firmness. A voyage to the Hebrides on the yacht develops an association with a black plastic bucket below decks for some, while others, finding themselves impervious to sickness, may be selected as crew for voyages to St Kilda and the Faroes. The University degree, which once seemed so all-important, pales a bit when padding five miles through the snow in the half-light of dawn, with Marie Christine's back some way further up the track, and the distance widening. That, too, has been enough to send more than one likely lad scuttling back to the soft under-belly of the South, and the fellow who was so convincing on interview in London looks a deal less effective than another who was shy and inarticulate in the city, but finds that deeds are more valuable than words in some situations.

But the real heart of the Instructors' Course is the team-building. Young men and women who nervously glance around the buffet in Inverness station, then again on the train to Lairg, and finally identify the other members of the team on the mailbus to the West Coast, find themselves thrust into a way of life which will absorb all the waking hours for the next seven months – and from the nightmares, it seems some of the sleeping hours too. The first couple of days can show gaps in the armour of self-reliance. There are those who think that dishwashing, bed-making and clothes washing are things done by Mother and a machine. Sweeping a floor is suddenly made to look like a method of spreading dust into the air instead of the dustpan, and Lance goes about muttering darkly that "Them young buggers 'ave never done a day's work in their lives." Paint merges in dribbles of red, white and blue on the boats, and brushes are found stiff and uncleaned – another Congo Hamilton ruined. The intense young Socialist from South Wales, keen to practise man-management for a year between school and university, just can't stand the fellow in the bunk

73

above him whose Daddy drives a Bentley around Guildford. But alone together on a pitch dark night in the middle of seventy-five square miles of wilderness by Cape Wrath, they discover they have much in common. We have found personality more import-ant than a great knowledge of clog bongs and chocks and pitons, and the fellow who has already persevered sufficiently to pass the entrance exams for university is more likely to succeed at Ardmore than a drifter with some vague notion of "changing the world" but who can't stand the people in it.

Richard Shuff had spent the winter cutting bananas on a kibbutz in Israel, where he'd befriended a young Swede by the name of Krister Nylund. At six foot two, with the easy grace of a good middleweight, and a huge blond Afro hairstyle, Krister created quite a stir in Lairg, as he waited for his friend to pick him up in the Land-rover. What he'd missed on the Instructors' Course, he more than made up with his enthusiasm and charm; a fervent pacifist he'd come to Scotland rather than return to his homeland for the draft – or another stint in the aluminium smelter in Sundsvall. At nearly four, Rebecca thought Krister was wonderful. She'd never seen anyone who could do a standing jump over a fence keeping both legs together.

The Easter courses came and went, wrecked by the mail strike. We were given a fine "Shetland Model" boat with a lugsail rig by a man in Suffolk who'd enjoyed reading my book *Journey to Ardmore*, and Richard and I had towed it all the way up on the trailer.

Then we sold our ex-RAF launch to a road-haulier from Conon Bridge and looked for a suitable boat to become the flagship of the dinghy fleet, something with an inboard motor which could be the safety boat in case of capsize among the smaller boats. In a cupboard I came across a simple brochure for a traditional wooden clinker built "Shetland Model". It looked just the thing and was bigger than the one from Suffolk, but the problem was, I'd picked the leaflet up at the London Boat Show ten years before. Nevertheless I called the operator and asked her to try and connect me with the number in Hamnavoe in the Shetland Isles. Old Walter Duncan came on the crackling line. He was rather deaf and said he was in his seventies, but he chuckled when I told him about the boat we were looking for. "My wife's just read an article in one of her women's magazines about Ardmore. I'd be more than pleased to build a boat for you," he said. "Of course I'm

74

getting on now, as I told you, reckon I've got more boats to build than I've got years left . . .''

The upshot was a fine boat, made from a rough pencil drawing sent in the post by Walter for approval and then built by eye and very good hands. She was shipped to Aberdeen and from there she came up on an empty fish lorry. Nineteen foot of pleasure, we called her *Rebecca*. She was built after the style of the old Viking four-ern, and although sudden lack of funds prevented us from having mast and sails made for her that first year, Walter kindly sent another sketch for Lance to build from the following year. Her tan lugsails have graced Laxford ever since. I tried to get Walter to build us another sister ship, but he was right, he hadn't enough years left.

One afternoon in that summer of 1971 the telephone rang in the croft. It was Chay Blyth speaking to me from his yacht, *British Steel*, in the Bay of Biscay. He had been alone for 285 days and was nearing the end of the first non-stop single-handed voyage round the world against the prevailing winds – I was filled with envy, and thrown into turmoil again. This was a different feeling from the need to get out to the Amazon, it was more the waking of a bogey. I had really hated my fifty days alone on the yacht which ended in Brazil. Tensions within me brought me to tears on almost every single one of those days. But at the back of my mind I knew I could never be at peace with myself until I had obliterated that failure with another achievement. It had been heady stuff for both Chay and me to row across the Atlantic, but there is a price to pay for everything, and to have rowed the Atlantic meant a lifetime of being introduced: "Have you met John Ridgway? He rowed across the Atlantic, you know."

This is an effective conversation stopper, and nine times out of ten the response is "Oh. What are you going to do next?" So I've found myself on a sort of roundabout of other people's expectations at a rather superficial level. With my broken-up face, strangers would say how tough I looked, but I could always assure them the man they really wanted was the fellow who did it to me. The aftermath of the rowing unsettled me. While I loved to hear the sound of the applause, the limelight burned rather than warmed me, and I seldom felt at ease with myself. Marie Christine disliked the glib veneer I developed to cope with the unaccustomed pressures of public engagements and lecture tours for the Army, and the failure to achieve another success in 1968 still rankled in my mind, just as I imagine it must have done with Chay.

Now, here was Chay, having laid the bogey for ever with a colossal voyage round the world against the wind – what everyone else had thought of as an impossible voyage. It speaks volumes for my own shallowness that I should think everything else counted for nothing, and that I must mount some similar exploit of my own. It was something which was to haunt me for more than long enough. I have always seemed to need to invent worries if I run out of real ones. Life at Ardmore could offer sufficient problems to keep five men happy. But I couldn't settle for that – there had to be some giant concern to wake me up in the middle of the night, or I felt I was just wasting time.

By the autumn we had completed our third season at the School. The BBC television film *Journey to Ardmore* had produced a rush of interest in the one-week Businessmen's Courses. 1972 was going to be a big year for us; we wanted to make some improvements in the facilities, and we had the coming winter to put them into effect. Lance and Hughie were doing great works in the cedarwood house, down by the edge of the loch. Since the Liddons had left it had undergone a complete conversion, with a large open-plan dining room overlooking the loch and the mountains beyond. There was a small kitchen for Marie Christine, as well as six bedrooms of various sizes, showers and wash-basins. The days of the tented camp on Paddy's Isle were over. The Businessmen's Courses would be housed in future in the Wooden House and a selected "few" would share with the Atlantic dory the pleasures of the "Museum", which, with its bunk-lined walls, now assumed the atmosphere of an accommodation hut during the Battle of Britain. Barging in, clutching the teapot in the early light of dawn, my cry "Cuppatea, cuppatea!" sounded to some rather more like "Scramble!" for the early morning run.

At a dispersal sale on the east coast Lance and I bought nine small timber huts of various sizes, including a fire station, for £500. At last we had a stock of good huts for stores and instructors' summer accommodation. The winter saw me become Lance's "marrer" as we dug down through the peat in search of hard for foundations. Tons of gravel and sand were recovered from the beaches at low tide, and the bubble on Lance's level seemed always to be finding out the poor quality of my work at concrete block laying. However, I got higher marks for tea-making during

76

snow showers, and the concrete set, even though the work was carried out at temperatures perilously close to freezing.

Communications between the School, over at Skerricha, and Ardmore had for the first three years been by ex-Army tele-L sets, bought from a surplus store in London. A caller from the School would vigorously wind the handle on the side of his set, sending a signal along the wire running for three miles under sea and over land round the loch before miraculously ringing a bell in the croft at Ardmore. Unfortunately, this system, which might have worked fine in the trenches of the First World War, was not designed to cope with our local hazards. The tide abraded the wire on the rocks at the edges of the loch, the heather fires in the spring burned it, the wind chafed it wherever it was in the air, and the blinking sheep seemed to have taken over the chewing side of things since the sale of the Gaffer's cattle. We decided to go for a wholly undersea wire, straight down the middle of the loch, cutting the total distance to little over a mile; two new sets still wrapped in their maker's air-proof wax containers arrived from our Army-surplus man in London. Pristine Army-green paint shone prettily, and their bells tinkled crisply as Lance screwed them down to smart wooden shelves by the door of the kitchen cabin at the School and by the front door below the outside telephone in our croft No.76. The wire was buried under the ground on its short overland route to the shore from the School and up the hill from the loch at Ardmore. On the beaches at either end, it was protected by lengths of alkathene pipe. We were in contact as never before.

During the long winter we got to know Sinclair Mackintosh, the factor of the Westminster estate, whom I had met first on the Shelter walk. He worked from the estate offices in the little village of Achfary some seven miles inland from his house, which is strategically sited at the mouth of the Laxford River. Achfary village is entirely made up of estate workers' houses painted a uniform black and white, and it is famous for having the only black and white telephone kiosk in Britain. I would pick Sinclair up at Skerricha at dusk on a Friday afternoon, and we'd take the boat down the loch, stopping to pick up a couple of lobsters for supper from the undersea store-box on the way. We fought out some terrific battles at Scrabble by the fire that winter. Next morning, if the swell permitted, we'd take a boat along the shores of Loch Laxford and hunt for driftwood for the kitchen stove.

Sinclair likes a bit of excitement. He seems to come into his best form in the early hours of the morning; I've never met anyone who could thrive on so little sleep. In deep mid-winter the days are short and the north-west Highlands sparsely populated. It's a time to find out who your friends are, and Sinclair was never found wanting in time of crisis.

Big gales at the beginning of December blew down a tree near the waterfall, so Marie Christine, Rebecca and I set off to saw it up. It was mid-afternoon by the time we got to the shattered willow and darkness was drawing in, on a short, still, gloomy sort of day. There was nobody at Upper Ardmore and the atmosphere there was like a sepia illustration from the past, in dead silence. There is a timeless quality about a place like Ardmore. I often expect to bump into a crofter from another age wandering through the wood.

We cut quite a bit of wood, everyone helping with the task, and by the time we set off for home we needed our torches to get back up the waterfall and on through the wood to Lower Ardmore. Laden with logs of different sizes in our rucksacks, Becca carried the hammer, Marie Christine the axe and I had the bow-saw. We staggered into the house and turned on the radio as we lit the Tilley lamp. We heard on the news that a lobster boat had gone down out of Kinlochbervie – it was the Morrison brothers again. The boat had finally sunk in a rocky inlet, and the boys were left clinging to floating wreckage under the cliffs in the December-cold sea. At that precise moment, Cathel Campbell just happened to be passing the inlet on his way back to port, and by chance he saw the orange buoys which made up a large part of the flotsam from the sinking. Buoys are an expensive item, so Cathel turned the boat to have a look and see if he could pick up any for himself. The brothers were more than pleased to see him.

Hughie was still having some success with the lobsters himself and working away at the Wooden House conversion whenever he could find the time. He often came in for supper and never failed to make us laugh with his tales of what it had been like to be the last child at school at Ardmore nearly forty years before. But he wasn't quite the last child to go to school at Ardmore. Becca was nearly five now and in the New Year Mr McLeod, primary adviser to the Sutherland Education Authority, walked out along the track to discuss how Rebecca should be educated. There was no chance of her going to and from school in Kinlochbervie each day, because of the condition of the footpath and the winter weather, but after seeing how she enjoyed spending the day up with Ada at the Blue House, he suddenly came out with the suggestion that perhaps Ada might become a primary teacher. Ada looked stunned; in all her years at 32, Park Avenue in Thornaby, she had never once thought of becoming a school teacher. It was true that Lance had asked her to marry him in part because he so admired her skill as a foundry crane driver during the War, but to be a teacher was something of a surprise. Nevertheless Ada found herself being driven by Mr Marshall, the headmaster at Kinlochbervie, to Dornoch on the east coast for a short teacher's course. In the summer Mrs Bell's Academy for Young Ladies opened its door to its first and only pupil, in the Blue House. The three Rs were pretty thoroughly covered there for the next three years, and neither pupil nor teacher will ever forget those happy times. At Christmas a present always came for Rebecca from the Sunday School at Kinlochbervie, for she was on the school roll although she didn't attend the classes there for the first three years.

We had now been involved at Ardmore for eight years, and we knew quite a few people from the time we'd spent working on the pier at Kinlochbervie; but Ardmore is cut off from any sort of connection with the local area by its situation. The geography of the north-west corner of Scotland is such that many people born locally live all their lives without ever visiting the more remote parts like Cape Wrath, Sandwood Bay, or for that matter Ardmore. There are no roads to these places and when you do finally get there, to a local, the scenery seems much the same as anywhere else on the coast. For our own part, the reverse applies. It is such a business to reach the mainland that we usually go far away if we go out at all. We probably visit Kinlochbervie three or four times a year. Geographically, Ardmore lies between two spheres of influence: Kinlochbervie to the north, and Scourie to the south; the councillors elected for these two communities serve them well. Funds are scarce and quite logically, Ardmore is not on their visiting rota. A result of all this is that we are quite voluntarily out of touch with what goes on locally, and I was to find out in 1972 that this is not a good thing at all.

One day we heard a road was to be built out to Ardmore, along the route of the existing public footpath. This rumour was not quite correct, for the road was to be built only halfway – as far as

Portlevorchy – but the idea was that it would be built with public funds to service the township of Ardmore (a crofting community is called a township). Plainly, if the road were to end at Portle-vorchy, the remaining switchback path of one and a half miles to Lower Ardmore would prohibit any movement of stores, and to all effects Ardmore would hardly benefit at all, except perhaps in winter, when it could be helpful to leave a vehicle at the new road-end in case of emergency. Foolishly, and as it was to turn out quite unforgivably, I dashed off a hasty letter to the County Council, saying that while we hadn't come to Ardmore expecting to live on a road, one a mile and a half distant would be useless. I suggested piers be built at either end of the loch instead. We were in full swing with the courses, which were overbooked that year, and I was going full tick. I suppose I expected a reply to the effect that the County Council would consider holding a meeting of the residents of Ardmore to discuss the value of the proposed expenditure of the funds being made available – nothing more; it really wasn't top of my list of concerns. I was in for a surprise.

The BBC telephoned first, then the *Daily Express*. They both wanted to know what I had got to say in my defence. To my amazement, what I had thought of as my private letter had been read out as a public release at the Council. I was pretty naive in matters of local government. In fact the only story I'd ever heard concerned a famous meeting held in the Rhiconich Hotel, when after a long harangue from the newly elected councillor, a voice from the back of the hall called, "We know ye've the neck, Kenny – but have ye the head for it?" The reporter from the local paper had seen a gem of a story in my blunder, one which could rumble on for ages, with lots of local interest to stimulate circulation. The essence was that an English incomer had objected to the poor people of the township of Ardmore getting their long-sought-after, and richly deserved, tarmac link with civilisation. I had no idea of the depth of local feeling this would stir up. Shocks are really an admission of failure to foresee things. They come like a kick in the lower stomach. I felt like a refugee who had found a home, only to discover he wasn't welcome at all. There was only one death-threat, and that was from someone in Perth more than 200 miles away, and I suppose I was too sensitive about it. Perhaps it was a good lesson: no man is an island. The building of the one and a half miles of public road went ahead, and we have done

English Rose VI heads for St Kilda.

Ardmore Rose under the stack of Handa.

English Rose VI hard on the wind.

Sandwood Bay, where I take the Businessmen to hunt for bits of Spitfire.

our best to turn it to our advantage. But of course it has never solved our transport problem, and because of the funds already expended on the road, we are unlikely ever to be provided with an alternative system of piers at either end of the loch.

That year we brought over by boat 2,000 concrete blocks for Hughie to begin the huge task of rebuilding the ruined shell of the stone croft house which was No.78, home of Heckie's child-hood hero Simon Mackenzie. More than thirty years had passed since a light had last shone from its windows. Sadly for us at Ardmore, Hughie had lost his heart to a nursing sister in Inverness and was going to live a hundred miles away. It was the only practical thing to do, for his elder brother Heckie was the crofter of No.77, so Hughie had no home to offer his bride on Ardmore. Small-scale lobster fishing and the occasional painting job miles from home which wasn't his anyway, were no substitute for a proper job and a new house in Inverness, particularly as Elizabeth was keen to continue with her nursing. All the same I think he was sad to leave Ardmore, and I felt I had lost a kindred spirit.

So the great stack of concrete blocks by the roofless ruin were to obstruct Willie the Post for several years more. A couple of trees thrived inside the walls at one end, and Lance used the other as a place to pile useful bits of plumbing, which were quickly consumed by voracious bramble bushes. The sheep walked along the moss-covered back walls of the house, where it was set close into the hillside, and each year, sheep's hooves and the action of the frost caused a few more chips to fall from between the large stone blocks which had once been hewn from the hill it-self by a "knacky" stonemason from Tarbet, beside the Sound of Handa.

Anyway, as Lance pointed out, the whole front wall was slowly bulging out, and would in time collapse. For a while we kept a hive of bees in the shelter of the ruin. Our idea was that bee stings might help Lance's arthritis; but they didn't flourish.

We had a busy season that year, and felt we were consolidating. Also people had heard of us. Sometimes this had curious conse-quences. In the middle of the Young People's Courses we had a visit from a writer and photographer from a well-known German magazine. They brought with them two models, one blonde and one brunetted to a fairly extreme level. The girls were to join the eighteen to thirty age group and be photographed taking part in the various activities. This did seem a bit unusual, but it certainly

81

put a little extra zip into the group, and the journalist had a nagging persistence which helped him get his way. After a couple of days of photographing the girls out sailing, canoeing, surviving, and cowering before lobsters, it was suddenly announced that they had all they needed and would be leaving for their next assignment the following day. I was quite relieved, and I could see no objection to their retaking a few photos on their own in the wood and out towards Ardmore Point, while our course was able to get on with canoeing without further distraction.

Several months later, a bulky envelope from the British Travel Authority came in the post. The compliments slip had no message, and there were several pages of poorly Xeroxed copy, which I could just make out as German. Scanning quickly through the pages, I returned to the front and was about to put it down and open the next letter of the day's mail, when my eye caught something faintly scrawled in English on the top right-hand corner of the article – the Xerox had hardly reproduced it at all – "What's Ridgway up to?" I could barely make it out. "What do they mean, 'What's Ridgway up to?'" I said, and Marie Christine leaned over to have a look.

She burst out laughing. "Those girls are naked!" I peered closer, and then it dawned on me what the four had been up to on that last afternoon at Ardmore Point! This, I observed, would go down well in the *Northern Times* – next to one of those letters about the Ardmore Road.

Bobby Clunas, a young boat builder from Elgin, worked with us for a season. It was his ambition to own his own boat and make a quiet living at the lobster fishing in the Moray Firth, close to his home town. He'd really come to Ardmore to spend a bit of time on the west coast and see if lobsters were as plentiful as he'd heard tell. Bobby was a great hand with the boats, and he became firm friends with Lance, but at the end of the season he managed to get a job with the British Antarctic Survey as boatswain in South Georgia. Months later, he was whiling away the permanent darkness of the Antarctic winter, thumbing through some old colour supplements, when he suddenly recognised a photograph of Lance's hand on the tiller of the old black lobster boat, the *Ada Bell*. Looking closer he realised he was looking at a fashion article in the *Telegraph Colour Magazine*.

June McCullum, fashion editor of the magazine, was looking for a location in Europe in mid-summer where she could have the photographs taken for a feature on "Fake Furs"; being furs, the atmosphere would have to be wintry. Someone suggested Cape Wrath and it certainly sounded suitable. June knew we were somewhere up that way, and that we had the boats which she felt were necessary props for the scenario she had in mind. Without a lot of thought – without enough thought – I agreed to this new experience on the telephone. June hired Helmut Newton for the assignment.

Helmut is an unusual figure to be seen at Ardmore. He is a naturalised Australian/German, based in Paris and California, an internationally famous fashion photographer, with several books to his credit – notably *Porno Chic*. He selected a German model, Mercedes, from his stable of girls for this particular piece; and June put them both up in the Dorchester while final arrangements were made for the flight to Inverness and on by hired car to Ardmore.

The whole idea seemed to fit well enough, down in Fleet Street, but when Helmut and Mercedes arrived at Skerricha, and saw the loch and the little boat which was waiting to take them over to Ardmore, they threw a bit of a wobbler, and poor June wondered if it was all going wrong. They wanted a hotel – a luxury hotel – but it was already late afternoon, and there was only Ardmore in prospect. When they finally straggled up the hill to the house, Helmut's immaculate safari outfit was looking a little less crisp than when it had come out of the Dorchester that morning, and the giraffe hair bracelet glistened with perspiration on his wrist. They didn't like the house. Mercedes was around six feet tall, a human stick-insect with a trombone left hand like Ernie Terrell; there was no chance at all that she would share a bedroom with anyone – and certainly not another woman. We only had the two bedrooms and Rebecca's little *Tierra del Fuego* under the roof. I stood around awkwardly, while the artists did their little bit. It had been a long day. I was thinking that a crashing right hand might do to Mercedes what Muhammad Ali had done to Ernie Terrell back in '67.

Finally it was agreed: Mercedes should have the spare room to herself, June could have Becca's little cupboard, and Becca and Helmut would have to sleep up at the Blue House. Richard Davis – "I do everything for Helmut, when he comes to Britain" – had to sleep on the floor in our sitting room.

It was not a happy party which sat down to supper in our

kitchen. Marie Christine dished up a steak and kidney pie, which the girls over at the School had said was too old to be given to the course. Helmut loved it, and began to settle down a bit, though I didn't like the way he looked at my wife.

Next morning, Granny Ross had never seen anything like Mercedes, as she sat out on the path between No.76 and No.77, doing her make-up at a rickety folding card table; but she had plenty of time to look, because Mercedes took the best part of an hour to carry out this operation. I thanked my lucky stars it wasn't raining. It was the hottest day of the year, and absolutely flat calm – where could we possibly go to make it look wintry? June was getting into quite a state. She had three huge suitcases bulging with the world's most fashionable fake furs and a project which looked doomed to failure.

When Mercedes was finally ready, Lance and I loaded the four of them into the *Ada Bell* and set off for the towering rocky stack at the north end of Handa, towing another boat to photograph from. Helmut announced the stars of the show were to be Lance and Mercedes.

It was still flat calm when we arrived under the cliffs an hour later, but now Helmut's eyes were brightening with anticipation. Inky darkness in the narrow V-shaped channel at the back of the Stack between it and Handa Island, promised just the atmosphere he was looking for. With the long low swell, the jet black water hissed and sucked gently at the foot of the soaring cliffs. Most of the birds had already left the island; the eggs had hatched, and parents and young were on the way to their distant winter feeding grounds. But there were still several hundred fulmars circling around, and water dripped loudly from ledges far above. Best of all Mercedes was beginning to look pale and interesting; she was soon going to be sick – in Helmut's view this heightened her beauty, and he splashed sea water on her carefully applied make-up to bedraggle her.

Mercedes spurned the hamper of pâté, sandwiches, cake and white wine which Marie Christine had prepared for us. June and Richard were performing rather mechanically too, but Helmut was in his element, keeping up an incessant flow of sweet talk to Mercedes, encouraging, bullying, flattering, and goading by turns as he fired hundreds of pictures with his battery of cameras. Mercedes was entering the survival section of the project; Lance's eyes were like saucers as she fired the elegant clothes on and off her skeletal frame, without pretence at modesty. I wondered if Lance would have to strip off and change too. Christian Dior catsuits were zipped and unzipped. Nothing was left to the imagination, and June fumbled in the bilge for the fluttering furs. By late afternoon, we were finished, to Mercedes' tremendous relief, and Helmut proclaimed the event an extravagant success. The supper party in the kitchen went much better that evening, but Mercedes was enthusiastic to be on her way as early as possible in the morning – she didn't keep in touch.

An earlier and more harmonious visitor had been Eric Shipton, one of my heroes, who came to stay for a few days. The legendary mountaineer looked a rather mild, retiring sort of person of average height and medium build. With thinning grey hair and deep-set eyes beneath bushy eyebrows, his face as often as not seemed to wear a shy, apologetic smile. He admired frankness, and we shared a peculiar sort of dread of wishful thinking in others. "Give me the man who knows something of himself, and is appalled," his look seemed to encourage. I admired his simplicity: he and Tilman had reckoned to plan a six-month expedition to the Himalayas before the War in half an hour on the back of an envelope. His quiet voice always made it clear that it was the actions, not the words, which counted with him.

On a raw March afternoon, we walked up over the top to the loch where the drinking water comes from, and then down through the heather to the house. Eric was a fit-looking sixty-four and I an under-confident thirty-three. By his standards I was a pretty moderate performer on the land, and I felt awkward asking his advice about the Patagonian trip Marie Christine and I had been thinking about ever since our return from the Amazon. I needn't have worried, for he couldn't have been more helpful, even offering to come himself. As he saw it, I should concentrate on some problem which required small boat work, the sort of thing we encountered every day at Ardmore, but which most mountaineers would avoid because it was out of their element. I had no maps of the area better than a large atlas, and those contained in his rather daunting book *Land of the Tempest*, but he brushed all this aside and said he'd give it a bit of thought. The best maps available were a set presented to him by the Chilean government for his help in settling a border dispute with Argentina, and he'd given them to the Royal Geographical Society in London. Before he left Eric suggested we meet again in the Map

Room at the RGS, and I felt as if I'd been asked to tea by David Livingstone. Now our expedition was taking shape. Marie Christine was coming and this time we wanted to take a couple of our instructors as well. Richard Shuff was an obvious choice for his climbing skills and when our old friend Krister Nylund, the skiing Swede, came back again to help with the instructing in 1972, he was just the fellow to complete the team.

Before autumn came, Francis Chichester died. It was the inspiration of his book *The Lonely Sea and the Sky* which had helped me so much to find my way forward from mending fish boxes on Kinlochbervie pier, where I'd read it back in 1964, to running the School of Adventure at Ardmore. I think a lot of his letters, in the bad times.

The geese were flying south over Ardmore, honking their way in from Greenland and Iceland, by the time the season ended. All the courses had been full, the School was looking good, and we left in buoyant mood. Becca seemed not in the slightest bit perturbed as she waved us off from Skerricha with Lance and Ada, who were holding the fort once more while we were away. I could tell from the grip of our handshakes that the place would be safe.

Greatly encouraged by the success of the season, Marie Christine and I visited the Camper & Nicholsons boatyard in Southampton before we flew out to Chile. It happened to be one of those unforgettable occasions. The October sun was just setting in a clear autumn sky as we watched the sleek Nicholson fifty-five-foot sloop *Adventure* slip silently up the river towards us. The Royal Navy had taken delivery of her that very day, and she looked magnificent: immaculate Navy blue hull and twin whip aerials on her stern, she looked all set for the first Whitbread Round the World Yacht Race. We were completely bowled over by the sight, and decided there and then that we must gamble everything and have one built for the School – to race round the world with a crew of instructors. It was to be a long haul.

7

Looking eagerly from the window of the plane as it approached the bleak Chilean settlement of Punta Arenas, on the northern shores of the Magellan Straits, we could see the place was still in the grip of the southern winter. I was remembering the fascination of gazing at the snow-covered peaks of the Andes around the headwaters of the Amazon. Now Marie Christine, Richard Shuff, Krister Nylund and I were about to find out what it was like to live at the southern tip of these same snowfields, for we had come to try and make the first crossing of the Gran Campo Nevado (Big Snow Field). Indeed we would be the first people ever to walk on it. I was apprehensive: mountaineering on this scale was something new to all of us.

We were a team of four who knew each other quite well, compared to the team on the Amazon. In both cases there was a tickle of fear for what we might find round the next bend, but in Patagonia we were entirely alone; there was no chance of meeting with other humans for many weeks. Richard at twenty-eight was the one to suffer most. He decided to use the expedition to help him give up smoking, and by the time he actually ran out of tobacco, he'd realised he really was dependent on the stuff. We were all under considerable strain, but poor Richard found the lack of a good smoke almost too much to bear. For Krister the expedition was a series of scrapes which suited the big gentle Swede's lighthearted approach to life at twenty-three; he always managed to remain cheerful and was to be a tower of strength throughout.

Marie Christine was finding the trip somewhat different from the heat of the Amazon, but we had a really good life-support system going in our tent – except when freak tides pushed the sea in to join us.

Apart from our continuous concern about the progress and safety of the expedition, we two had probably never been happier. The wilderness and the steady rhythm of physical effort needed to move through it offered a chance to stand back for a minute and take a good look at how our life together was really going; and for me to check again if I was making full use of the bonus time I'd been granted after the Atlantic row.

It took us five weeks just to find an approach to our ice-cap, and this included an eighty-mile voyage in vulnerable, heavy-laden rubber dinghies through the Magellan Straits, past tide races and narrows, sheer ice cliffs and calving glaciers. We were harassed by killer whales and nuzzled by porpoises, and visited at night by pumas. We pitched our tents for the last bid at the ice-cap high on a gently shelving beach of golden sand at the edge of the forest. It was a magical spot. Richard took a day to make a visual recce of the best route forward. His plan was to approach the ice-cap by a ridge running along the western side of the glacier valley. Marie Christine had now read Shipton's *Land of Tempest* two and a half times and, as she pointed out, Shipton always went up a glacier. I'd have given a bob or two for a word with him just then. But we followed Richard.

On the second day our progress was stopped by a blizzard white-out. On the third morning Richard and I set off along the ridge to recce the next bit of route before bringing up any further loads, and what we found was a point where the ridge fell sharply into a saddle and rose on the other side as a cliff.

"Scrub it," Richard said, and it sounded to me like a death sentence on a whole year of preparation. "I wouldn't follow anyone on that, let alone lead it." Richard had made his decision. There was about half an hour of weather left, and he began to make his way back to the tents.

I had less practical climbing experience to enforce caution, and I felt a kind of elation. After forty-six days we were poised to achieve success. Everything had been stripped bare and the prize lay before us. No man had ever stood here, where a thousand years was but a yesterday. I was determined to have a go at crossing the saddle on the following day.

Richard emphasised his point next morning by making his own way back down to the camp at sea level. Five condors shadowed him, growing bolder when they decided this lone figure was about to die. Their enthusiasm increased still further when he began lowering his pack on the red Kernmantel rope, which looked like entrails, and the long primary feathers at the tips of their ten-foot wingspan riffled like eager fingers. Richard fought back with a rage, hurling rocks at their ugly staring bald heads. Then he put up his tent in the forest and waited. Nicotine deprivation, inability to sleep, added to the cumulative strain of isolation, had got through to him in a way that had affected him, he frankly admitted, far more than he had expected.

It was Marie Christine who saved us. "I'd rather put a pistol to my head – I'm sorry, Johnny," she said through her tears, as the three of us stood above the saddle at which Richard had turned back. Krister was game to go on, but we couldn't leave Marie Christine alone on the top. She suggested we try the Shipton method of following the glacier instead.

With the benefit of fifteen years' hindsight, I realise I was wrong. As in so many situations of this sort, human factors crept in along with the stress. What had been too far forward in my thinking was a trial of wills with Richard: he had come because he enjoyed climbing; I had come because I wanted to achieve the first crossing of the ice-cap. When the enjoyment stopped, Richard had been brave enough to admit it, lose face, and make his own way back to the forest floor. I, on the other hand, was letting my heart rule my head. There was probably (we shall never know) no way that Krister and I could have climbed the cliff on the far side of that saddle. Luckily, we turned and made our way back down to join Richard, who was feeling broken and alone, far below. When he heard our voices, he thought he was going mad – then he felt a great surge of relief that we were all right.

We made a recce of the glacier, and the bottom part was an impossible formation of sharply pointed towers of ice, marching to the sea. We had nightmares. Marie Christine woke screaming that the tent was sliding down the mountain, Richard found diggings at his tent door – where he had been stabbing the ground with his shovel in his sleep – and Krister said he'd hardly slept at all. I recognised an old companion, Fear, but I knew I had to give it a go.

The food was fast running out. We no longer had time to spend on fishing or trying to shoot ducks and geese, and the glacial deposits on the shore seemed to deter mussels. Spring was slow in coming, and the valances on our tents were filled with hail stones which bounced down through the trees. The grumble of avalanches from above was never absent for long.

It was agreed that Krister and I should take the two-man tent and make one final attempt together. We packed sixteen days' rations, ate a huge curry lunch and set off in one of the Avon dinghies up the milky waters of the short glacier river. My goodbye to Marie Christine was hurried and left a good deal unsaid. She and Richard were to wait for three weeks. Then, shortage of food would force them to start for home with the other Avon and motor. In the meantime they each had a tent, a little food, and unlimited time to listen to the roaring of the avalanches above the forest.

Krister and I were carrying a maximum load. When either of us fell as we struggled through the brush to the edge of the glacier, there was no getting up; we lay like an upturned sheep at Ardmore, waiting for outside help. We surprised a small deer fawn, a huemul, but it let us walk right up to it, showing no sign of fear at the first humans it had encountered. The wildlife was plentiful and marvellous, so was the flora along the edge of the glacier, but the ice-cap loomed over everything in our minds.

Neither of us had been on a glacier before, or used crampons and jumars. Five days later, after many false starts in the icefall and twenty-nine hours pinned down in a blizzard, we at last managed to get on to our ice-cap. There were avalanches to left and right. But here, the snow was frozen hard enough to walk on without the exhausting breakthrough of each step, which had been such a feature of the journey so far. Then came another "white-out". Krister ran round me in a circle on the end of thirty yards of rope and when he didn't fall over anything we put up the tent, well pleased with ourselves. The snow blocks we cut for the platform made a good wind-break wall. Camp 5 was a real beauty. Our partnership had been going a week, and it seemed like a lifetime; I couldn't have asked for a better companion. Krister was neat and precise, completely at home in the snow, he made so few mistakes that he was constant reassurance. We worked well, just like Chay on the Atlantic and Elvin in the Amazon jungle. Such constancy doesn't come often: I feel a great bond with all three.

In the tent that night, I thought of the storms sweeping in from the Southern Ocean: what would it be like sailing towards Cape Horn on such a night? I wanted to find out.

Dawn brought a window in the weather. It was so cold, as if time itself had frozen. There were giant views in all directions, and we were in the middle of a huge sloping snow field. We reckoned it was only four miles across the ice-cap to a point above some narrows where we had had such trouble with the rubber dinghies in the rapids exactly a month before.

Roped together, we moved very fast across the hard surface under a still blue sky. Every 400 paces, Krister gave a shout, and I stuck a stick in the snow. These markers were tipped with a strip of red polythene to back up the compass on the return trip. We wore blue plastic biscuit wrappers tucked under our goggles to keep the sun from our noses, and thick smears of glacier cream. At the halfway mark, the visibility began to go. The rising wind started a whirling cloud of drifting snow at ankle level, and we felt we were running on a giant mattress. We kept on, watching the compass carefully, and at 1130 we were at the northern edge of the glacier which leads down to the narrows.

"We made it!" Krister shouted, pushing his goggles on to the top of his forehead with one hand, and pushing the other out for me to shake. "I never thought we would, you know, not after we went down from the ridge!"

The wind was rising all the time, and after some biscuits and tinned cheese, we set off back in another "white-out". The whirling powder snow engulfed us like dense smoke, erasing our outward tracks, but compass back-bearings brought us on to the red-topped markers as Krister counted out the paces. We were going home. The big diesel inside me was running smoothly, and shining like a beacon in my mind's eye was the pot-bellied Romesse stove in the kitchen at Ardmore.

Marie Christine and Richard were stunned to hear the sound of our outboard motor coming down the glacier river ten days after our parting. My heart lifted as I saw the small figure of my wife at the edge of the trees, then Richard appeared and Krister slowed the engine. He stood up and waved his right arm as if signalling the advance of a Grand Army. The figures at the water's edge began jumping up and down with joy. It was nothing, yet it was everything.

"I gave you up for dead when you didn't come back on day six," was the first thing she said, and I noticed her brown face was thinner. It hadn't been much fun.

Together, we tore up the plan she'd drawn of a tea-shop she was going to build on the main coast road at Ardmore – the John Ridgway Adventure School would be going on after all.

8

I got great satisfaction from the expedition to cross the ice-cap in Patagonia; it remains in my memory as an individual island of fulfilment. I had that clean feeling of achievement which is so hard to find in life.

On the flight home aboard a DC8 from Buenos Aires to Rome, crossing the Atlantic coast of Africa, dawn came rushing to meet us across the sandy wastes of the Sahara Desert. The shades of red, yellow and blue in that vast emptiness exactly matched my dreams of the great open skies which had lured me from Ardmore to the Amazon and Patagonia. The Desert must be the next place I should go and see, but Rebecca was on my mind as we headed for home, and in that dawn the world seemed a wonderful place. I fell to wondering if there might be some way for Marie Christine, Rebecca and me to go and see the Desert together – to show Becca that there are places where it doesn't rain quite as much as at Ardmore. Some sort of practical geography lesson would be the thing, before she had to go away from Ardmore to School. Ardmore was the only place she had ever known. Now, if we could sail out from Ardmore, and on down the west coast of Europe, I'd be able to show her those big open skies – the way the colour of the sea changes and the sun warms your back . . .

We arrived back in London just in time to visit the Boat Show. The yacht *Adventure* dominated the whole of Earls Court. The fifty-five-foot dark blue sloop looked every bit as beautiful out of the water on the Royal Navy stand as she had done coming up the river towards Camper & Nicholsons' yard in the dusk.

"We just can't afford it," I said to Marie Christine, with the dark shiny hull towering over us.

"What if we sell the house in Farnham and the car?" she replied, helpful as ever.

Before we left for the north we placed our order for a Nicholson 55. It was a heady moment. Sanity reasserted itself a few months later and we converted it into a deposit on a Nicholson 32 without an engine, instead. To help pay for the thirty-two-footer we sold the small terraced house we'd bought in Farnham in 1965, when I'd returned to the Parachute Regiment after failing to settle at Ardmore. We had really gritted our teeth to buy that house, struggling to recoup the Scottish failure. And now in 1973 we found it had more than trebled in value. This kind of windfall always gives me twinges of doubt, for I'm the sort of person who feels sure that beyond every silver lining there lies another dark cloud. Nothing easily gained is really worth having in my book. Happily Marie Christine feels none of this sort of nonsense.

We had been away from Ardmore for a little over three months. The thick stone walls had chilled right through, and for the first few days, when we awoke in the mornings, the blankets were soaked with dew. But the pot-bellied stove glowed red, consuming basketfuls of dark peat blocks, and slowly the old place warmed up.

Lance and Ada arrived back just before a cold spell which laid a fourteen-inch carpet of snow right down to the edge of the sea, and Becca kept us out on the toboggans for much of each day. Rocking back and forth in her chair Granny Ross wrung her hands with anxiety while Marie Christine raced down through the crofts on her skis, executing neat stem-christies.

Lance and Ada often came down after supper for a game of Scrabble, or we would go up to the Blue House. Some evenings we all helped Marie Christine assemble a pile of brochures which would help her through the next couple of weeks' enquiries. The brochure, designed for us by our friend, John McConnell, had a large sepia cover which unfolded to reveal a thirty-three-inch photograph of Loch a'Chadh-fi and the mountains beyond. Details of the courses were separate inserts, varied from year to year. It was so successful that we kept the same format for ten years.

Rebecca spent her days up at school with Ada, trotting to and fro with her satchel, and Ada sometimes went over to Dornoch for further teaching instruction.

In the winter, Lance usually travelled over to the School at the other end of the loch by boat at first light, which was around eight o'clock in the morning, and he came back to beat the darkness at four. His workshop was at first only a small shed next to the cookhouse/instructors' cabin. But then he built another boatshed across the front of his workshop so the *Rebecca* and *Ada Bell* could be brought in, one at a time, in the winter for painting and repairs.

The boatshed has a floor made of short larch planks, each two inches thick. These lift to reveal a four-foot drop into the foundation, and part of this space is used for storage of paint; we keep stocks of emulsion for the inside of the School, as well as red, white and blue paint for all the boats each year. The harsh winds and driving rain are hard on the timber skins of the buildings, so we paint the outsides with Cuprinol every year as well. If a Land-rover needed a new exhaust, Lance lifted a few boards and got to work on the underneath of the vehicle from his garage pit; if welding was needed, he donned his goggles and set to work with the oxygen and acetylene bottles he kept strapped to the walls of the workshop.

Lance could never entirely forget that his old man didn't reckon much to his son's workmanship, but Ada, Marie Christine and I reckoned Lance's Dad had got it pretty wrong. Lance would give a wry grin and say only Adam was indispensable. But as the years passed, I realised we never ever had to send anything away for repair. Whatever the job, Lance would shake his head – say it was impossible – and then go right ahead and do it. His creed is that nothing is as efficient as one man with his back up against a wall, and that the best kind of monument a man can build to himself is his own work. Slowly but surely the whole School was becoming a monument to Lance's work. We began to call the boatshed the "Chapel". Instructors lived in fear of his wrath – he had little time for "them young buggers", as he called them collectively. All the same they were always welcome up at the Blue House for a glass of Ada's home-made beer, and the parties Lance and Ada gave during the season became legendary. If a young fellow showed any aptitude, Lance would go to endless trouble to show him how to do something, but touching any of his precious tools carried a near death sentence. Saws and chisels lived in countless dark hand-built wooden chests of drawers, each wrapped in its oily cloth to prevent rust. Most of the tools were generations old, but kept sharp as a razor; others had been made by Lance himself, like the massive metalwork drill, every part of which he had made from molten metal.

On a winter's day, walking towards Ardmore along the footpath above Portlevorchy, the snow-covered buildings lay long and low on the far side of the loch, hugging the shore below the hills of Ardbeg. Everything was still, but a keen ear could just pick up the steady single cylinder thump-thump of the heavy Lister generator. Lance would be there, prodding about, alone at his bench, a small electric fan heater whirring quietly in the background. Paraffin heaters were not allowed, because the water vapour from the fuel rusted his tools. His windows looked straight down the loch to Skerricha, and around lunchtime the burly figure of the Gaffer often came stumping down the track with his sheep dogs, for a cup of tea. Inevitably, there would be a strong smell of burning rubber: Lance always heated his boots upside down over the Primus stove. When they finally collapsed from this treatment, the soles were either converted into self-closing hinges for the small gates at either end of the flower garden in front of the Blue House, or the entire boot provided a major charge for the Rayburn, when a good oven temperature was needed on Ada's bread-baking days. At the end of a short winter day, Lance would bring the boat back up the loch to a running mooring in the lee of the Annait, and walk back up through the wood to the Blue House for a glass of Ada's home-brew before supper. If the loch was frozen over, he'd drain the water-cooling tank on the generator at the School before walking the three miles round the loch. Mostly he worked alone, and the tally of his production mounted with the days.

We were well into the Instructors' Course in the middle of March when Heckie's dogs began killing sheep, with lambing not much over a month ahead. It was an agonising decision for the solitary shepherd, but there could be no delay – all three: Scottie, Bessy and Spot were shot and buried.

Heckie cut a sad figure, out on the hill alone. His next dog came half trained, but he ran away. We scoured the shoulder of Foinaven up by Gualin after sightings in that area. But we didn't find him, and after a while Heckie got another very shy dog called Mona, which bolted for cover under the kitchen table whenever we went in to see Granny Ross. Mona was a slightly built collie, her face black down one side and white on the other, giving her a quizzical expression. She kept her distance on the croft, with one ear cocked and the other floppy, but she was rather too nervously keen to be a first-rate dog. She and Heckie got on very well indeed, however, and one was seldom seen without the other.

Ardmore had once supported 250 sheep. Heckie kept his flock to about 100, but he and Mona still had the same 1,820 acres to cover. Brother Hughie would come up from Inverness to help clip the wool by hand. Dry weather is essential for this, so inevitably there were many wasted journeys in a wet August. Donald and Angie Corbett drove their own small flock from Portlevorchy to the fank at the bottom of the waterfall, for the "dipping", and sometimes the Gaffer came over from Skerricha to give a hand, but it was a much reduced gathering, both of sheep and men, from the busy times past.

Around mid-November each year, the tup arrived to run with the ewes on Paddy's Isle until the end of December. Usually the weather was at its foulest for the powerful ram's arrival in Heckie's little green and yellow boat from Skerricha, but one way and another the beast always got ashore without accident, and each spring another crop of lambs was born.

Sometimes as I walked up the hill from the shore, I wondered what the old fellows from the past would have thought about the way things were falling into disrepair on the crofting side of life. Granny Ross often told us how she used to turn the whole of their croft by hand each year, with the help of one other woman, and she also spent a good bit of each spring standing in the icy water, cutting seaweed to carry up the hill and spread on the land. In those days she expected eighty sacks of potatoes in the autumn. Long ago, before her, other people had cleared the hillside of stones and piled them in huge cairns, then they'd dug deep furrows and laid dry-stone drains.

In the past, the place supported large families and everyone played their part in keeping life going. The men worked on the land and sea, the women on the land and in the home, and children carried water and peat. Today there are many fewer families, but boats have engines; a rotavator can do the work of many people in a day. Lime and fertilisers improve the ground, and wire fences are much easier to erect than the dry-stone walls of old. Marie Christine loves flowers and Lance can't go for long without his vegetable garden, but for me the grass is everything. It is a bright, hopeful symbol of the fruits of that unending struggle which is the enduring appeal of Ardmore for me.

Seen from the top of Ben Stack, the tiny green patch of Ardmore inbye land is an emerald oasis in a barren wilderness of rock and ocean.

When Hughie came up to help with the lambing, from mid-April to mid-May, we got to talking of scallop farming in the loch. The idea was to suspend ropes from rafts to gather the scallop spat from the tide. They would always be in the water, unlike the great colonies of mussels clothing the rocks around the loch, which spend much time exposed by the falling tide, when they have nothing to eat. Kept clear of the bottom the scallops would be out of reach of their deadly enemies, the star fish which writhe around on the sea bed. Scallops are a valuable shellfish which could provide a crofter with a bit of extra income, without much capital expenditure and no food bills at all. The scallops sift their own food from the passing tide. Hughie was interested in the idea and took my diving manual with him when he returned to Inverness. Skin diving would be useful for checking moorings and rafts, but the idea of simply diving for scallops for a living didn't seem attractive to either of us. Diving boats come occasionally from further south. Usually converted small seine net boats with considerable range, they clean out the small scallop beds and move on like vultures.

I was always looking for some means of adding to the meagre living the shore-side crofts could provide. My time at Kinlochbervie pier had given me an insight into the fishing industry and its similarity to Stone Age agriculture. There was an ever increasing harvest being won from the waters by more boats with better equipment, but there was no real conservation of stocks.

The times when crofters went sailing out to fish the small lines were long gone. In those days Angie Corbett, from Portlevorchy, fished from a twenty-foot double-ender called the *Queen*, and Hector, Heckie's father, sailed the *Victoria*. Together they raced out to the fishing grounds under sail, tacking to and fro across the loch, and rowing back if the wind failed.

1927 and 1928 were "The years of the big herring", when the German Klondikers anchored in Fanagmore Bay on the southern shores of Loch Laxford and the masters of the *Queen* and *Victoria* had a real bonanza. Loch Laxford and Loch a'Chadh-fi were solid with herring, and in one fortnight in December 1927, Angie and Hector scarcely went to bed, they fished so hard. A boat worked six drift nets, each 150 foot long and fifteen foot deep and anchored at either end. Hauling the net up and across the boat, they extracted the herring trapped by their gills, and then let the net down into the water on the other side of the boat. Shooting their nets in this fashion through the December ice, on one day alone in the narrows between Portlevorchy and what is now the School, they filled forty-four round baskets each brimming with a hundredweight of silver herring. Sometimes they were knee-deep in rotting herring, which piled up on the shore from other drifters, fishing from even smaller boats which just couldn't handle the weight of their catches.

The German Klondikers took all the herring they could get from the people of Ardmore. Shipping them direct to the continent was a bonanza for them too – not for nothing were they called after the Yukon gold-rush town of 1896. The skippers sold salt to the crofters and they had stocks of precious tobacco and brandy too, to help business along.

"Were you in the War?" one grim sea-captain asked Hector, handing down a bottle of brandy from his ship.

"Aye, I was that." To this day, there is a little brass plaque, engraved H.ROSS, screwed to the door of No.77, from Hector's Royal Navy ditty box in the Great War.

"Well, so was I, and I'm as acquainted with this loch as you," the German laughed drily. "I took a fat sheep off here once, but then a seaplane interrupted us. It tried to torpedo us, but we submerged and got away into the Atlantic."

When the herring at last moved out of the lochs, the Klondikers followed, never to return. And the crofters of Ardmore returned to their lobster fishing, until they were needed again to man the North Atlantic convoys in the next great War, barely ten years later.

Angie would leave Portlevorchy at five o'clock on a summer's morning and walk round the loch, up the waterfall and through the wood to Lower Ardmore. By five thirty he was calling up the stairs at No.77, "Are you woken, Hector?" They once took 166 lobsters in twenty-four hours from thirty creels, each baited with a small haddock, and hauled every quarter hour at the back of Handa Island. They even caught an eleven-pound lobster which got tangled in the bottom of a herring net near the shore under the Ardmore wood. But the prices were so poor that subsistence was the order of the day, and there were no more bottles of brandy to pass round. By the time the boxes of lobsters reached Billingsgate Fish Market in London, the damp bracken had often dried out on the train; and the merchants' claim that the lobsters were dead on arrival could never be queried by the crofters far away in Scotland.

Angie and Hector had to look beyond the summer, and think of feed for the cattle and sheep in the winter. So, on a June night when the tide was right, they'd sail silently out of Laxford to land on the inshore side of the Black Rocks, just north of the Whale-Back Rock. The murmur of the tide covered the noise of their landing, and with stout tiller in hand, they crept over the rocks in their stockinged feet, stalking a bull seal which could weigh anything up to eight hundred pounds.

A crashing blow on the skull killed the beast before it could slip into the water. The two friends quickly skinned the animal and cut off the blubber with a knife, stowing it away in a sack.

When they got home a black pot was put on the fire with a little water in the bottom to prevent it cracking with the heat, then they fed the blubber into the pot in chips. Once the fat was rendered to oil, it was stored in whisky bottles for the winter. The hardest time for a sheep at Ardmore is in the early spring, when the store of fat lining its stomach has been melted away as fuel for the beast during the cold months after New Year, and the new grass has not yet come up owing to bitter dry easterly winds. Nowadays we feed our sheep with enriched ewe nuts before the lambing, but in those days a quarter of a whisky-bottle dose of seal oil in March served the purpose. A cow got half a bottle, and sickly humans were fed a small dose as well. Angie's uncle even wore a sealskin waistcoat. Seal oil may sound unappetising, but Angie was used to such things. As a boy of eight or nine he and his brother would chase the nanny goat barefoot on the croft at the back of Portlevorchy. Once they had it cornered they'd cockle it over and one would suck the milk straight from the animal while the other held it still.

From the mouth of Loch Dughaill (the Blue Loch) at the Rubha Sgeir a'Bhathaidh (the Drowning Rock) the wild shores of Ceathramh Garbh (the Rough Quarter) take a turn to the north. Here, hugging the coast and rising 118 feet above the sea, stands Eilean na Saille (the Island of the Salt Spray). This island is a favourite nesting place for fulmars and shags, and their droppings have ensured it is covered with a mantle of lush green grass, suitable for wintering a few strong sheep. The constant surge of the ocean makes for a tricky landing, and the fence protecting the sheep from a cliff has rusted away – indeed Heckie told me the last time he recalled landing on the island was on the occasion of George VI's coronation. One day I should like to repair that fence and fatten some sheep over a winter on the phosphate rich grass.

A little to the south of the island and a bit to the west of the

Drowning Rock there is a small patch of clean ground, a pinch too small for a seine net boat to shoot its gear without fouling; a good spot for fishing small lines for haddock from November to January. The first line is laid straight out to sea from a plumb rock just to the north of the Drowning Rock. And when a mark on the far shores to the north, up by the white sand beaches of Oldshoremore, comes into view through the narrow channel between Eilean na Saille and the Ceathramh Garbh, more lines are laid NNE–SSW. They need hauling every hour, or the dogfish will eat the catch. Fishing only takes place on the flood tide, for it's Angie's opinion that no fish will feed on the ebb, not lobsters nor even trout in the hill lochs. Baiting five hundred No.19 haddock hooks with mussels at nine-foot intervals was a job which needed plenty of preparation at home before ever putting to sea in mid-winter. The mussels were gathered from the dense colonies around the shore of Loch a'Chadh-fi and carried up the hill in pails. Angie kept a few roasting in the ashes of the fire while he worked away with the others at opening shells with a short-bladed knife. His father hated to hear cooking shellfish whistle, for it was an ill omen, and bad luck was not the thing when fishing off the Drowning Rock.

With the onset of spring the sheep ticks began to attach themselves to the cat as it roamed through the heather. Tiny insects not much larger than a pinhead, they burrow into the flesh and then swell grotesquely with the blood they drink. Marie Christine and Becca were for ever pulling them off and throwing them into the fire. We've had a series of short-lived cats at Ardmore. Their job is to catch the winter invasion of mice which rattle around between the lining boards and the stone walls of the croft. The mice will eat anything at all. I got really upset when they started eating the cork handles of my fishing rods. I think the cats were more concerned with their own survival than killing mice; every time the trap went off with a loud "click" in a kitchen cupboard, they'd do no more than twitch an ear as they lay snoozing in front of the fire. The Rosses had a really ragged cat. They called it Scroggach, in the Gaelic, because it used to return from sorties to the wood in absolute tatters. One day it failed to return to base, and Granny Ross said it had probably fallen victim to the feral cats which lurked in the wood, relics of past crofters who'd abandoned their cats to run wild when they left Ardmore.

Our own first cat was killed by the same bandits which got

100

Scroggach, but the second one was part bandit progeny and born in the Rosses' byre. We gave it to Becca for her third birthday, a bright little kitten brought in from the dry-stone byre in a cardboard box done up with a ribbon. The mother had nursed it in a hen box, and it wasn't used to the light, so as soon as it got out of the box it ran off and hid under the sofa in the sitting room. Becca grew very fond of her cat which was strangely excited by bagpipe music, and always growled in a ridiculous manner over its food. One day the cat began hissing and raging on the kitchen window sill, so we put it outside. A few hours later we found the poor thing on the path, locked in a death spasm. There was a great commotion, and we traced the cause to a bottle of sheep dip which the Gaffer had unknowingly advised us to bathe the cat in, to kill the ticks. He hadn't realised it, but unlike sheep, cats lick themselves clean, and so it had poisoned itself.

The next cat was an amorous tom, whose stays away from home became longer and longer, as he searched for partners out on the mainland, until one day he never returned. His most alarming habit was to hide up in the roof, among the rafters above the lining boards; there was only one way up to this retreat, and this was where the boards had been removed in Becca's little bedroom, called *Tierra del Fuego*, to make more headroom above her bed. Sometimes visitors would have to sleep in this cupboard-like room, nodding off in the candlelight from the Wee Willie Winkie, under the solemn gaze of the stuffed alligator and piranha fish from the Amazon and the penguin from Chile. When the black cat leaped down from the rafters and on to their chests in the middle of the night it was quite a little test – there was no electric light to switch on and few brought a torch to bed with them. The attack had to be repelled in pale moonlight from the skylight and some people thought they were being attacked by the penguin.

One winter night, when the cat was shut outside, the mice were making an awful noise, and Marie Christine told me to get out of bed and do something. I was wearing a long red flannel nightshirt to keep me warm, and I fumbled my way across the floor, trying to find the torch which I thought I'd left beside the wash-basin by the door, but I couldn't find it. So in a fit of pique I flung open the cupboard door under the basin, determined to deal with the problem unaided by light. The mouse rushed blindly for safety straight up the sleeve of my nightgown. I lurched back, hit my head violently on the sloping ceiling and let out a bellow of rage which brought my wife sharply into a sitting position with the bed covers tucked tightly under her chin. I hopped about while the mouse ran across my bare shoulders in the darkness, then suddenly, I felt its feet scrabbling as it slipped down my chest. Things were getting desperate. Then it went into a free fall and I held my breath until it landed on my left foot. I jumped on to the bed and fell flat. "Don't bring it in here!" the wail went up. We couldn't find the torch, and for a while we just lay there twitching, wondering if the intruder had still been on my foot when I jumped on to the bed. Next morning the cupboard door was still hanging open. The survival rations from Horlicks had been chewed right through their white greaseproof boxes, and the spare curry bars were ruined.

Our next cat came from Scourie. A small grey tabby with some Persian in her, called Pussy Ridgway, she signed a peace treaty with the last of the bandits, a huge black and white tom who occasionally took a bite to eat from a saucer left outside the Rosses' kitchen window. We still had mice, of course. But they didn't win every round. One day Marie Christine found a dead one in the chest of drawers – the little chap had made the fatal mistake of nibbling a string of red beads I'd been given by the Campa Indians who had rescued us from the raft wreck on the Amazon. The woman with the painted face who'd watched us eat her awful fish supper, had warned me they were poisonous, but how do you test such things?

9

By 1973 Ardmore had occupied much of my thinking for nine years, and we had been living there full-time for four years, the School was beginning its fifth season and the courses were fuller than ever. I was thirty-five and in the prime of my life. I sometimes wondered if I hadn't already passed through life, and perhaps Ardmore was heaven. Walking through the wood at any time of the year on my own, the view across to the Foinaven Ridge often stopped me in my tracks. I felt very lucky. Everything I had hoped for had come true. I remembered the Atlantic again and still savoured every bonus day.

But there was never a time to relax, or I would go the way of my neighbours. The crofting system had taken such a beating that it had almost disappeared round the shores of Loch a'Chadh-fi, leaving a handful of old men living on their memories, neither enthusiastic nor sharply critical of my incoming foreign ways, perhaps resigned to age and the passing of the old order in which they had been brought up.

I do not know what they really thought of the pair of drunken doctors who ''borrowed'' bikes from outside the Rhiconich Hotel, hoping to wobble back to the Businessmen's Course after closing time, but only succeeding in getting as far as breaking the local policeman's window. What did they think of the occasional executive arrival by helicopter on the only spit of relatively flat grass at the foot of the Rosses' croft? Even there, passengers had to jump the last couple of feet. One fellow threw out his luggage in a gallant Toad of Toad Hall gesture before leaping after it, only realising too late he had forgotten the bottle of vintage port inside his suitcase.

The Businessmen's Courses allowed room for skylarking company directors to cut loose. But what became known as the IBM Course, was something different: it couldn't really be described as enjoyment at all. The aim was for participants to

103

discover how individuals behaved while tackling group tasks under stress.

Participants assembled at Inverness to board a coach for the hundred miles to Ardmore. But they weren't destined to get there so easily. The bus pulled off the road at Laxford Bridge, not a village where they could buy film for their cameras and have a pint, but just a bridge, a place to change and pack rucksacks with things they might need for a few days living rough in the hills. Next time the bus stopped each was handed an envelope as he stepped off into bleak coastal moorland. I watched through binoculars as envelopes were torn open and three separate groups of eight strangers staggered off each under the watchful eye of an IBM training officer (T.O.). Before meeting me they would go through "Timeplan" and "Tortoiseshell", two gruelling tests devised in collaboration with IBM and my old Parachute Regiment friend, Peter Mitchell, to help participants become more effective in times of stress. One of our own instructors also accompanied each group to ensure its physical safety and well-being, and there was an Army wireless operator assigned to each to provide the communications network which kept me in touch with overall co-ordination without showing my face. Nobody got introduced to anybody, and some of the groups became convinced that Peter Mitchell must be the elusive Ridgway.

"Timeplan" began at dawn after a night on an island under canvas, and was the two-day disorientation phase of the course, involving progress across rough country using map and compass to navigate from lochan to lochan. Next came "Tortoiseshell", designed to test leadership, participation, planning and organisational abilities towards breaking point. They were given a hypothetical disaster, such as a chemical explosion on Merseyside, and told their job was to undertake reconnaissance tasks for re-housing an entire town in the isolated Ceathramh Garbh area.

They found themselves stumbling about in the dark and the rain, building rafts, investigating hilltops for possible helicopter pads, anchorages for relief shipping, carrying telephone poles across country, and marching punishingly back again over the same ground. Their instructions were punctuated by "emergency" changes of plan and seeming breakdowns in logistics, resulting in shortage of food and sleep. By the time they had breakfasted on dogfish and walked across the hills to the bothy at Strathan several of them felt near to collapse, and more than a

104

few were spoiling for a showdown with the absentee Ridgway who was clearly responsible for all their discomforts.

The three groups left Strathan shortly after noon on the second day, taking separate routes for a move up to the north coast – the final area for survey, and from where they hoped to be evacuated by boat. A spell of rest, a piece of dogfish, and the unexpected clear weather helped the teams forward. Endless bleak moorland brightened in sunlight, the lochs were pools of blue, the bracken autumn red; away to the north-west was the stubby white finger of the Cape Wrath lighthouse. Snow on the mountains and a distant sight of the Orkneys helped lift the spirits. The teams really were teams now, each individual helping his comrades, trying to lose self-pity by thinking of the others, welded by the shared experience of the previous thirty-six hours.

Kearvaig House stands alone near the highest sea cliffs on the British mainland which rise to 900 feet a little to the east. Each group in turn reached this remote spot as darkness fell. They rattled hopefully at the door. A tall figure passed across a window. Relief – someone was coming! The door opened and a young man with a huge blond Afro hairstyle smiled shyly at them; he signalled for them to come through into the rough kitchen and handed the leader an envelope. Several of the group spoke to him at once, but he didn't seem to understand what they were saying. They tried with French and German, even a bit of holiday Spanish, but nobody could speak to Krister in Swedish, and he had inconveniently mislaid his English for the duration of the emergency.

The message in the envelope was stark enough – no boat, because there was no fuel. They were to be issued with a tin of sardines each and next day had to walk back to the head of the Kyle of Durness.

That night, all three teams slept for eight hours in separate rooms, and there was no communication between them. Next morning, they left Kearvaig at first light by diverging routes for the five-hour walk south-east to a rickety suspension bridge crossing the Dionard River where it flows into the Kyle of Durness.

The weather was kind, and the autumn chill kept the walkers cool. The first group, down at this point to seven men, shared the kit of the two weakest, who focussed their minds on reaching the bridge. As their leader pointed out, that bridge was right by the main coast road, so whatever happened, they'd all be able to get a lift back to Ardmore from there. Logically, the bridge must mean the end of the exercise, everyone was agreed on that.

From our position by the Dionard River suspension bridge, we heard over the radio when the group was crossing the Grudie River, just over a mile away on the far side of a low hill, that tempers were short, and they didn't appreciate being given a further sparse twenty-four hours' rations by the Grudie River. But they came across the suspension bridge on time, and were ushered into a bare corrugated iron hut close to the road. It looked as if it might have been some kind of store. A couple of rough trestle tables were fitted in an "L" at the far end of the hut, and the team sank gratefully on to benches by them. There were maps pinned to the walls and another table carried the paraphernalia for a detailed briefing. A mug of steaming coffee and a plate of biscuits awaited the arrival of someone.

The group sat quietly. The longer they sat, the less likely would they be to get moving again. Faces were drawn, but there was an aggressive team spirit about them, even though they were now heavily outnumbered by fresh-looking instructors and soldiers.

A Land-rover pulled off the empty coast road, and stopped in front of the hut, close to a camouflaged Army radio control vehicle. The driver went round and opened the passenger door for a mild-looking chap in a smart tweed suit carrying a briefcase. Everyone was suddenly very respectful. I walked to the hut, put my briefcase on the table, but stayed standing – looking down at the seated group.

"Hello. I'm John Ridgway; I'm sorry I haven't been on this course so far, but I've been down in Edinburgh speaking at the Festival." I sat down and took a sip of the coffee and a bite from the biscuit. Hungry eyes looked on but no one said a thing.

I took a long steady look at each of them in turn. One of them returned my gaze in a forceful manner. He was a high-stepping centre from a class rugby club in the south of England.

"How's it gone so far, Peter?"

"Oh, pretty good really, sir," Peter Mitchell sounded his most deferential. "This is Group 1." He introduced them by name.

"How have you enjoyed the course so far . . . Jones?" I asked firmly.

"Um – it's been very good," muttered Jones, scarcely able to believe his own voice.

106

I paused. "You don't seem to have shaved . . ." I looked directly at the rugby player.

"We haven't had time." He answered aggressively.

"Pity to be a sheep, following the poor standards of others," I said sharply. The rugby player bit his lip, barely able to control his anger, and for a moment we stared at each other. I asked one or two more questions relating to the aims of the course and then asked Peter to continue with the briefing. The group listened warily. I thought they were still holding up as a group, but they might go either way when they heard the next part of the task.

Peter covered the work they had done so far on the one inch map, complimenting them on their efforts and the standard of their written reports. Then he turned to a map of the north of Scotland, emphasising that the scale was now four miles to every inch. He told them the explosion at the chemical factory had turned out to be only a part of wide-scale terrorist activity across Britain, and as a result of this there had been a considerable breakdown in the supplies of fuel and foodstuffs. The relief situation had been expanded, a new Relief HQ was being set up in Thurso, some seventy-five miles away along the north coast.

The group was to make its way fifty miles across country, through the mountains, to the railway at Kinbrace, where tickets awaited them for the journey to Thurso. They were to report to the Relief Headquarters in two days' time. The going would be difficult and there was a snow warning. A fresh training officer, instructor and radio operator would be allotted to the group. They would have to carry tents and spare batteries for the radio. A fishing boat was leaving on the tide from Portnancon, some four miles across the hills to the east, in two hours' time. If they caught the boat it would take them across Loch Eriboll, saving them at least ten miles.

The group was told to go outside and make a plan of action, returning five minutes later when one of them would be chosen to give the briefing. The atmosphere was fairly fraught as they got up to go outside. Tents and batteries were issued at the door. The rugby player grabbed a couple of biscuits from the plate as he passed, but I smiled indulgently.

Presently they filed back in. They did plan to continue to Thurso, but the two weakest men were going to drop out as they couldn't go fast enough to reach Kinbrace in time for the train.

"What about food?" asked the rugby player resentfully.

"Weren't you given some back at the Grudie Bridge?" replied Peter Mitchell.

"Yes, but nothing like enough to get us across to the train."

"Well, you can have these four biscuits," I chipped in. "There's five of you – but then you've had two already, haven't you?" The rugby player was furious; he looked down at the floor.

"We've got another four eggs here." Peter held out a plate. Again one was left without. It was all too much for the rugby player. With a bellow of rage, he flung his egg at me – it missed, and smashed against the wall, sliding messily down the grey corrugations.

"Don't be so bloody stupid!" shouted someone. "Now there's only three!"

The rugby player jumped up, fists clenched. Then we were all on our feet, and I was thinking about my new suit. But they all filed sheepishly out.

Five minutes later they were gone, climbing grimly up the hill on the other side of the road, leaving the two casualties in the back of a Land-rover. The Signals NCO called from his vehicle to say the second group was just leaving the Grudie Bridge, but was moving very slowly. I asked for the third group to be delayed at the bridge. The tables were set up again and the driver and I went back to the quarry down the road in the Land-rover, to await the signal to come forward for the repeat.

On the hillside the fresh instructor, TO and radio operator were beginning to draw ahead of Group 1, urging them to catch the fishing boat. The group hung on grimly, nursing the last of their energy, determined not to be beaten.

As soon as they were out of sight of the group coming across from the Grudie Bridge, the TO called a halt. "That's it – you've done it," he smiled. "We all go down to the Land-rover in the quarry and then back to Ardmore!" A cautious silence followed. Then a great cheer went up.

The next couple of days were run by personnel from the Management Development division of IBM. They dealt with motivation and leadership, encouraging the groups to relate standard textbook theories to their own recent experiences in the field.

Finally there was the "Trust and Influence" exercise. Each individual gave each of the others in his group points for how much influence he thought they had exerted in the course of "Timeplan" and "Tortoiseshell" and how much he trusted them.

A similar score for each quality indicates a reasonable openness; a high score on both counts identifies the born leader.

High on influence but low on trust is a pattern which often occurs. The dominant and aggressive person can also be seen as self-centred, manipulating the group for his own ends. In some circumstances this influence may be acceptable, but in the situations the groups had been in on this course, personalities tend to become quite transparent; and then dislike and resentment creep in.

The "nice guy" usually scores high on trust but low on influence. The group often feels a strong loyalty towards the quieter personalities after the battles are over, and this note of appreciation is underlined with a pile of trust points. Whether this person is simply harmless to the others is what needs to be examined in the context of leadership. The course is not designed simply to reward decency: leadership is seldom a popularity contest.

Occasionally, after the six days, someone is ignored and ends up with no points at all. While in other scoring patterns the participant can draw something from the experience – at least he has had some recognition. But being ignored makes it important for the TO to help him constructively with this reaction.

Discussions between the eight participants in the group and their TO are quite sensitive. Only six days previously, none of them had ever met, and now they feel they have shared a lifetime. There have been situations which individuals may wish they had not shared with the others, while some have gained steadily in stature as the days passed.

The individual participant must feel he has gained something from the course. At best he will have developed a clearer view of any problem he might have previously had in his dealings with other people, and from this, discovered a way of modifying his behaviour to improve the situation. Simply winning through the traumatic experiences of the six days helps to lift the individual's self-esteem.

For the last phase we pile them back into the Land-rovers before midnight, with tents and rations, but they remain uncertain of their task and destination. Darkness limits discussion, and alighting from the vehicles, they are led to pre-marked individual isolation sites in moorland. Each person is equipped with a tent and adequate rations, and asked not to stray more than twenty-five yards from his site, close to a water supply.

The individual remains alone for the next forty hours. Once the tent is up, he can crawl into his sleeping bag and simply drift off to sleep. Most people wake up next morning, make some breakfast, then try unsuccessfully to go back to sleep. Few people experience real solitude in our modern society. Many people are lonely – but solitude and loneliness are different things.

Participants are asked to take no reading materials with them. It rains now and then, but they can be comfortable in their tents, surrounded by silence, and this gives them a chance to think over all that has happened so far. The discussions of the previous couple of days were something we hoped they'd consider.

Towards the end of the second day the TOs visit each person in their group and briefly discuss the course. Shortly before dark, instructors collect everyone together for a hot meal, and the final exercise begins.

The course has to form its own organisation structure and to split into many small groups, thus ensuring the destruction of the original eight-man group pattern. The choice of an overall leader poses some difficulties, and in the event a compromise leader is often selected. The task is complex, applying lessons from the earlier part of the course. Less emphasis is necessary on the physical side of things and success depends much more on the organisational abilities of the participants.

Everyone returns to the School in time for an early breakfast, and the course stands down until lunch. Then the afternoon is spent discussing the isolation and final course exercises. The remaining couple of days are devoted to the usual activities of a normal course: sailing, rock climbing and canoeing, but there isn't much call for hill walking. It is not an easy course.

The departure of the IBM party signalled the end of the season, and suddenly Ardmore was silent again. We turned our attention to roping things down for the winter gales, and puzzling out how to get *English Rose V*, our new special Nicholson 32, from Camper & Nicholsons' yard in Gosport up to Ardmore. Sailing it up straight after Christmas seemed the only solution and, in the event, this presented a test worthy of the most fiendish IBM leadership and planning exercise.

There were only three of us aboard: two young instructors, Francis Ash and Jamie Young, and myself. Jamie had been with us more or less from the start of the School. He had been among the boys from Dunrobin School who'd helped us replace the roof sections on the main building at Skerricha, after they'd been blown away by a south-easterly gale just before our opening. He was a good man in a tight corner. Which was just as well, since the first real life "emergency" which occurred, as if straight out of a teasing IBM sealed envelope, was young Francis' being stricken with suspected appendicitis in the Irish Sea, several days out of Portsmouth. We put hazardously into Portrush and a third of our crew duly departed towards Derry in a blue flash of ambulance lights.

The forecast for the Hebrides was south-east wind force 7 to severe gale force 9. As Jamie said, encouraging as ever, there's not much space in the Minch if it gets really windy, and it would be harder with two of us. But our luck held, and we acquired a crew replacement at Portrush. Brian Cunningham told us he had recognised the name of the boat through binoculars and had been trying to get a place on the IBM course for a couple of years. He was also an experienced sailor in northern waters.

Our next hazard was trying to home in on the Barra Head radio beacon accurately in a Force 9 in order to enter the Minch. Too late we caught a glimpse of the lighthouse behind us and with a rising storm 10 from the south were committed to an outside passage round the Hebrides.

It was an awfully worrying night. All these years later it would be easy to recall it as just another tricky situation, but it was much more than that. We were running under bare poles in an engineless boat before a winter storm, and there were close on eighteen hours of darkness in every twenty-four. The chain of islands which make up the Outer Hebrides stretches 135 miles from Barra in the south to the Butt of Lewis in the north. We were being blown close up the western side of this fearful coastline, without any firm idea of the distance we had travelled as we had taken in the Walker log to stop it tangling with the warp we were streaming astern to slow us down, and our radio direction finder had no satisfactory beacons in range for us to take cross-bearings.

At the back of all our minds too was the thought of the unlit islands of St Kilda, some seventy-five miles north of Barra Head, with cliffs rising nearly 1,400 feet sheer out of the Atlantic. Approaching them from the south-east, they would present a tiny four-mile frontage on our ragged night ride up from Barra. Surely, we comforted ourselves, if we had actually been aiming at them, we would miss them in these conditions. It was 0730 the next morning, and the faintest glimmer of a new day, when Brian, who was on watch, let out a thin scream of terror, which brought Jamie and me hurtling up from the cockpit.

For a moment we just stood there. None of us had ever seen anything like it – we'd never been so close to cliffs in such a sea. A black wedge, like the bows of some huge ship bearing down on us, it seemed already too close to avoid. The seas appeared to rise right up it and disappear in the clouds.

What it was or where we were, didn't matter. I had that awful sinking feeling of despair in the pit of my stomach. It was as if we were in the grip of a malevolent magnet, and it wouldn't matter if we tried to go forwards, sideways, or backwards – it had drawn us all the way from Barra, there could be no escaping it now . . .

"Get the spitfire up!" I shouted, and Jamie was already undoing the ties which held the scrap of foresail to the deck, while Brian braced himself against the mast with the halliard in his hands ready to haul up the sail. It was up within seconds, and I was winching in the jib sheet from the cockpit.

The "magnetism" of the rock maintained its grip on us. I let go of the trailing rope on the port side, hoping it would help us to turn starboard and away from the rock. We now had 720 feet of thick rope trailing astern in one long line; the sail was up and this increased the drag on the rope. I set about hauling the rope aboard, feeling as if it was somehow in the grip of the rock and we were pulling against each other – it was a desperate weight. I realise now that I should have let the rope go, but even in that extreme situation, the ingrained training that everything should be made to last for ever would not leave me. Lessons learned on the Atlantic rowing, and solo-sailing, the painful economic realities of building the School: all these things prevented me from ever thinking of throwing the rope away.

It would have served as a curious epitaph, for I have a feeling that heaven may be a place where the lucky ones are allowed to sweep floors all day, and if they're especially good may be given a go with the vacuum cleaner. Jamie and Brian came back into the cockpit and disengaged the Hasler self-steering gear, then Brian took the helm while Jamie and I strained to pull in the warp. We couldn't use a sheet winch because the new polypropylene rope was hopelessly kinked. Agonisingly slowly, it began filling the cockpit in a tangled mess.

Next thing I remember is the wind veering – or was it the

Portlevorchy from the Ardmore footpath, with the Adventure School across Loch a' Chadh-Fi and Ben Stack on the horizon.

Canoeists go through their paces with the Foinaven Ridge beyond.

Mucking out Lone Bothy before the Ladies take up residence.

Masthead view of Ardmore, looking south-west.

boat responding to the helm as the rope shortened in the sea behind us? I really don't feel I'm the sort of fellow for whom the wind would change just when I'm stuck right in the jaws of death.

We swung to the north of the rock, and I was completely done in. I crawled below and tried to orientate myself with the chart. We had all but wrecked ourselves on Stac Levenish, a six acre, 185-foot high pyramid-shaped rock. The main island of St Kilda lay a mile and a half beyond Levenish and we were going to clear it all right. The wind was rapidly veering to the south-west and falling away.

We rounded the Butt of Lewis, on the northern end of the Outer Hebrides, during another night of storm force winds from the south, but at dawn the wind eased again, and we could see clear across the Minch to what looked like a scatter of sharply pointed, snow-covered islands. These were in fact, individual mountains along the north-west coast on the Scottish mainland, and un-known to me, just to seaward of the easily identifiable Foinaven Ridge, Marie Christine and Rebecca were scrambling out to Ard-more Point to look for any signs of us. My wife was half fearing the worst, but Rebecca, with all the optimism of a six-year-old, was quite certain all was well.

"Don't worry, Mummy, they'll soon be here," she kept saying. But it wasn't until a quarter past eleven that night, that we finally found our way into Loch a'Chadh-fi.

The coastline is entirely unlit and we were conscious of the lack of an engine as we threaded through the rocks in a colossal swell. I'd never come in in the dark before, and there were the usual sudden squalls from the hillsides which are so easy to see during the day as they race across the water towards you – but in the dark there is no warning.

We had up the mainsail and No.2 genoa to ensure steerage way; there was nothing for it but to keep on at full speed. I trusted my memory for the ninety-degree turn to the left through the seventy-five-yard-wide channel, between the headland at the bottom of the croft and Chadh-fi Island. I was at the helm, with Jamie anxiously watching for dim signs of the mooring buoy, boathook in hand up in the bow. Brian managed the jib winches in the cockpit, alarmed at the sudden speed and narrowness of it all.

High up on the hillside, close on our left and tucked out of the wind, I could see the white sides and black, unlit windows of the two old croft houses.

"All asleep, the bleeders!" I muttered uncharitably.

Past Heckie's lambing pen, and the potato patch – just a black square on the steep grassy slope – then the peat shed and the Annait headland itself. Dead ahead lay the island.

"Here we go!" I called to Jamie, pushing the helm away and pulling in the mainsheet at the same time.

"Tighten the jib a bit, Brian!" He raced the winch handle back and forth, adding the sound of the clickety winch to those of the wind and rushing water in the night.

Marie Christine heard the thunder of the sails as we rounded up on the mooring buoy under the wood, and an oil lamp appeared in our bedroom window a hundred feet above the sea. Dragging on some clothes, she called to Becca to stay in bed while she went to pick up Daddy in the Dipper. Next thing she was trying not to slip on the nearly vertical wet grass of the hill, and waving her torch in welcome. The old sixteen-foot timber rowing boat moved easily downwind to the yacht. We three were delighted at not having to inflate the Avon dinghy in the dark.

"Hello," squeaked my wife. "How did you get on?"

"Some trip!" I replied, catching the painter.

10

Our friend Willie the Post retired that winter. The Gaffer took over the job and for a while our mail came by sea from Skerricha instead of on Willie's old bike-and-foot route along the track and up the waterfall. Jamie Young saved the Gaffer from drowning one winter day after he'd capsized his tiny pram dinghy on the way out to board his ancient black lobster boat, the *Dove*. A few weeks later the *Dove* broke her moorings and ended up high and dry on the top of Fionn's Rock on the southern side of the channel near Portlevorchy. Again Jamie came to the rescue, and the boat was refloated on one of those extraordinary January high tides caused by storm surges. We had never seen such tides. They turned the "museum" into an island, and another three inches would have flooded the building itself.

This was the winter of the fuel crisis and once again the future of the School seemed in doubt. At least our Rayburn was fired by peat not oil and Lance was positively enjoying the idea of a siege economy. Already he had plenty of vegetables from his gardens on Upper Ardmore. The loch shore was encrusted with mussels, and we could easily shoot shags which are often eaten by islanders at the southern end of the Hebrides.

One January afternoon, Ada saw a strange figure in a long brown overcoat slinking down the long hill from the top of Gentle's Brae towards the rickety gate in the Ardmore boundary fence. At a distance he appeared to have a stick across his shoulders, over which both arms were draped like a chained convict. By the time he came into view over the lip of the waterfall, Ada had the binoculars out – it was a young man, and it wasn't a stick but an iron bar. She wasn't really afraid, but nevertheless she wished Lance wasn't over at the School. Knocking at the Blue House door, the visitor asked politely in a pronounced Italian accent where he might find John Ridgway, and Ada lost no time in pointing the route on through the wood to Lower Ardmore.

His name was Aldo, and he had come from Milan to the north

of Scotland to practise winter survival. He told us he was carrying the long starting handle from his vehicle, in case he should be attacked. He was living in a short-wheelbase Land-rover with canvas sides, parked three and a half miles away, on the high ground near the Rhiconich River just above Mrs Fraser's Post Office. Aldo lived off the mussels he gathered from the shore nearby, but just at the moment he was supplementing his calorie-controlled diet with a sack of maize dog food. He got on very well with Rebecca right from the start, and he was certainly something entirely new to her. As it was getting dark Marie Christine suggested he stay the night, but she insisted he should have a bath before supper, and no sooner was he in the bathroom than she collected his socks and underwear from the spare bedroom and tossed them on to the burning peats in the Rayburn. Then she washed his shirt and trousers, so that for supper Aldo was entirely clad in my gear. Only the heavy brown overcoat escaped burning or washing. Lance and Ada came down to supper, and afterwards we talked a bit, but Aldo's English wasn't that good, and Marie Christine and I were anxious to avoid Lance starting up on the subject of the three-day week because it only upset him. The home-brew was beginning to flow, so we decided to try and divert the energies into some sort of game, but Scrabble would be out of the question for Aldo and he didn't look too keen on dominoes either.

"What about 'Happy Families', Mummy?" asked Rebecca, and we all agreed this was probably the fairest solution as it was such a long time since any of us could remember having played the game, that we'd all have to learn the rules together. In the event Aldo proved very quick on the uptake, and he was so pleased at his success that whenever he came out to Ardmore in the future, he would knock on Ada's door and call "Ees Mrs Bunn at 'ome, please?"

Aldo stayed by the Rhiconich river all that winter. He said he planned to sail round the world, but we never really got to the bottom of what it was that he was trying to achieve, and he left just as suddenly as he had arrived.

One Saturday morning Marie Christine, Rebecca and I went into the ruin next door and began once more to clear away the brambles. I got a bow saw and cut down a stout rowan tree which was growing in the middle of one of the rooms. Since Hughie had married and moved to Inverness the plans for rebuilding No.78

116

had been shelved, and the stack of 2,000 lightweight concrete blocks was beginning to crumble after repeated winter frosts. Lance and I had often discussed ways of bringing the rest of the building materials up the steep concave slope from the shore, but we never could agree. He thought some form of windlass, hauling a cart with large wheels, was the only solution. I saw only the irretrievable damage this might do to my precious grass. Our topsoil was so fragile, we'd soon find ourselves living on a bare rock.

In the spring of 1974 we took on the first of several instructors we have had over the years from Australia and New Zealand, and most of them have come as a result of the influence of Stafford Morse. Staff as he was always known was a short, cheerful fellow of twenty-one; longish fair hair and a bushy beard concealed some awful scars resulting from climbing accidents. Long spells in hospital, with a broken neck and a crushed skull among other things, had developed in him an unquenchable enthusiasm for life and excitement. Staff's verve and example were to inspire so many people at Ardmore in the few remaining years of his life.

In the short interval between the Easter courses and the start of the Businessmen's Courses that year, we made the most of the driest April since records were begun two hundred years before. The biggest ritual at this time is peat cutting. Lance still manages to cut a few from a number of small banks up above his house, using aerial ropeways to swing the bags down to Ada, who waits below in the bushes by the byre. This is all rather disturbing for the chickens as the heavy sacks hurtle past their coop and into the restraining wire at the bottom. Lance's years in the foundry have given him a fluency with the spade which discovers peats where others have long thought the ground worked-out. The Macpherson family must have given up working there generations before, as other shallow scrapes for peat can be seen far out towards Ardmore Point. The desperation for peats in a harsh climate is measured by a story Robert Ross once told me. Robert is another of Granny Ross's sons, and with eight children in the house, tasks like fetching water up from the well and carrying peats down from the hill were soon taken care of. But this was not the case for old Simon and Kate in No.78. "Kate gave me my first contract," remembered Robert, "a bag of peat down from the hill for a shilling – and she only got ten shillings a week pension!"

In a countryside bare of woodland, and hundreds of miles from

117

the coalfields, peat banks are much sought after resources, handed down through the generations with the crofts. Since the rise in oil prices in the early seventies the area has seen a marked return to peat, and many crofters living by the road who had gone to all the trouble of converting their Rayburns to oil in the late sixties have gone back to the peat again. There was, of course, never any conversion to oil out on the Ardmore peninsula. When the peats were worked out on Ardmore itself, the Rosses simply took to their boats and rowed the three hundred yards across the loch to Ardbeg, where they worked two good banks close to the sea. The only snag with this lay in the handling. The peats had to be bagged in large hessian sacks, carried down the steep shore some fifty feet or so, and rowed across for unloading at Ardmore at the foot of the croft. Everything burned in the house then had to be carried a hundred feet straight up from the sea. As the saying goes, "The peat warms you three times: when you cut it, when you carry it, and when you burn it." I've always thought that old Hector Ross was sustained into old age by his interest in shepherding and his daily exercise. Even at eighty, he was still carrying a sack of peats up that hundred foot hill every day.

Our three peat banks came with the croft, each fifty yards long but they're far from Ardmore – three miles down Loch Laxford on the southern shore, in a sheltered bay more than half a mile off the coast road. We tie the boats to the same iron rings which moored the sailing ships chartered from Bristol in the last century to take the victims of the Clearances away to the other side of the Atlantic.

The first step is to ensure the drainage is in good condition from one year to the next. Working ankle deep in mud is disheartening. A couple of days before the cutting itself, the ground is prepared: the heather is marked out in squares with the rutting spade along the length of the vertical face of the bank left from the previous year's cutting. Then the "flatter" is used to skin the heather squares off the top of the peat, and these are carefully laid down to provide a fresh carpet of growth where the peat was removed from the previous year. It's rather like strip mining.

The day of the peat cutting needs to be fine yet cool, and a good big box of food and drink is loaded into the boat. We aim to cut something over 5,000 peats before dark. The party splits into teams of three or four. Each has a man with a "tusk", who stands on top of the bank slicing the peats into just the right size and nudging them into the hands of the fellow in the trench below who stands on the heather squares cut from the top of the peat strip on the previous day. Each soggy peat is handed on to another person who lays it gently on the heather beyond.

It all gets a bit competitive as teams race to complete their strip first, and begin cutting a second layer, and this is where the advantage of laying the first layer well back from the edge comes in. It's a back-breaking event, but with plenty of sandwiches and jugs of tea, the whole year's stock of peat can be cut in a single day.

The weather plays a large part in the next step, because the peat needs to dry and shrink before it can be built into little three-sided towers with one on top; and these are later moved down into a large stack on the shore for loading on to the boats towards the end of summer. We store our peat in a shed at the foot of the croft and bring it up the hill a sack at a time as it's needed. Good peat is black and heavy, but we have to take the good with the bad, which is light and full of fibre like straw. This poor stuff burns quickly and produces much less heat. Peat is certainly an invaluable free fuel in a subsistence economy, but there's an awful lot of work in it to stop you from feeling too lucky.

One Saturday in May I was confronted by a ladies' tea party in the Wooden House. We were embarking on our first Women's Course and I don't know quite what I expected. Certainly not handbags at tea time. I felt distinctly out of my depth, but noticed Marie Christine and Ada were really enjoying themselves, and the ladies were loving Ada's cakes. The trouble with Ada's cakes is that they look so good people think they must have come from a shop, but there aren't any cake shops within seventy miles.

The ladies ranged in age from thirty to nearly seventy and they were at Ardmore for a week. For some, it was the first time they'd been away on their own since they were married. I would never have believed at the time that I'd be seeing some of those same faces round the same table ten years later. Perhaps they did take a little longer over some of the activities, but the ladies made up with determination what they lacked in physical strength, showing they could do just the same programme as the men. I think they got more from the scenery and the bird and plant life than the men did, and they certainly beat them out of sight when it came to making packed lunches after breakfast.

The ladies especially enjoyed sailing to Handa Island and, now
we had *English Rose V*, we had two boats and could take the whole
course on the same day. Jamie skippered *English Rose IV*, the
thirty-foot sloop in which I had sailed to Brazil and which we
now hoped he would sail in the 1976 Observer Single-handed
Transatlantic Race.

Handa is derived from a Norse word meaning "sandy", and
the island is a massive wedge of Torridonian sandstone lying less
than half a mile off the much older and harder Lewisian Gneiss
of the mainland. It is roughly one and a half miles from east to
west, by a mile wide from north to south. 400-foot sea cliffs rise
sheer on the north and west sides and their weathered sandstone
ledges provide nesting sites for more than a hundred thousand
guillemots and razorbills from April to July each year. They share
the cliffs with large colonies of fulmars, kittiwakes and shags, as
well as a few hundred puffins.

Until the middle of the last century a small community existed
on the island. It had better grazing than the mainland, as well as
an inexhaustible supply of eggs and birds which were pickled for
the long winters. In the eighteenth century the feathers were
bartered for wool, weight for weight, with the mainlanders. They
had their own queen, who was the oldest surviving widow, and
a "parliament" which sat at eleven o'clock each morning. It took
a potato famine to drive that little community from their island
home in 1841 and most of them emigrated to Canada. The grave-
stones that remain largely belong to mainland dead, brought over
to avoid having their graves disturbed by wolves whose hungry
diggings made short work of the shallow topsoil.

I have sailed round Handa Island well over five hundred times
in the past twenty years, and in that time the sea has killed six
men there. So hazardous are these waters, that I try to treat every
voyage as my first. Each time I am inspired by the perfection of
the bottle-green combers breaking on the flats off the south-west
corner, or the heaving sight of a great whale's back as he comes
up to blow, or maybe the explosion of a flock of kittiwakes, the
sunlight pale white through their wings, as they lift off together
when we pass close to their rocky perch. Sometimes it's the élan
from a charge through the overfalls in the narrow southern end
of the Sound, or a rush along the white beaches with a free wind
in the sails. With the autumn gales comes a majestic tramping
run, close in under the cliffs, booming home with black squalls

120

on our tail and at a speed which would take us to Greenland in under a week . . .

> To suffer woes which Hope thinks infinite;
> To forgive wrongs darker than death or night;
>   To defy Power, which seems omnipotent;
> To love, and bear; to hope till Hope creates
> From its own wreck the thing it contemplates;
>   Neither to change, nor falter, nor repent;
> This . . . is to be
> Good, great and joyous, beautiful and free;
> This is alone Life, Joy, Empire and Victory.

When I start thinking like Shelley, then I know the air is doing me some good.

Sometimes I walk from the visitors' stone bothy on the southeast corner, up a green hill and across a stone-walled meadow to visit the RSPB warden who lives on the island from April to September. But often I never do get to see the warden with my sandwiches and his cup of tea. The sights and sounds of the meadow are so wonderful I just sit down in the sun with the old wall to keep the breeze off me and drink in the perfection of it all – that meadow is one of my favourite places in the whole world.

At first I was a bit sceptical about confining visitors to a circular marked route, as the Society did when they took over, but a substantial breeding group of great skuas assembles in the centre of the island each year now that visitors are kept away from their nesting area, which more than justifies the RSPB intervention. The Handa warden is often a shy, gentle sort of fellow, happier on the island than the mainland, fit, broke, bearded and deeply tanned, in a shredded Barbour jacket and old wellies. Occasionally he might own a car, but that seems to be about the limit of his material possessions. Weeks may pass without Old William the Boatman bringing across a visitor from Tarbet. The man who takes a second season on Handa is an exceptionally self-sufficient person, but his knowledge of everything from lichen to golden eagle is impressive. Whenever a warden has come up to visit us, he has always left us better informed about the woodland and shore life around Ardmore.

The climax of the Women's Course is the two-day expedition to climb Ben Stack, Arkle and Foinaven, or any permutation of the three which suits them. Before attempting the Foinaven Ridge on the second day, they spend a night at the remote Lone bothy.

It was a strong team of fourteen which left the bothy with me at seven thirty that fine morning on the first course. There were eight ladies on the course, plus Kay Price, our sixty-year-old secretary, the two instructors and myself. Marie Christine and Sinclair Mackintosh's wife Sandee had also decided to come along in case the ladies proved too much for me!

The first part of the walk took us into a small plantation of firs at the bottom of the Allt Horn burn, less than a quarter of a mile from the bothy. The entrance to the plantation is between two halves of a solitary boulder some twenty feet tall which must have split as it came to a halt after a ride on a melting glacier a long time ago. A stout wrought-iron gate is set into this cleft, and it's said that one of the dukes had planned to build a lodge by a nearby waterfall and the plantation was intended to form a windbreak. It would have made a grand site, well away from the main road and with a tremendous view of Ben Stack. Now the little stand of pine trees is like a scented oasis when you come off the mountain.

The real climb begins at the gate in the deer-fence at the top of the plantation. From this point the path follows the Allt Horn burn up its steep-sided valley and round the back of Arkle to its source on the flanks of Meall Horn, whose summit is a couple of hundred feet higher than Ben Stack. I have climbed Foinaven more than a hundred times, in all the seasons of the year, and the approach up the Allt Burn early on a good spring morning is as uplifting as anything I found in the Himalayas.

The path is barely eighteen inches wide, but beautifully constructed, with skilful drainage on the up-side and sturdy culverts to allow tributaries to pass unheeded on their way down to the main burn below us on our right. The rainfall on the mountains can be sudden and savage, and these clear, elegant streams rapidly turn to raging torrents. I had learned from the track we'd built from Skerricha to the School that a path is only as good as its drains. This old path beside the Allt Horn was built for ponies to carry down stags shot on the hill. It has needed little attention over the years and the springy heather has curled in from both sides almost obscuring the yellow strip of firm gravel which runs three miles up from the Lone Bothy to 1,750 feet on the shoulder of Creagan Meall Horn. We should be leaving it there to strike north, but the path winds on down for a further eight miles to Gobernuisgach Lodge over to the east.

I was hoping to see the golden eagle in the Allt Horn valley. I'd often seen him there before, soaring like a black plank in the sky, but we were out of luck. There were plenty of deer, though, and they moved warily over the skyline on the far side of the valley as we made our way steadily up the path. The larks sang loud and all seemed well with the world, apart from the forecast of rain in the afternoon. Already the cloud was banking over Lewis, forty miles across the Minch, away on our western horizon, but for now the mile and a half north to the cairn on the first peak was perfectly clear.

After the firm surface of the path, the plod across moorland bog with its gradual ascent for nearly a thousand feet took a bit of the steam out of even the fittest ladies, but they cheered up a bit when I told them we should be moving on rock for the three miles to the far end of the Ridge. All the same I could see one or two of them were thinking to themselves that the high point of Ganu Mor looked as far away as ever.

We passed round a flask of hot tea while sheltering from the rising south-westerly wind, in the lee of the cairn, and I split the party so that the four slower ladies needn't feel harassed about holding up the faster four who were hoping to reach the Rhiconich before closing time. If the men could do it . . .

I set off with the faster team. Marie Christine was really enjoying her day away from the office and Sandee was going well, though I wondered how her golfing gear would stand up to the rain. Kay Price was insistent on coming on with the fast group, too, and I just hoped I'd be able to cut the mustard with such style when I got to sixty. I had no doubts at all about the four ladies, except that they might leave me behind. We moved swiftly across a tricky curve round the head of a valley, disturbing a few ptarmigan along the way.

Next week or the week after, I'd find a nesting bird out on those stony flats, and a few weeks on from that the mother would hobble about trailing a wing to lure me away from the chicks hiding among the crevices in the rocks. Or maybe the story wouldn't end so happily, and all I'd find would be a few yellow-stained broken eggshells to show where a predator had fed.

Near where we joined the Ridge proper, it falls sharply for some five hundred feet down a sort of staircase in a deep "V", then rises almost as steeply up the other side. This is Cadha na Beucaich (the Pass of the Roaring), that fatal coughing bellow in the rutting season that gives away the stag's position to the approaching stalker as he comes up the hillside into the wind.

After the briefest of rests we cut round the side of the hill into the saddle beyond, in order to avoid the "Shed", a slippery, steeply sloping wedge of rock with a sheer drop of hundreds of feet. The sky was dark now, but to our right lay the Dionard Valley, a completely deserted moonscape whose rock floor is 2,300 million years old, among the oldest rocks exposed on the surface of the earth. Northward of the valley lies Loch Eriboll, a ten-mile gash in the north coast which had served as a deep-water forming-up place for many an allied convoy bound for Russia in the Second World War. The Navy christened it Loch 'Orrible, and it looked none too cheery through the rain that day either, as we huddled in the shelter of a great pile of boulders just half a mile short of Ganu Mor, the 2,980 foot summit of the Foinaven Ridge.

"We're almost there," called one of the ladies over the wind, taking off her rucksack. "I've got a Mars bar here. We can share it out." And she dug into a side pocket in the rucksack, while someone else looked for a pen-knife.

"Oooooh!" screamed our benefactress, throwing the chocolate bar to the ground.

I reached over and picked it up.

"Look," said the lady. "It's been all chewed!" I looked closer. One end had the unmistakable marks of a mouse's teeth – through the brown paper and deep into the caramel and chocolate.

"It's gnawed right through my rucksack, too!" she wailed, pointing at a hole in the side pocket. "And I was using it as my pillow last night at Lone . . .!" The rest of the team paled.

"Oh, come on," I said. "The businessmen would never make a fuss over a little thing like a mouse!"

We plodded on along the Ridge, heads bowed into the wind and horizontal rain, each person lost in their own thoughts, just keeping the heels of the person in front in view. I kept looking back, but no one seemed to be flagging too badly, although Sandee was beginning to look a bit wet through the old golfing jacket and trousers. We each added a stone to the cairn on Ganu Mor, and then turned to retrace our steps a couple of hundred yards before swinging north again for the last half mile to Ceann Garbh on the very end of the Ridge, still with a fighting chance of reaching the Rhiconich before it closed, but not many of the party looked as if they were going to drink a lot of beer.

Nearly eighty, and chewing a fat cigar as always, Old Johnny McLeod – everyone's old at the Rhiconich – seemed to have owned the hotel for ever. His wry sense of humour astonished many of his guests, but late at night in bad weather with nowhere else to go for miles they had to be pretty upset to leave. "How are you?" people asked the old man, kindly.

"None the better for seeing you!" he'd snort, chomping down on the cigar. He kept a few donkeys in a field by the hotel, and one day he was driving them up the road waving a birch stick at them. Some tourists stopped their car and began to photograph the rustic scene. When Johnny drew level with the car he leaned over towards the driver. The passengers listened intently, wondering what piece of folklore they might hear. Poker-faced, Johnny spoke very slowly. "Is this the way – to Jerusalem?"

He liked to act the mean old man, but the locals knew differently. I remember the time Rebecca was on a sponsored walk with children and parents from the Kinlochbervie School; it was a bitter day around Easter time and the empty road seemed to stretch on and on for ever. The children were beginning to look a bit disheartened, and we were only halfway from Scourie to the Rhiconich. Johnny McLeod turned up just at the right moment, sweeping into a passing place by the roadside with hot sausage rolls and tea for everyone – such treatment is usually reserved only for closing time on Auld Year's Night.

After the ladies came the businessmen and for the next ten weeks I seemed to eat all my meals standing up, dashing around collecting the plates from one course and reappearing with the next. There are two separate worlds in the Wooden House: the one with twenty men seated round a long table overlooking loch and mountain is a relaxed, jovial, peaceful sort of place. But just through the door, in the kitchen, is like the engine room of a damaged warship in action. The room in the early years was far too small for a start, scarcely larger than you might expect in a caravan; somehow Marie Christine managed to cook for thirty people on two little household Calor gas cookers placed side by side. At the sink stood the unlucky duty instructor, wreathed in steam; another fellow was jammed against the wall trying to dry mountains of plates with a series of sopping tea-towels and fitting them into an impossibly small storage space beneath the sink. As the weeks passed, kitchen rows became increasingly violent and frequent, while for me, life sometimes seemed to be a long list of things which instructors kept saying we needed, and an equally long list of disasters I thought were about to happen.

It was at this time of full pressure that Marie Christine and Becca decided they really did need a pony! I took advice from Sinclair Mackintosh and from Willie the Post's brother, Doy, who looked after the ponies used for collecting the deer from the stalking on the Reay Forest. It looked doubtful if a pony could be brought up the "Waterfall", never mind ridden on the steep rocky Ardmore peninsula, interspersed as it is with bogs. But I was over-ruled and a great Connemara gelding named Boy Blue joined the team. He walked the three miles in from the horse-box, which wouldn't leave the main road, and Staff, the farmer's boy from the Australian outback, set about coaxing the unenthusiastic creature up the "Waterfall" and into his new home in the tiny field in front of the Blue House. Lance felt sorry for the poor beast standing alone by the fence, so he let him out, thinking he would wander about on Upper Ardmore looking decorative. But Boy Blue had a mind of his own and when he didn't receive enough attention from Ada and Rebecca, who were often distracted by boring things like school, he emphasised his presence by chewing lumps from the windowsill of the schoolroom. Lance was less than enchanted by this performance, and when the monster pony took to leaning on the fences round the gardens to get at the vegetables their friendship deteriorated. Poor Boy Blue went on to lose more friends one dark night when a team of thirsty instructors walking up through the wood to a home-brewed welcome at the Blue House suddenly heard a noise like thunder up ahead. With no way of escape other than to take to the trees, everyone leaped into the bushes on the down side and rolled helter skelter down the nearly vertical hillside. Crazed snorting and a blaze of sparks marked the passage of the monster pony on his way to pastures new at Lower Ardmore, and a new era of chewed laundry and sundry vandalism had dawned on the old place.

An old era was also coming to an end. The Ross family was going to leave Ardmore. Granny Ross was now over eighty, and Heckie felt they must live beside the road at Foindle in his brother Robert's croft across Loch Laxford, now that Robert and his wife had moved over to Ardgay on the east coast to keep their large family together during their children's secondary education.

Heckie kept on with the sheep and came over by boat several times a week. But it wasn't the same without Granny Ross and the cups of tea. It was the first time anyone could remember when there were no Rosses living out on Ardmore.

11

I loved Ardmore in all its seasons. I loved the way I disturbed the old buzzard from his roosting perch along my morning run, and the muted rumble of the Crocach Burn as it spills into the sea. I loved the winter willows burned red by frost against the hillside and our precious patch of inbye land standing out bright green against the darker shade of the gorse, testimony to generations of labour. I knew it was all I had ever hoped it would be. But I still had this need to get away sometimes and find a different challenge, just to make sure I was still able to cut the mustard. That's the reason I admire Muhammad Ali so much, for coming back from enforced retirement to beat George Foreman, against all the odds, for the heavyweight title in Kinshasa. He described the source of his willpower as "borrowing from the future". I get a tremendous uplift from that sort of unquenchable spirit and try to remember, and gain strength from it, in my own tight corners. The Spirit is everything.

I was also very aware that Rebecca, who would soon have to go away to school, had not lived anywhere else or known any other world than Ardmore. It was time to widen her horizons with a family expedition. The memory of the voyage planned on that dawn flight over the Spanish Sahara as we returned from Patagonia the year before was to be translated into a reality now we had *English Rose V*. We sailed the engineless and heavy-laden thirty-two-footer due south through the October storms of 1974, from Ardmore to Madeira in fourteen days, with Jamie, Krister and Staff. Under Marie Christine's guidance, taking over from Ada, seven-year-old Rebecca was supposed to have finished all thirty-six "Peter and Jane" reading books by the end of the voyage. But I like to think she learned a lot more besides as she and I rode the stainless-steel frame of the pulpit up in the bows, watching the great clouds of spray fly back either side of us, making delicate rainbows each time the bow dropped on a wave.

We clipped the outer side of the Canaries on our way to the

Spanish Sahara and stayed a while at a seldom visited island among the Cape Verdes, where it hadn't rained for seven years, and where Rebecca was the only child without a coal-black skin. We called at the Azores in early December, then headed for home. In a storm on Christmas Eve, a couple of hundred miles off the Irish coast, we were swamped by a big wave which came rolling over our stern. Down below, in the cabin, with icy water up to her waist, Becca announced "This is the horridest Christmas ever." That night we slept five in a bunk for warmth.

We reached Barra, the southernmost island of the Outer Hebrides, on Boxing Day, and after a night at anchor, we set sail for Ardmore. There was another big gale in the Minch overnight, which kept us all in life-jackets and safety-harnesses, but as we sailed safely into the calm waters of Loch a'Chadh-fi next evening, two small boats came out of the mist to greet us. Heckie was coming in with his lobster creels, and Lance was returning from another lonely day over at the School. Within the hour, we were all safely up in the warmth of the Blue House with glasses of Ada's beer.

I hoped Becca would find something from the trip to lift and build her spirit, to help equip her for her new life at school away from Ardmore. Ten years later, in Peru, she was to have the chance to show us what she had learned.

From the day we sailed out of Boa Vista in the Cape Verdes, it had been our plan to get home for the New Year. It was against everybody's advice, but we had managed it, making landfall at Castlebay on Barra on Boxing Day. There wasn't much going on there, but then Christmas is of little importance on the west coast – New Year is the main event. The New Year, by a cunning juggle of old and new calendars can be made to last for the best part of a fortnight. The celebrations are peculiarly suited to the west-coast personality, sometimes rather reserved and shy until a wee drop of whisky gets into the system.

For us New Year is the time for calling on the people who live around Loch a'Chadh-fi. Portlevorchy is the first call for an exchange of drams on the way out to the main road. Donald, Angie, Ruby don't go far from the house. After a while Ruby appears with tea and sandwiches and her delicious cakes; the hours slip by until it's suddenly already mid-afternoon and the whisky fumes are threatening to bring proceedings to a halt before they've even begun. The Bells and the Ridgways usually extract

Ardmore today, above. Below left, the salmon farmer. Right, loading the boats at 0600 hours before crossing for the start of the morning run.

Looking across Loch a' Chadh-Fi to Foinaven from Ardmore.

A summer evening on top of Ardmore, Ben Stack in
the distance.

Gone fishing.

themselves in some disorder from Portlevorchy and make a feeble attempt at beginning the rounds between Kinlochbervie and Scourie which may have to be spread over several days. This is the civilised way of bringing in the New Year – there is, however, another way.

You go to the public bar in the Rhiconich on the evening of 31 December, around nine o'clock, and you will find assembled there just about everybody. And everybody is charged up for the beginning of it all. The air is thick and the drinks are giant clusters of glasses: big ones of MacEwans and little ones surprisingly deep in whisky. It's a time for goodwill, and the stuff in the glasses brings the goodwill on a real treat. When closing time approaches the management stumbles into philanthropy yet again, and out come the soup and sausage rolls. The first priority after closing time (scrupulously observed because the policeman lives across the road) is to decide where to be when the New Year comes in, and for the Ardmore people there is no doubt but that the best place to be is at Skerricha with the Gaffer. The Gaffer is usually in pretty good heart by this stage.

Being neither Scottish, nor dark haired, and having no ready access to salt or coal with the Gaffer, our team is not required for any curious ceremonies. The Gaffer moves into centre stage.

He can call on such wealth of experience that he assumes increasingly gigantic proportions as the night wears on. Usually Achriesgill is the centre of operations, over on the north shores of Loch Inchard towards Kinlochbervie. The Gaffer is welcome everywhere, knows everyone, dominates, almost fills wherever he is. As time moves on towards dawn mobility becomes a problem. Ice and snow make driving a tricky business, and sometimes the Gaffer is hard to find. I once had to go searching for him when the word went round that he was missing. Thinking he might be outside, I stumbled into the snow and tried a few weak calls; but hearing no answer I stepped off the path into what I thought was some kind of garden. I could just make out a wall as my eyes grew accustomed to the darkness, and I thought he was unlikely to have gone beyond that as there was a bit of wire fencing running along the top. I suppose I must have been thinking of what to do next, because I tripped over a pile of snow and fell. Thinking the obstacle surprisingly soft I went back to examine it. At first I was sure he was dead. Dead people are inclined to have their eyes open and stare at you, after all – but he wasn't. With a

129

little bit of help we got him back into the house, and after a bit of a pause, sat in front of the fire, he went on as if nothing had happened.

The worst part of embarking on this latter method of seeing in the New Year is the walk back into Ardmore, usually around dawn on 1 January, and there can only be a couple of hours' sleep before it's time to be off again on the next round.

The Gaffer's boat was out of action for the winter, and so he was doing the postal deliveries on foot. One February afternoon he limped out with the usual heavy mail we get at this time of year from all over the place, but I noticed a blue envelope from the village of Durness just fifteen miles up on the north coast. Small, precise handwriting proclaimed that one Arun Bose was starting the Cape Wrath Boatyard and there was one particular sentence which struck a chord in me. "I do hope you will support my new venture." "Sounds like us ten years ago," I said. I felt glad I wasn't starting all over again on this miserable February day.

"Why don't you and Lance go up and see what his work's like?" Marie Christine replied. "Maybe he could build that new dinghy you're wanting."

And so it happened that a couple of days later, Lance and I drove into the ex-RAF camp, now serving as both home and workshop for several families who have come to the far north-west of Sutherland to make their living at craftwork. Lance's years in a Teesside iron foundry had left him with little regard for candle-making and tie-and-dye. I didn't expect him to be enthusiastic. The fifteen-mile drive through the rain hadn't been particularly cheering as Lance had been quite definite in his views that "them 'irsute buggers should get back where they came from and get on with some proper bloody productive work." I began to think that if Mr Bose managed to convince Lance of his workmanship then we'd really be on to something.

We found Mr Bose among the jumble of narrow concrete ex-bunkhouses, and I could see that Lance wasn't much impressed with the tiny eight-foot pram dinghy lying on its side among a heap of tools in a room with polythene sheeting over the windows to help keep out the cold. It looked as if this was all that Mr Bose had ever made. Lance spared the man hardly a glance. Instead he turned his attention to an ancient black band-saw; this massive construction soon had the dour Teessider talking nineteen to the

130

dozen about his favourite topic: iron foundries. This was lucky in a way, because Mr Bose was painfully shy; he was small and neatly built with long, straggly black hair and bright, dark eyes behind round spectacles. His beard reminded me of Sikhs I had known at Sandhurst. It looked as if it had grown wild, and never known the edge of a razor. I put him at about twenty-three and half-Indian by his complexion. The small black-rimmed spectacles gave him a curiously studious look for a boat-builder. My own efforts at conversation were hopeless; I couldn't hear his replies.

"Shall we go through to my mother's shop?" he whispered at last, and we followed him along a low corridor in the cold, dark building, and into an open area at the far end; this was set up with a couple of intricate wooden looms at which Noelle Bose, a lively Nottingham widow of striking appearance and firm opinion, was weaving the tweeds she makes for a living.

"Arun made these, you know," she said proudly, as soon as we'd been introduced. Lance looked at the precision work of the looms, and then back at Mr Bose, as if seeing him afresh. We were on to something.

The idea of the "Big Boat" had been pushing in and out of my mind for a long time now and recently refusing to go away. We had weathered the worst of the economic crisis and our savings were in a building society. But with galloping inflation we had been advised to take them out, buy something on a housing estate in Inverness and lease it to a tenant. This idea seemed so pathetically tame it didn't deserve to succeed.

"Put it all into the Big Boat then, and to hell with it. Anything to stop you going on about it," Marie Christine said finally, after I'd raised the subject for the umpteenth time.

Arun came down for a trial week, to help with preparations for the new season. We got to know him as he stayed in our house. Inevitably talk came round to the "Big Boat". Just how big, I wasn't sure. Arun had already agreed to build the fourteen-foot loch boat we needed, and I had a feeling he was the man for the "Big Boat" too.

Spring came slowly as ever. Krister returned from Sweden and set about organising the Instructors' Course. Jamie had stayed with us since the end of the Cape Verdes trip and he was deeply involved in preparing for the 1976 Observer Transatlantic Race. His entry had been accepted and he was going to do the qualifying 500-mile solo sail out to Rockall and back in *English Rose IV*, the sloop I'd sailed to Brazil. If this went all right he'd do the Atlantic race in her too. Having the boat below us on the beach gave him something tangible to work on. Staff came back from his tour of Europe, and Neil Scobie and Jim Marland returned safely, but a little older, from several months in Africa where they had had some narrow escapes. Steve Leger and Murdo MacEwan joined us for the first of several years. It was a strong team for a busy year.

With the coming of spring Noddy was brought back from his winter quarters in the field at Badnabay, on the southern shores of Laxford. Noddy was what Boy Blue had been rechristened by those of us who didn't appreciate him as we should. Getting him up the "Waterfall" was as difficult as it had been the first time, but Staff did at least know that it could be done, and that was a help. Noddy was as wilful as ever, and he showed no interest in staying up by the Blue House right from the start this year. Maybe he liked the idea of having more people about down at Lower Ardmore, I don't know, but when Krister decided to show us how a true *gaucho* from the pampas would ride such a pony, Noddy let out a pretty fierce whinny – some say they saw flames from his nostrils – Krister just saw the sky, and then he crashed down on the grass. For an instant it looked as if the rearing animal would bring its hooves down on the unfortunate loser, but once again the Swede showed himself to be a quick mover when he had to be. He was out from under like an eel, and Noddy set off at full tick up the steep grassy slope of the croft.

"I think we should just let him settle down – for a few days, John," Staff said in his usual earnest fashion. Nobody disagreed. Noddy had again established the pecking order. He was a splendid creature to look at and fitted well into the general atmosphere. But steadily he began to let us know he was running the place. The washing line at the back of the Wooden House is frequently used by the businessmen to dry their clothes after they have been immersed somewhere. Noddy showed a remarkable liking for smart striped shirts and not everyone thought they were improved by the chlorophyl green patches after he had chewed them for a bit.

All through March I wrestled with the figures to see how we could possibly afford to build the kind of boat I had in mind. While we tramped along the Foinaven Ridge on the hard-packed snow with the Instructors' Course I was trying to decide just what would be the right size of boat to bring the best advantage to the School. Deep in the septic tank, shovelling the residue into black plastic buckets, I could only think of the boat. The idea did have a bit of a set-back, however, when we decided to make an overnight trip to Stornoway in the thirty-two-foot Nicholson which had so recently been our home. Murdo MacEwan was the first to succumb that bumpy night, and the awful familiar smell from the black plastic buckets soon had us all retching in the dark. But once we got home and the sun shone, and the world looked fresh and new in the light of spring, the whole "Big Boat" dream came flooding back. Buildings were Cuprinolled, boats launched, and canoes set brightly on their racks: the only way to live was to look up and press forward. We were all standing in the mud, but some of us must look at the stars – as Oscar Wilde would have it.

This stirring sentiment was given a boost by a letter I received from New Zealand. One of the nice things about the School as the years go by is being kept in touch by former instructors and hearing about their own subsequent achievements, inspired, I like to think, by what they discover they are capable of at Ardmore. Nick and Julie Grainger's achievement was one of the most outstanding. Nick had been a successful oarsman with Thames Tradesmen before he and Julie came to Ardmore first in 1973, but with us he learned to sail a dinghy, fell in love with and acquired a twenty-one-foot Orkney clinker-built boat which he called *Aegre*, and talked Bobby MacInnes down the coast at Scourie into modifying her so that he and Julie could sail to the West Indies, which they did in time for Christmas after a well-executed forty-four day crossing from the Canaries to Barbados. They had set the gaff-headed trisail upside down as a square sail while running before the north-east trade winds, which had pushed them over a hundred miles a day on more than one occasion – good going for a heavy boat with only a seventeen-foot waterline.

In Barbados they were persuaded of the feasibility of sailing through the Panama Canal and on across the Pacific to New Zealand. I had shared this last piece of news with Bobby MacInnes in 1974 and we settled down to a long wait. We heard again when they reached the Marquesas and set off for Tahiti. But it was the last leg from Tahiti to New Zealand which we knew would be the real test. Now I had Nick's own account of it.

The *Aegre* capsized and was dismasted in a storm just two days out. They loaded their sextant and most of their rations and

133

survival equipment into their inflatable dinghy but it drifted away in the night. They were obliged to sacrifice precious drinking water in order to use the empty cans to regain buoyancy. Their remaining dried foodstuffs were ruined. Starvation was some time away, but so was land.

The storm lasted seven days. On the eighth it eased enough for them to sail again with a flying jib forward and the gaff trisail set aft of the jury mast they had managed to rig out of the boom and the stump of the old mast. In the capsize they had not lost the American Pilot Charts of the Pacific, and they had a sodden Nautical Almanac and Julie's chronometer watch, which, miraculously, was still working. With these three things and their own university mathematical training, they could find land.

But by the twentieth day they had sailed through and missed all the Cook Islands. It was imperative they didn't miss the Tonga group too. Refusing to give up hope, Nick worked at latitude sailing by the stars, the method of the old sailing ships. When he felt he had established their latitude he made a courageous decision. They would sail on almost to Tonga, then turn north for Samoa. It put days on their voyage, but the Samoan islands are higher and closer together than the Tongan group and don't have the same offshore coral reefs. If Nick's navigation was correct they'd have a better chance of making landfall there.

They were now very weak from lack of food, plagued by salt-water sores, and Julie was being sick, losing precious body fluid she could ill afford. But in the dawn of their thirtieth day since the capsize and 1,600 miles on, they saw a rocky headland through the cloud and rain. They had reached Samoa. "We feel a lot older and wiser since we left Scotland," ended Nick's letter. I was stunned. They had shown tremendous resource to arrive even at the point where they capsized. Their performance since the capsize had taken qualities beyond simple resourcefulness. I felt proud to have known them.

Nick and Julie's story inspired me to spend a day with Jamie and Krister scuba-diving in the snow to lay moorings for the "Big Boat". A little voice kept saying: come on, it's the only way to be alive again. You witter on about a fourth dimension to living, but the spark's gone out of you!

Not everyone was so keen on the idea. Lance had a shrewd suspicion that it would only involve him in new problems which he had no real confidence he could solve. I suppose his opposition only made me more stubborn. One night Heckie and Hughie came in for supper with us, and the Bells came down from the Blue House for the evening. There was plenty of home-brew flowing and Heckie was telling us of a crock of gold supposedly buried at a certain spot beside Loch Glendhu not far from Kylestrome, about fifteen miles down the coast from Ardmore.

"Well, that'll be no problem when we get the 'Big Boat'. We'd be down there in a couple of hours," I laughed.

"Bloddy daft. Ye've no slip, no moorings, no pier. I don't know, the whole place has changed from the first year we were here. You're getting carried away with yourself."

There was an uncomfortable silence. No one wanted to get Lance really going after he had had a drop of beer. While I had an uncomfortable feeling he might be right, that same uncomfortable feeling is just the thing which helps push me along. Becca suggested we all might like to play dominoes, and the moment passed.

Arun came to the School quite often, and one day we both met with Mr Williamson from the Highlands and Islands Development Board who had come up from Inverness to discuss the idea of a twenty-eight-foot sea-angling boat. Fitting it out for us would help establish Arun as a boat-builder and there was a possibility of a grant from the Board.

"You know," I pronounced unconcernedly, "what we really need is a proper sail-training yacht – a Nicholson fifty-five-foot – like the *Adventure*, which won three of the four legs in the Round the World Yacht Race last year. It would extend our range to the Hebrides and it would mean employment for a skipper, too."

Mr Williamson looked up from the sea-angling brochures in surprise. Arun looked startled as well. Half an hour later Mr Williamson was promising to sound out the Development Board for assistance.

The Development Board confirmed a loan offer for £11,400. Instead of a Nicholson fifty-five-foot sloop we decided on a Bowman fifty-seven-foot ketch, with double the accommodation for the School. I signed the contract – and then I could sort of forget about it until the end of October. That was the day when the hull was to be escorted from Alresford to Emsworth in Hampshire. Bowman Yachts had agreed to Arun fitting out the ketch at their yard during the coming winter, then we could sail her up to

Ardmore in January 1976. I hoped it wouldn't be like the time we brought up the Nicholson thirty-two-footer!

The summer was in full swing, and when the Young People's Courses began, Noddy was greatly admired by the children as usual. He still had to be watched if he got near the clothes line. The croft is so steep that when he decided to come down from under the cliffs at the top he often began to skid and sooner or later he would decide to overtake the slide by going into a gallop. At the bottom of the hill there is a narrow shelf of flat land which terminates in a sheer earth bank some eight feet above the rocks of the shore. By the time Noddy reached the shelf he would be going much too fast to stop, so he had got into the habit of making a tight racing bend, parallel with the sea. The shelf is also the natural route for anyone walking from the Wooden House to the museum. More than one person made the quick decision that discretion is the better part of valour, and dropped over the bank at the sound of thundering hooves.

One day in early July, when all was quiet on the crofts, Noddy was grazing along the shelf. Head down he followed his chomping teeth until his nose came right up against the concrete block foundation of the museum. The canoeing group were due to start an expedition towards Cape Wrath in late afternoon; their twenty rucksacks were neatly stacked in a corner of the museum and in the centre of the floor lay three cardboard boxes containing the rations for twenty people for two days. It was eleven o'clock in the morning and the last person had forgotten to shut the door behind him.

Noddy went through the open door as if he owned the place. We keep the windows open at the top to counter the effect of the sun on the black felt roof, and soon after Noddy got in a breeze blew up and slammed the door shut behind him. But this sort of thing was of no concern to a beast of his regal outlook. Much more interesting was the stack of rations. He began at the beginning and finished at the end with the boxes of matches. Then he had a nap. He was discovered some hours later lying stretched out on the wooden boards in a scene of total chaos, piles of gently steaming ordure adding character to the show. Outside the happy cries of the returning canoeists carried across the loch.

I don't think Noddy realised his time was running out. That December when I was tottering up through the wood towards the Blue House, with a bale of hay balanced on my head for him, the

136

sharp pricks down the back of my neck prompted me to wonder if this really was the way to keep a pony. Surely, the whole idea was that he should be carrying things about for me, not vice versa? This train of thought was developed further when Lance took a bowlful of Pony Nuts out to feed the poor creature on a really foul day. Rather than see the animal suffer outside Lance tried to entice Noddy to follow him into the byre, but Noddy was having none of that – he thought the idea was to deprive him of what was rightly his. Quick as a flash he turned right round and kicked out with both legs at Lance, who luckily swayed aside just in time. This was Noddy's last error, in a long chapter, as far as I was concerned; we had further discussions and at the ballot the workers came out heavily in favour of dismissal – Noddy must go! So plans were laid for his departure to the home of Hughie Nedd's grand-daughter on the east coast where he would find green fields, flat ground, and other ponies to talk to. I think we were both on good terms at the last farewell.

Jamie took advantage of the settled weather early that July to sail out from Ardmore to Rockall and back as his 500-mile qualification for the Transatlantic Race the following year. I made too much of the sunshine myself on the balmy trips down to Handa. The cool sea breeze chilled the lower part of my back and by my thirty-seventh birthday on 8 July I was moving like a ninety-seven year old. These attacks sometimes lasted for up to a fortnight and reduced me to a point where I was either in bed or only just able to crawl about. I'd suffered the discomfort for so many years that I had just learned to live with it, thinking it was part of the reason the Army had paid me seven and six a day extra for parachuting – I would be earning that pay for a great many years to come.

The Durness Highland Gathering is held on a Friday afternoon in high summer, and on a fine day on that grassy field, high on the cliffs overlooking the deep blue waters off the northern coast of Scotland, the event takes a lot of beating.

Caber tossing and hammer throwing attract a small band of giants from all over the country, and the sight of one of these kilted monsters rushing headlong down the slopes towards the cliffs with a toppling telephone pole adds something to the occasion. For many the Highland dancing or the pipe band or chance to win a goldfish in a glass bowl is memory enough. Strange and unforgettable sights can be seen in the beer tent, too. Sometimes a session here is a necessary part of the final training for the tug-o'-war. The Kinlochbervie fishermen usually battle unsuccessfully in the final with a near professional team from Bonar Bridge, but if support could swing the day the locals would win every time.

As with the heavy Highland events, the track races attract entries from outside the district, mostly students who pay for their holidays with the cash prizes won on a tour of Highland Gatherings around the north and west coasts. My eyes are set only on the hill race, the last event of the day. I know the course better than any other entrant, better even than Marie Christine, who is the only female ever to have run in the race. My chances of winning the open event rely on a major catastrophe occurring to the main body of the field up ahead of me; I was at Aintree the day Foinaven won the Grand National at 500–1 on the Tote, and I do sometimes dream of some similar crash bringing me to the front in the closing stages. I'd love to drive home and give that mountain a wink as I passed.

The nearest I've ever got to winning is a little ploy called the John Ridgway cup . . . Winning does seem to be the point when you're running the hill race. The start line is the first real inkling of the competition. People of all shapes and sizes are milling about in the relaxed atmosphere which comes right at the end of the day when the beer tent is littered with bodies and the smell of ale and crushed grass levels everybody and everything. Competitors eye one another, weighing up form based on performance in the other shorter races on the track. With a bit of luck the *victor ludorum* type is pretty much at the end of his tether. Unlike Muhammad Ali he won't feel that to lose will mean much to him. His success on the track will prevent him from "borrowing from the future". Not that this concerns me. He would be able to lend a bit and still be home before I come into sight. No, my concern is for the grey-haired fellows, who come out of the crowd nonchalantly peeling off a track suit, trying to look as if the whole thing is just a spur-of-the-moment decision. They don't kid me: they've been training just as hard as I have since January. They're after the John Ridgway Cup for the Hill Race – thirty-five and over.

I smile, eyes like a snake, trying to look relaxed, feeling sick. Marie Christine looks around, hoping that Jumbo, the telephone linesman, will be as good as his word and give it a go. She's beaten him before. Our instructors look like greyhounds in their slips, hardened by a full season on the hill; there is much prestige to be gained at the School from winning the hill race at Durness. But they're worried, too. Should they have made that deadly effort in the 880? Was the obstacle race really worth the effort?

Then there is the local champion – Tattie. Goalkeeper and inspiration of the Kinlochbervie football team, a man of giant heart and buckets of saliva; my great friend at the pier, where he works loading the lorries as I did in '64.

The starter, a dapper wee fellow who sometimes wears earmuffs when he's driving the JCB, fires the pistol – and we're off. No hint of any line-up or anything. A few, including Grey Hair, are not ready, and I'm delighted. I'm tuned to the second – how I love a five-yard start.

We have to do a full lap of the track before leaving the field. The pace is far too quick, but I must make sure of a moral ascendancy over Grey Hair before we set off out into the country. My entire life has shrunk into this one race. I'll die for it. Hundreds of spectators are leaving the Highland Gathering now. There is nothing left that's worth watching. We bob and weave our way through the cars, choking on unaccustomed fumes on the rough track to the Durness road.

"The first cup is taken without sugar. It is bitter, like Life." I was remembering the words of the tea-drinking ritual we'd been introduced to by Arab nationalist students in the Spanish Sahara, last stop before the Cape Verdes.

The course now is steadily uphill, past the entrance to the Craft Village where Arun is working away at his plans for the Bowman. I'm finding my rhythm, forcing the pace – nothing clever – simply running from the front like "Yifter the Shifter", my all-time hero from Ethiopia. When I say running from the front, I mean running in front of Grey Hair. There are only the two of us in my race. The road descends towards Balnakiel. I must be careful not to overstride or my breathing will get out of rhythm. No sign of Grey Hair. Only an amateur would look back to see where he is – I imagine he's just behind me and lift the rhythm a bit: got to drop him. Jumbo is flagging and I take him before we reach the road-end at Balnakiel beach. He gasps something as I go by. It sounds sort of friendly. I can see Tattie is well placed, his football jersey is far ahead up on the long green hill towards the distant concrete coastguard hut on the cliffs. The instructors are up there too, but Tattie has outwitted them – it's his first race of the day, and he's making them pay for the money they won earlier on the track. Their colours are fast running dry. If they're behind Tattie at the high coastguard turn, they'll be pushed to catch him – did he visit the beer tent? That's the big question.

"Concentrate, you twit!" I curse myself. Grey Hair is bound to have gained a few yards with that mental wandering.

"Encourage the old machine – don't curse it!" I remember the Yoga book. Rhythm is the thing. I go up the short springy turf on the hillside, rising like a lark. "The second cup has a little sugar in it and is bittersweet, like Love."

Coming through the five-barred gate just short of the coastguard hut I hold out my right wrist for the checkpoint dye-stamp and my rhythm goes. The grass is suddenly a lot longer and my breath starts to saw like a broken horse. I get round the hut, and as I start down the hill I look back across the slope coming up. There's Grey Hair flowing like syrup up the hill, legs going like a metronome.

I remember how Hampton, the Army champion, opened the first round with a confident straight left. Pivotting from the hips, my right hand snapped through the "V" between his left glove and shoulder, crashing on to his chin. Hampton sat down, the stadium stood up. "I coulda' been a contender."

What a lot of guff – Hampton got up to win the fight on points.

"I'll show the blighter!" I lengthen my stride as I descend, trying to relax and work up a bit of bite for the uphill on the far side of the valley. But the young fellow ahead, who looks too stout to be a runner, is pulling away from me, no doubt about it. On the upturn on the valley floor the going seems to get harder than I remember it; my approach to the gate is lumbering and I clamber over, dropping like a stone on the other side – never mind about the vault. It's all such a drag, the pain, how many more minutes have I got to keep going for . . . must be less than ten.

Grey Hair goes by with an eviscerating burst. It's no contest. I never saw him coming. How could an ancient wreck like that go so smoothly? He's ten yards clear and I'm out of contention. I don't deserve this, I weigh only thirteen six – just a shadow of my former self.

We're on the long narrow straight track now, running parallel with the arena just a few fields away to our left. I overtake a figure collapsed on the verge. Grey Hair didn't stop, so neither shall I.

140

He's thirty yards clear now but not pulling away any more. Maybe he'll collapse too? There are a few spectators at the gate leading on to the road. "A fellow's down – back there!" I gasp, begrudging the effort. On the road I concentrate on holding my form. Relax the shoulders, loosen those clenched fists, get that breathing right down to the bottom of the lungs, I think to myself.

It's only a few hundred yards back to the Durness junction, then off along the track into the arena. I reckon I am no worse than sixth in the whole field of nine or ten. Maybe I'll get a lift when I get on to the grass track itself – there's nothing I respond to better than clapping. Downhill towards the cliffs I mount a charge on Grey Hair, but he's already halfway along the up-side of the track, and by the time I reach the bottom bend he's entering the home straight, half a lap clear of the field, in a different race. The long haul up the empty side of the track stretches for ever, I feel as if I'm keeping the pipe band waiting. Rounding the final bend at the top of the field, there is nothing to make that death-defying sprint for, but I make it as a matter of form – I might not have it next time unless I unleash it now! The finishing line slips by and I collapse on the grass. What they call done in. "And the third and last cup has much sugar and is sweet like Death."

For a while I don't care about much except recovery, then I ask the instructors how they got on, and Marie Christine goes by on her final lap and the pipe band starts up on the last phase of the Gathering. Hoar-headed old piping judges in kilts clamber on to the dais for the prize-giving. Marie Christine crosses the finishing line and flops down beside me, exhausted. "I wasn't last!" she gasps. Becca congratulates us and hands out the tracksuits. "Tattie won!" chortles Ada.

I look around for Grey Hair. He's on his feet looking composed, so I get up myself. "You did well," I say, trying to sound sporting, saliva tasting like hemlock.

"Yes, it went OK. I thought you had me in the first half – you started so fast," he smiles, trying not to look too pleased, but his wife looks absolutely delighted beside him.

"Where do you live?"

"We come from the south. I'm a marathon runner really. I'm very pleased because I broke three hours last month – my first time."

"Well, maybe you'll try the south of France for your holiday next year," I grin. "Be sure and send my cup back."

141

In the evening there is The Dance in the Durness Hall, a wild and uproarious affair with Neil Scobie leading our team into the Highland dancing and Krister a dashing second. Jamie fresh back from his trip to Rockall, Steve Leger, Staff and Murdo, Jim Marland and Mary, Jane and Pam. The drink flows, Tattie will take a while to come down from the stars – a legend in his own lifetime.

Hours later Marie Christine and I find ourselves in Kinlochbervie Post Office, making sandwiches and tea with Kenneth Morrison, an old shipmate from our days on the salmon coble a decade before. It's getting light as we make our way back to Ardmore along the path. Becca and Arun's little sister, Percy, have been asleep in the back of the Land-rover, but they make a brave effort on the walk in, and are rewarded by the entertaining sight of Kenneth trying to keep upright on the narrow footpath.

At last we reach the top of the Waterfall. It's still only half light, and as we pass the front of the Blue House, Kenneth peers in through the kitchen window. Never entirely positive about his eyesight in such situations, he is astonished to see a figure padding about in a long khaki shirt (the white sergeant's stripes tell me it's an old one of Chay Blyth's). His hands are full of beer bottles and so Kenneth knows he need go no further – all that nightmare wrestling to get forward along the path has been worthwhile. Lance is equally stunned to see people passing his window at four in the morning; unable to sleep he's been bottling his beer. Never one to miss a party he beckons us in. We leave Kenneth with Lance and stumble wearily to bed.

At the beginning of November Arun and Jamie Young began rigging the Bowman 57 at the boatyard in Emsworth. My long dream of a Big Boat, which had been recurring since the sight of the Royal Navy's *Adventure* at the 1972 Boat Show, was at last coming true. They were exciting days. As we drove back north from Emsworth Marie Christine was busy drawing colour schemes for Ratsey spinnakers. The spending spree was already under way.

We arrived at Ardmore in time to help Lance and Ada move furniture across the loch and up to the Blue House. They had sold their home in Teesside after eight years' absence. Lance was now the crofter at No.80. We were lucky to have a lull in the weather, and as we passed Fionn's Rock in front of the School, the boat laden to the gunnels with chests of drawers and chairs, our silver wake made a broad "V" across the loch and a pair of curious seals raised their whiskery heads to see who was moving in.

Another piece of good news that winter was the return of Granny Ross to No.77, next door to us in Lower Ardmore. Now well over eighty she had been pining away for her home on Ardmore for eighteen months. The croft across on the other side of Laxford was on the road, but it held no memories for the old lady who had been born in our house on Ardmore and married the boy next door. And what memories she had: she bore nine children, one of whom had died in infancy, but the little croft house had long been filled with the noise and music of her family, and that is where she wanted to be. Her sons, Hughie and Robert, carried her up the hill from the boat in a chair. Wrapped up in her shawls in the rocking chair once more, she soon recovered her spirits and most days we would call in at separate times for a chat and a cup of tea to make her feel welcome back. She was particularly fond of Becca, who once again took in little bunches of the nearest thing she could find to flowers in the wood on winter weekends home from school. This habit, which gave so much pleasure to the old lady, also gave the child an abiding interest in the wild plants, which a gruff fellow like her father might pass by un-noticing.

The only time Granny Ross had been away from Ardmore before was for short spells in her youth, when the local womenfolk travelled as far away as Lowestoft in special trains which took them to wherever the shoals of silver herring were being landed from the North Sea, and there they worked at curing the fish. It was on one of these forays from home, when she was just eighteen, that people began to think Robina had the second sight. She was in Fraserburgh in 1912 when she went down with jaundice, and during the illness she had a vision of the cooper climbing on to a barrel and tying a rope securely round a beam in the roof. Then he stepped off the chair and hanged himself. Robina fainted and a doctor was called. He declared she was so sick that she must be taken home as soon as possible. Two weeks later the cooper hanged himself in exactly the same manner.

Granny Ross herself preferred to talk of the more exciting times, like when in 1942 a German submarine stole quietly into Loch Laxford, coming right into Loch a'Chadh-fi between Ardbeg and Paddy's Isle. The skipper had been with the Klondikers in Fanagmore Bay back in '27 during the year of "the big herring", and he knew where to look for sheep to replenish the submarine's larder.

In mid-November Marie Christine went off to hospital in Inverness. Now we had the Bowman we could think seriously about that other old dream of mine – a non-stop round the world trip. So as a practical precaution we had decided to take advantage of the winter at home to have our appendixes out. It was Marie Christine's turn to go first. It was when she came out of hospital smiling bravely without her appendix that I realised the time for theory was over. The plan had to be serious.

12

Ten of us brought the Bowman back to Loch a'Chadh-fi in the new year of 1976. The big white ketch creamed north through the Minch and we all knew she was destined to give us some great times at Ardmore and further afield.

I was still concerned about the moorings for such a big boat under the wood; the water is sixty foot deep, but the holding ground is not good. Diving in a wet suit to fix these new moorings in November had been no fun on my own. I found I could stay down for half an hour fiddling around with shackles, swivels and anchors in the gloom. The trouble always comes in the last ten feet to the surface. Chilled from the dive, I found I had little resistance left on entering the layer of near freezing fresh water which lies on top of the warmer salt water from the Gulf Stream. Lance had had to heave me into the rubber dinghy like beaching a whale.

I had tried to follow Field Marshal Slim's maxim, that "When faced by two alternatives of equal merit, a man should always choose the bolder course"; sometimes it is quite tiring though. These days I was stretching dangerously near my limit, mentally and financially. Permanent tiredness and frequent yawning became a feature of life which blurred the edges of my memory. My fears were reinforced every time Lance warned me of the folly of aimless growth and expansion. In his view the most efficient machine invented is one man with his back against a wall. The idea of a big boat like the Bowman, without the essential facilities to maintain it, could only lead to disaster. Cranes just aren't a feature of the west coast. The nearest slipway was fifty miles across the Minch in Stornoway, and when it came to anti-fouling the bottom of the hull, there was nowhere else to lay the boat alongside while the tide went out.

Poor Lance well knew that when the problems began to occur, he would be called upon to come up with a miraculous solution, and this time he seriously doubted if he could manage it. On the

145

other hand, I believed we'd find a way when we had to. I saw the advantages the boat would bring the School: quality, range, flexibility and all-weather reliability.

Lance was feeling his age, and he was sorely troubled with arthritis in his hands and feet which made agony of every step across the rocky shores in and out of the boats. Time and again we clashed as our paths diverged, but always he saved us when problems seemed about to swamp us. "What you don't realise is . . ." was the preface to every solution, but our intentions were gradually growing further apart. Lance and I were an unlikely couple brought together by chance rather than design. Evidently we must both have got something from our relationship or it wouldn't have survived, but the arrival of the big boat did put that relationship under severe strain.

Unfortunately the new pressures coincided with the break-up of the team of instructors who had been with us for several years. Krister Nylund had gone back to Sweden. We gave him one of the Rolex watches we'd had on the Patagonian trip to the Gran Campo Nevada. On the back I had inscribed GCN KN/JR 1972. But for him I'd still be sitting at the bottom of a glacier. When Jamie set off in May to join the solo Transatlantic Race there was at first nobody to step in as anchorman for the general day-by-day running of all the boats until Tony Dallimore arrived.

Short and powerfully built, with a strong neck and stubby fingers, taciturn and effectual, Tony had recently come to us from the Glamorgan College of Education with his new teaching degree. Competent and well qualified in sailing and canoeing, he rapidly made his mark with a natural, forceful style of leadership. While Jim Marland rose to the occasion as chief instructor, and led the mountain walks, Tony and I took the Bowman across the Minch each Thursday, spending the night at anchor in places like Port of Ness and Stornoway, and sailing home the next day. It was valuable experience: we were working the boat up for future longer voyages.

Bob Burns was another man in the right place at the right time. Hale and hearty, after twelve years in the Royal Navy, he graduated naturally from erecting giant television masts round the country to working high on the North Sea oil rigs. Once with us, Bob's imagination was fired by the chance of sailing round the world, and he turned his considerable energy and enthusiasm to securing the post of bosun on our non-stop circumnavigation.

146

Arun was working away all the while up at Durness, making pieces for the Bowman and bringing them down to fit whenever the boat lay at Ardmore. As he fitted a new hatch cover one day he made a suggestion. "I was wondering if you wouldn't be better entering the Whitbread Round the World Race in August '77 to April '78. It would be so much more interesting stopping at Cape Town, Auckland, and Rio de Janeiro than going non-stop."

I discussed the idea with Marie Christine.

"Oh, I'd love the three stops," she cried. "It'd make up for all the misery in between!"

"I don't think we could afford the time!"

"You always say that. What's the point of living? You can't spend all your time denying yourself."

The television company who were going to make a ninety-minute film of the voyage also found the three stops attractive and before long we had adjusted our sights to the new, more competitive project.

As the pressure built up I found my relaxation in another world that was still close to home. I discovered it while diving to check the various moorings around Ardmore. Instead of going up to bathe in the warm shallow freshwater lochs in that hot airless summer, I took to exploring the depths of Loch a'Chadh-fi when the sun shone and the tide was at its lowest. Hughie and Donald Corbett had both told me they'd caught lobsters in the old days among the tumbled cairns of rock under the Ardmore wood. At first I was rather nervous swimming alone through the streaming seaweed, but diving is rather like flying, and I found that with careful use of weights to control buoyancy I could stay some distance above the bottom and observe, without having to touch, the obscene-looking starfish writhing their way on to the huge horse mussels which litter the bottom. Deep in the centre of the loch and well beyond the weed, I was pleased to find the yacht mooring had buried itself in the mud. This would slow the rusting of the chain cable considerably. Once I'd checked these essential facilities I could use the rest of the air in my tanks for pleasure. The shallow, well-lit places, around thirty feet below the surface, were warm and yet still beyond the outer edges of the weed.

After three or four days of exploration I finally came to the place which I have come to regard as my garden. A secret, hidden world to which I can fly when I feel the need for solitude in the midst of a busy summer. Many people treasure a place where they can be alone. Marie Christine has a favourite beach on the southern shores of the Ardmore peninsula. But I prefer to slip into the water at low tide on a hot summer's day, by the museum running-mooring, and slowly work my way out along the edge of the Annait until I am on the bottom of the 150-yard-wide channel between it and the south-west corner of Chadh-fi island. The tide flows quite strongly here, scouring a bar of fine gravel between the incoming arm of the loch and the deep pool under the wood. The tidal stream falls slack for an hour either side of low water, and as I cruise over my few neat scallops, weeding out the unwanted starfish, I think of the barn-door skate out in the deep water beyond. Slack water is the time when these monsters stir themselves to feed. Then, when the tide begins to flow again, they turn themselves to face the new direction of the stream and, fluttering their ugly triangular wings, they dig into the bottom to prevent being washed away.

Marie Christine makes a delicious dish of poached scallops with a white wine sauce, and several times each year I harvest a few from the gravel bed. The sack grows heavier and the air tanks become lighter as time passes, so it's possible to stay down for half an hour or so without much problem of buoyancy. Lance has made me a short trident from a foot of broom handle and a welded three-prong fork with barbs, but the dabs always seem to be somewhere else when I have it with me. I do see lobsters now and then, but I couldn't really be sure of finding one. They are always hidden at the mouth of a lobster-size cave in the rocks, and as I approach they suddenly look a great deal bigger than they do on the fish-shop slab. I'm never short of plans for swimming down and grasping the creature firmly from behind, but I haven't yet tried it, and somehow I always seem to find a compelling reason for avoiding the ordeal.

Diving calls for concentration, but having to think simply and accurately on a subject so far removed from my other daily preoccupations provides a very necessary relaxation. Yet I think it is the unspoilt natural beauty of the underwater world which helps most in the mending of my spirit, combined with the sensuous pleasure of "flying" through the landscape.

One evening, early in July, Jamie rang from Newport, Rhode Island. He'd managed to cross the Atlantic in thirty-nine days and eleven hours in *English Rose IV*, our thirty-foot sloop. His gruff voice was as matter of fact as ever. Given a couple of days he

148

planned to set off again, racing himself this time and confident he could knock a day or two off his outward journey. But I knew it would be a different, more self-confident man who would arrive back at Ardmore.

As summer passed, Becca helped Heckie with the hay-making, the peats were brought across the loch, the sheep were gathered and dipped and the lambs sent off to Lairg market. Early in September the first frost nipped the bracken and another summer turned to autumn as the IBM course filled our days.

We decided to make a trial voyage with the Bowman and a crew of fifteen to the Azores at the end of the season. The instructors would be tried out for the Whitbread Race. Arun, Marie Christine and Becca came along as well. But it was the end of a long, hard season. Everyone was tired and the weather was grim, so I cut the trip short. Was my bonus time since the rowing running out? I hated giving up.

However, sometimes fate does seem in control. Maybe we are not really in command of our own destiny quite as much as I would like to think. Had we not been at Ardmore that winter, the whole future of the place would have changed.

During the summer, we had noticed people with binoculars in hired Land-rovers who seemed very interested in Loch a'Chadh-fi. But I'd learned my lesson from the Ardmore Road saga, and anyway life is too short to become paranoid about every stranger you see near your home. In the autumn, we were asked to help scientists from a marine laboratory to survey Loch a'Chadh-fi, as we owned the only boats on the loch. I thought it a little odd, however, that the scientists could only come on a weekend in the middle of winter, as I've always thought the whole idea of being a civil servant was to have your weekends free. I did suggest they stay overnight with us at Ardmore, but they decided to stay at the Kinlochbervie Hotel eight miles away, even though it was closed. The two surveyors duly walked out along the path in the late morning on a cold, blustery November Saturday. At the Blue House they asked where they could find the boat, and Ada directed them to Lower Ardmore to discuss the project, but they said they were in a hurry and went straight down to the mooring. We had recently installed a telephone extension from the Blue House through the wood to us at No.76. This Ada used promptly to say she thought the scientists were wishing to avoid us. Conditions were rapidly deteriorating into a really miserable day as

I made my way down to the shore and called to them that we had some hot soup on the Rayburn and they'd be welcome to come up and join us. Eventually the weather became so squally they were forced ashore. Then it was a question of either standing out in the sleet and waiting for things to get better, or coming up to the house for soup and shelter – it would have taken a good man to choose the former course.

They explained that the Laxford River system was of considerable scientific interest as it is completely free from interference by man. They were testing the salinity and acidity of the water in Loch a'Chadh-fi, information which would be useful for the marine biology lectures on the Young People's Courses. The scientists said they'd be able to finish their work inside the afternoon and so wouldn't need to come out the following day. And that was the last we ever heard from them.

The following week Dr Marshall Halliday and his wife Ann came to dinner out at Ardmore. Arriving just before dark Marshall was bubbling with enthusiasm – about how the loch would make a grand site for a salmon farm. As the manager of the new salmon farm just south of Scourie, I was sure he should know. He was rather surprised to learn that salmon farming had been our first plan for Ardmore, back in 1964, and as a new neighbour he said he would be pleased to help us start our own small farm at the foot of the croft. I suggested we might try and make a co-operative with the crofters around the loch, rather like a sheepstock club except that where they would use a vet for the sheep maybe we could enlist Marshall's help in technical matters. By the end of the evening we were all as enthusiastic as Marshall.

"Loch a'Chadh-fi? Oh yes – there's going to be a salmon farm there, surely you will know that already?" The curt voice on the phone from the Highland Development Board offices in Inverness sounded authoritative.

"No, this is the first time we have mentioned the idea to anyone – it's not going to be very big. The idea is to have a crofters' co-operative and begin in a small way to start with," I replied, beginning to sense something was wrong.

"Oh, well, I'm talking of an outside commercial scheme – there's a meeting here at the Board's offices next Wednesday. Perhaps you'd like to attend?"

"I certainly would!" We had just a week to act. It was quite clearly going to be us on Loch a'Chadh-fi, or some helicopter-

150

leasing firm from the south of England. We knew the only place deep enough for salmon cages was right at the foot of our crofts. The Land-rovers in the summer and the weekend survey had been from this firm. I kept telling myself this was standard business practice and that we must come up with counter measures.

Within three days we had formed our co-operative: Angie Corbett for Portlevorchy, the Gaffer at Skerricha, Lance for Upper Ardmore, Heckie Ross for No.77 and myself. Together we could deny shoreline access round the loch to anyone, and a few phone calls reassured me that the opposition would have to come some way by sea every day if they wanted to work on the water in Loch a'Chadh-fi.

I developed an awful cold, but Marie Christine and I set off for Edinburgh in the Land-rover. There was deep snow on the A9 south of Inverness and the road was reduced to one narrow lane. Abandoned cars littered the verges. It was a long, dark night, but I knew we had reached another watershed in our lives. What happened in the next few days was as important to me as survival on the Atlantic with Chay or in the Amazon rapids with Elvin Berg. I knew full well that we could expect no quarter from any developer from the South; as the telephone voice from the Development Board had so coldly put it: "If it comes to a choice between recreation and food – I know who'll win!" All we represented after a dozen years of struggle at Ardmore was a pale listing in a government file under "recreation". I chuckled to myself.

"What are you laughing at?" I didn't realise Marie Christine was awake. We seemed to have been driving for hours; it must have been around three in the morning.

"I'm just thinking this is the biggest single battle we've ever faced at Ardmore – it's a good thing we turned back from the Azores trip!"

"I know – that's why I can't sleep."

Next morning at nine o'clock, after a quick shave in a transport café loo, we were knocking on the ornate door of the Crown Estate Commission in Charlotte Square where I made a formal request on behalf of the co-operative for a lease of the sea bed where we wished to site the salmon cages. Next day, at the Development Board offices in Inverness, the officials expressed some surprise at the presence of Ian Smith, our long-time friend and solicitor.

On the other side of the room sat our adversary and his assistant. He looked a reasonable sort of fellow, if a bit solemn. I felt the familiar tingle of excitement that comes before stepping into the boxing ring. I knew what losing would mean to me. I remembered the business of the Land-rovers and the survey, how close he had come to getting the lease of the sea bed in the loch without our even knowing about it. No, the rules were probably not quite the same as in amateur boxing. I stole a quick glance at Ian and felt pleased he was with us. I had great regard for his fighting spirit and his ability.

"This application by the crofter's co-operative is very sudden," opened the official from the Development Board's Fishery department.

"No, we applied to do this in 1964," I countered.

"Well, that's a moot point," the official shrugged and smiled expansively.

"There is nothing 'moot' about a written application," snapped our solicitor incisively. Everyone stiffened. Years in the criminal court had enabled Ian to sound pretty cross.

"But the crofter is not the sort of animal to run a successful salmon farm," protested the official, clearly stung by the turn of events.

"Describing crofters as 'animals' is hardly appropriate for employees of the Development Board," came Ian's frosty reply. I couldn't see it winning many hearts in the local paper myself.

The argument became more heated than I had expected, and it was clear to me that we had only stumbled on the scheme after a lot of preparatory work had already been done. After an hour or so we seemed to be achieving nothing, and the deputy chairman of the Board, a retired Admiral, was asked to intervene. It was decided that each party should put its case to him in private during the afternoon.

At the end of the day the opponent agreed to look for a site elsewhere, and I felt sorry to have caused him so much trouble.

The co-operative met next day at Portlevorchy to work out plans for the farm, and the bottle of Grant's whisky was dead in under ten minutes. We decided to buy our first crop of smolts in the spring of '77. This gave us five months to obtain cages and moorings and put them in position on the sheltered site tucked under the wood at the foot of the crofts. No ocean swell ever penetrates that far, and there is little fetch for any wind to build up the kind of sea which might destroy the cages. For our pilot scheme we bought four small cages, each only sixteen feet square, from Marshall's salmon farm at Badcall near Scourie. He was just changing over to twenty foot cages, and he asked us down to have a look at the Badcall farm. The first thing Lance, Angie Corbett and I noticed about the site was that it was a good deal more exposed than Ardmore. Although protected from the full weight of the seas by a scatter of islands lying on the outside of Badcall Bay, it must take a beating in a north-west gale, and we agreed that if they could cope with the conditions there, then we should surely manage at home. The burden of putting all the equipment together, and fabricating the special parts our own situation demanded fell on Lance, but with Marshall's specialised knowledge and his optimistic approach, I really felt we'd be ready in time for the spring crop of 5,000 young salmon.

The crisis over the salmon farm had demanded our complete concentration. But preparations for the Yacht Race continued to go ahead on various fronts over the turn of the year. The television film was finding a shape and I had a contract to write a book of the trip.

One day Lance was nearly trapped on the yacht by advancing ice out on the winter mooring behind Paddy's Isle. The short winter days leave little time for error at the end of the afternoon. If the ice had closed round the yacht we would have been unable to reach him until the following morning – if then. For several days the boat was stranded out in the loch, out of reach until the ice melted, while on the shore great rafts of ice piled up with the rise and fall of the tide.

After this escape, Lance set to and designed and built a pier of telephone poles set in a wall of sandbags filled with concrete against a sheer rock wall on the sheltered side of the Annait. Leaning against it at low spring tide, the yacht dried out completely. No longer would we have to cross the Minch for the annual anti-fouling.

Two friends came to stay for a weekend in the New Year, Hughie Nedd and his "colleague", Old Murd. They had been helping us for a decade with the building and maintenance of the track to the School. Hughie had been foreman of the County Squad and Murd a member of the gang for many years before their retirement. The solid support they had given us, and particularly the "crack" we'd have together during hard winter days when they came up to Lance's workshop for their lunch, was one of the bedrock reasons why it was such fun to live at a place like Ardmore.

I picked them up in the Land-rover and we drove to the road-end at Portlevorchy where I'd left the boat down on the shore. Murd had his glasses up on his forehead, tied at the back with a string. His old blue mac flapped around him in the breeze and his "things" were in a small brown paper parcel tied up with baler twine. He was having a bit of trouble with his hearing-aid as the three of us picked our way down the hill to the boat. I think the noise of the diesel in the Land-rover must have affected it.

"Ach, that thing. It'll only go in the box along with your teeth," cracked Hughie; his "things" were in a tiny brown attaché case and he had a thin aluminium stick to help him over the rocks. His sheep dog followed obediently close at heel.

"Well, we'll both be able to use it then – you'll not be far away," replied his friend with a loud, not-got-it-tuned-yet cackle.

"You'd better not have it on too loud, I'm saying, or you'll be hearing what's not in it at all!" Both of them were clearly excited by the idea of going away for a weekend. Murd hadn't been across to Ardmore for thirty-three years. But when it came to the crunch, Hughie's dog wouldn't get into the boat, so he elected to walk round the loch rather than upset his four-footed friend.

Settled in front of the peat fire in the sitting room with a "mooth full o' feathers", from the Famous Grouse whisky bottle, they were soon in great form, remembering tales from the past.

Hughie told how he looked forward to Marie Christine's post-cards from the expeditions like the Amazon and Patagonia. "I always mark in a few hugs and kisses, you know – then I take it up to 'Donally' over the road to show him, make him jealous – he's a Seceder you know, went over to the Free Presbyterians from the Church of Scotland."

Supper was slightly spoiled by the corn on the cob which Murd couldn't really deal with. He'd never had it before and his teeth were not part of his "things" for the weekend.

Next morning breakfast was a little later than usual owing to the heavy night before, and when we did eventually begin Marie Christine asked Hughie what he would like.

"Och, I'll have a wee toddie," came the reply, quick as a flash and old Murd nodded hard beside him – no trouble with the hearing aid on that one.

154

Sad to say we never saw them again. Too soon they were both "in the box" as Hughie would say. But they are not forgotten.

1977 was different from the normal routine at Ardmore, and it wasn't just that we were starting the season earlier so we could sail down to Portsmouth for the start of the Race in August.

More subtle than this was the difference between the type of young person whom we were used to meeting each spring on the Instructor's Course, and the older and more complex personalities who were so keen to gain a place on the boat for the Race.

With hindsight, it is easier now to appreciate that a young fellow enchanted by the wild Highlands and looking for management experience to help develop himself, is a much more straightforward proposition than the unusual fellow, in his late twenties or older, whose personal and business life allows him to take the best part of a year away from his responsibilities. I believe my misunderstanding of this basic difference was the nub of the difficulties I had with the instructors and later the crew during the next eighteen months. Added to which the potential crew quite naturally looked no further than the Race, while my own plans for the boat ran many years beyond it. We'd had her built primarily for use at the School and I jealously guarded her for her future role.

However, as time passed, the eight men who were to make up the crew, besides the two-man film crew, Marie Christine and me, gradually emerged from a great number of possible choices.

The season got into full swing and still the yacht was alive with the sound of hammers and power tools whenever she was at her moorings. Sea trials continued every week, as we tested techniques for setting spinnakers and other rigs on the two-day voyages to the Hebrides.

Funds were running dangerously low now, and the whole boat project was looking as if it might be going to run away from me when rescue arrived in May from an unlikely source. We were out cutting peats when the smooth team from the chain store arrived. I took them on board. The boat was in chaos and Arun had spots of white paint on his glasses and in his wild black hair.

We were in the heads compartment adjoining the skipper's cabin when one of them said, "What would you think about naming the yacht Debenhams, John?" I looked down at the loo and imagined what twenty-five thousand used one-pound notes would look like piled up in it.

"It does have a certain romantic ring to it – Debenhams." I rolled the word off my tongue and grinned hugely. The deal was struck.

As well as working on the boat and building the pier Lance had been assembling sections for walkways and cage frames for the salmon farm and setting up the mooring system under the wood. The next drama came with the arrival of 5,000 smolts from a hatchery in South Uist. Smolting is the stage when the baby salmon is ready to make the change from fresh to salt water. It's a particularly vulnerable time and our smolts had been sixteen hours in transit, including two ferry crossings. It was obvious we were in deep trouble when we opened the lids of the tanker. The precious smolts lay belly-up on the surface of the stale warm water in the tanks while we raced to transfer them by net and dustbin to the waiting cages. 1,401 were dead in the first twenty-four hours and hundreds more continued to die during the first ten days of their new life in the sea cages. It was a far from auspicious beginning for the salmon farm co-operative, but it was a beginning. We would learn from experience and make sure that when we took delivery of the 1978 crop we were in control of the process. By that time, if things went to plan, we should have sailed right round the world.

Pussy Ridgway chose the busiest possible time to have her kittens.

Every time Marie Christine looked like leaving the croft to go down and cook the evening meal for the Women's Course, Pussy would set up a heart-rending miaowing to prevent her departure, and eventually the three small kittens were born. They were the result of a liaison with the bandit in the wood, and as we were shortly to set sail for nine months they really couldn't have arrived at a more awkward moment. The ladies on the course came up to see them after supper and thought they were just lovely; I wondered what we would do with them.

Heckie came in as he was passing and told a tale about a man from Avoch on the Black Isle. "I could never drown kittens," says he. "I was on a frigate in the North Atlantic when our sister ship was torpedoed. The men were drowning all round us – it was a cruel afternoon in February – we just couldn't go to them all at the same time. The cries were something I'll never forget . . ."

Drowning kittens didn't seem the thing to do when we were just about to set off ourselves. We gave one to the VAT inspector,

156

who took him back home to Wick; and another went south to Hampton Court with a London solicitor, who shocked us all by announcing he was a cat lover and calling it Ridgway. This left one unfortunate kitten selected by neither party, which Marie Christine and Becca insisted be taken into the family – much against my will. He grew up to be a big black and white tom with many of the less attractive traits of his renegade father. Becca decided to call him Oliver and because I thought him too fat, he became known as Fat Oliver. Together he and Pussy Ridgway have become an effective force against the mice, even though they are inclined to be importers, and the doorstep is frequently littered with corpses. They are put out at night, whatever the weather, but their revenge is to practise jumping from the bank at the back of the house on to the roof, and pacing up and down to make sure we can't get to sleep. Although they spend much of the day asleep in front of the stove in the kitchen they do follow us down to the shore and, when we go off in the boat, they sit waiting at the mooring for us to return, sometimes many hours later.

The last few days at Ardmore rushed past and I found I was already missing the place, even before we set off. Frantic loading of tools and materials for running repairs by Arun and his assistant, Colin Ladd, took all night, and made the yacht lie a little down by the bow when dawn came on 2 August. Lance and Ada would cope with everything that happened between now and the following April, including feeding the salmon and Pussy Ridgway and Fat Oliver. Ada is fond of Pussy Ridgway and Lance has a sympathy for her son. He keeps admiring his soft black and white coat, and I wonder if he isn't thinking what a nice rug he would make stretched out on the bedroom floor.

We went in to say goodbye to Granny Ross and told her we would be back just as soon as we could. There were a few more games of racing demon with Becca who would be going off to boarding school in Brighton and staying with her grandmother in the holidays. All the while endless stores continued to be loaded.

At last, at eight thirty in the evening we slipped our mooring and headed silently out of the loch bathed in shadow. As we passed the headland below the croft, the eldest group of the last course gave three cheers which rolled back from the surrounding hills. Then on the far side of the loch, way up on top of the hills, still golden with the evening sun, the two younger groups appeared like rebel tribesmen, and they too gave three cheers. I found myself blinking back tears: it was one of the most moving moments of my life.

There was something tremendously romantic about the first leg of the Whitbread Race, sailing down the Atlantic to Cape Town. Channel weather gives way to giant blue skies, the water takes on a magical colour, and there were days of perfect sailing in which to tune the boat as we ran south under the spinnakers until we reached the nerve-jangling Doldrums, beat into the south-east Trades and picked up the Westerlies for the final thousand-mile run in under Table Mountain. We made it in forty-six days and came in eleventh of the fifteen boats. I was sorry we had to make a landfall. I was in the mood for sailing on and on.

Eleventh was where our cruising boat was expected to come, experienced skippers on the other fourteen told us. But, of course, I had hoped to do better. However, the next leg to Auckland offered a chance to pull up our position if we took a calculated gamble. The Great Circle track, the shortest possible line from Cape Town to Auckland, leads over the Antarctic continent. But by sailing further south than the rest of the competitors we could cut as much as 800 miles off the 7,500 miles to Auckland. It would be uncomfortable sailing and the hazard, of course, is the pack ice, but we would probably be the only boat coming up the east side of New Zealand.

We saw our first ice eighteen days out. "Only a bergy bit," said our Antarctic expert dismissively, but it was the size of a block of flats. We saw more and more of them: jagged, luminous whites and blues of every hue, with crashing waves and hundreds of birds feeding on the krill trapped at the foot of the ice cliffs. The boat rocked in the backlash of waves from these majestic islands, just as she does coming from Handa when there's a big sea running. But unlike these unstable bergs, Handa never seems in danger of capsizing. At dawn we were embayed among a huge area of loose ice and motionless bergs. Ahead lay a great blank wall, some ten to fifteen feet high, stretching to the north and south horizons. This was the pack ice, the most inhospitable lee shore in the world, and there was no way through.

We eased our way north, through lanes of brash ice and growlers. Even though our gamble was beginning to come badly unstuck, I was irrationally seized with the same elation I have tacking among the overfalls of Handa: there was the same thrill of feeling the boat come alive in my hands.

158

Once clear of the pack ice, something began to go badly wrong with our navigation. After a couple of days, we realised we had been sailing too much to the north and not enough to the east. We had squandered our Great Circle advantage and were only level with the other boats which had an advantage over us on handicap. It was a bitter discovery. And as a result we abandoned our plan to sail up the east coast of New Zealand where winds were strong and favourable. We followed the others slap bang into a flat calm in the Tasman Sea, on the way up the western side of the islands.

I had allowed myself to be talked out of the unorthodox and become just another sheep. We were eleventh of the fifteen into Auckland, and to all of us aboard *Debenhams*, that spelt failure, after all we had gone through in the freezing fog of the Southern Ocean. The film crew were certainly finding material for the psychodrama they wanted to make. In Auckland I had a mutiny. But in the end only two men left the crew before we sailed on for Rio and Portsmouth. The experience was a very real test for me: it needs fire to make steel, and I hoped I had gained from being in that particular crucible.

The final leg to Portsmouth saw us finish last after getting caught in the Azores High, so we finished up thirteenth overall in the Race. This was not much to my liking, but at least we could console ourselves with the thought that our time would have earned us fourth position in the first Whitbread Race only four years previously.

As we sailed into Loch a'Chadh-fi on 15 April 1978 we had completed my dream of fourteen years. We had sailed all the way round the world from Ardmore to Ardmore in 255 days (174 at sea). It was a warm, sunny morning once we came under the shelter of the hills and, flying bravely from our rigging, we had every flag from the locker.

We sent up a great shout when we saw Heckie Ross appear on the clifftop of Ardbeg. He waved his stick in reply and was so moved by the sight that he picked up his dog Mona so she could see us better. Granny Ross, near on ninety, was sitting in her rocking chair with the rug over her knees, just the same as ever.

"Well, Ridgway, so you're back. 'A good neighbour close at hand is better than a brother far away.' I came out again today to wave you back. I don't suppose I'll go out again."

13

We were home just in time for the lambing, which is like a renewal, a promise of hope for the future linked to the coming of spring. We had now lived at Ardmore for ten years. The decade of struggle to gain a foothold on that inhospitable shoreline had been successful; our new approach was consolidation. In our absence Lance had built the foundation for a huge new workshop at Ardmore, then he and Ada had brought over all the construction materials by boat and fabricated the sections. He only needed us to prop up the sections while he bolted them together. Now all the small boats could be painted at Ardmore each autumn and Lance could cut down on his winter crossings of the loch. We installed an electric generator to power a dishwasher for Marie Christine and tools for Lance. There was even talk of the distant possibility of an EEC grant for the introduction of electricity in isolated rural communities. But the most far-reaching idea came from Marie Christine: to build a new bunk-house for twenty-two people down on the shore, with ten double rooms and two singles, together with its own showers and facilities.

Tony Dallimore, Steve Lenartowicz and Peter Brand from the Round the World crew formed the backbone of the instructing team for the season which began only two weeks after our return. Peter, the tall Tasmanian, went off to Kirkwall in the Orkney Isles with Lance to bring back the spanking new fishing boat we'd had built while we were away. She made a grand sight steaming into the loch one beautiful May morning with her shining red hull, gleaming white upperworks and a bone in her teeth from the 60 hp Lister diesel throbbing below decks. I had high hopes for this new Pride of the Fleet nearly thirty foot long with a spacious wheelhouse well forward, complete with cooker, sink, bunks and all, and a proper derrick and hydraulic lobster-creel hauler above her broad, open after-deck. *Ardmore Rose* was to be the symbol of the New Approach at Ardmore; she spelled Consolidation.

Another thing I had been planning was a new port of call

in the Hebrides for the two-day cruise with the Businessmen's Courses. Poring over the chart on the saloon table as *Debenhams* began the long haul back up the Atlantic, I had found a little place called Mariveg, a bit to the south of Stornoway. The Pilot warned me it was difficult to get into if the wind was from the east, but it looked perfectly sheltered once inside. I particularly liked the look of the surrounding lochs. There was sure to be some good brown-trout fishing if I could slip ashore with a rod of an evening.

It was a misty evening as we made our first landfall at Mariveg, just the very thing I wasn't looking for. I lined up the green island and the black island, interpreting from the Gaelic on the chart, and slid cautiously towards where I hoped the narrow entrance would be. Out of the mist loomed a small dinghy with a sheepdog in the bows and an old man sat in the stern doing a bit of handlining for early mackerel. From the wave he gave us I could see he was willing to pilot us into Mariveg. It was a good twenty-minute run through the twisting channels, and it would save him a bit of fuel if we gave him a tow.

And so it was we came to know Fido Macdonald. After supper at anchor below the scattering of crofts which surround the sea-loch, I went ashore in the dinghy, safe in the knowledge the yacht would be secure whatever direction the wind might blow up from. I found Fido's neat little house almost directly above where he moored his boat. Although it was still misty, I could tell he had a commanding view of the whole loch. His wife, Cathie, came in bearing a tray laden with tea and cakes, and what with one thing and another, there was no fishing that night. In any case Fido was quick to tell me that he held the record locally with a six-pound trout he'd caught only the previous year. Cathie laughed, and said he was desperate lest anyone should get a bigger one. On my way back to the yacht I met Morag Macdonald, Fido's niece, and she showed me the small salmon farm they were starting. It was much the same as ours at Ardmore, so I was interested to compare the feeding methods, particularly as we had got our first crop of smolts from the same island hatchery as Morag. Mariveg was to become my favourite port of call in the Hebrides.

At home we were getting ready for the arrival of 7,000 smolts for the 1978 crop. With Marshall Halliday's guidance we had installed four new twenty-foot cages and nets at the site under the wood. We improved the delivery a bit on the previous year by getting the road tanker bringing the smolts from the other side of Scotland to position itself on a grassy point directly above the loch at Skerricha. From there we ran the fish down an eight-inch alkathene pipe into the cages, minimising mortalities during the critical delivery phase from fresh to salt water. I had plans for picking the fish up next time at Laxford pier in tanks aboard the new fishing boat, but that would have to wait until we could afford the tanks.

We salvaged a massive wrought-iron anchor with the guidance of George Davidson, the harbourmaster at Kinlochbervie. It had lain deep in the mud for many years, and when Lance and I finally had it slung across the stern of the fishing boat, we hosed it down with the deckwash and found it good as new. It must have weighed the best part of three hundredweight, so when we got it back to Loch a'Chadh-fi I tied a number of plastic pick-up buoys to it. Then I put on my diving gear and got in the water beside the anchor, which was very slowly lowered until the buoys just kept it afloat.

My plan was to cut free a buoy at a time, so the anchor would slowly sink to the bottom some thirty feet below. Once suspended, just off the mud I'd swing it into its final resting place by hand.

Knife at the ready, I cut the first buoy free, foolishly hanging on to the anchor with my other hand. I never really knew what happened. Suddenly I was under the water and going down too fast. My ears hurt. I knew I must get clear of the anchor before we hit the bottom. A great cloud of mud sprang up, but I was free. My back hurt.

I hadn't realised that as the anchor descended, so the pressure on the plastic buoys would crush them flat, allowing the anchor to accelerate its descent.

We'd often talked of what we'd do "if I break my back". Ardmore would become an even more difficult place to live. Now, it really looked as if I'd done it. The pain lowered my spirits. We still went ahead with the building of the bunkhouse, bringing all thirty tons of material over by sea from Laxford Pier. We struggled through the IBM Course, and then we bought seven cast ewe sheep at the Lairg sale as planned. But I wondered if I was putting my head in a noose.

The end of September saw the end of the first decade of the School at Ardmore. The Bunk House was up and the builders departed. The instructors were all gone. Suddenly, for the first

162

day in eighteen months, I was no longer responsible for the safety of others. But I was turning into a cripple. A visit to a back specialist in London confirmed the worst and in the new year I found myself in the King Edward VII Hospital for Officers having a disc removed which was the consistency of soggy porridge. The others, they reported, appeared to be in good order. They needed to be.

On my release from hospital Marie Christine had to manage the boat as we returned up the bleak loch from Skerricha. While she was busy dodging the ice floes I spotted old Donald Corbett's bent figure, well wrapped in a long grey overcoat, fishing with his bamboo pole from the point off Portlevorchy. He put down the long pole as we came near. "Twenty cuddies," he chortled, holding up the chipped white enamel bucket. "Welcome home, boy – fish or no fish." I was feeling pretty battered one way or another, but that welcome was the best tonic for me – the orphan's accolade. I felt tears prick my eyes. I was home.

The snow clamped down, and the world stood still. Mice came to the traps in an unending line. Small birds got caught in behind the wooden lining and the rough stone walls of the croft, and the sheep made a fearful row as they rushed for the maize from the bucket each morning and evening. A high pressure system over the Highlands at 1,017 kept the loch frozen solid for a week. I had got home just in time.

This was one of the worst times of my life. Mostly I lay on the bed of boards Lance had made me. I felt diminished, done for. Marie Christine saved me.

As the hard weather continued, birds like herons and shags, which normally get their food from the surface of the loch, fought a battle for survival. The herons flapped out to stand in the less sheltered shallows of Laxford, but the shags developed a fatal fascination for the salmon in our cages. In spite of the new heavy-mesh predator net George Davidson and Danny Mackenzie had helped us lay just before Christmas, they still continued to try and spear the fish. Becca called them the "nightriders" after the sinister creatures dreamed up by Tolkien. Jet black and cruel beaked they dive some distance from the net, then choosing a place where predator net and cage are pressed together by the tide, they come up from beneath the fish, spearing them through the mesh. Helplessly the beautiful salmon can only dive to the bottom of the cage, for they are blind below: the set of their eyes only enables them to see upwards.

Lance and I realised the only solution lay in a deeper predator net, say ten feet below the fish cages themselves, but I was too crippled to do anything. There was no future in shooting shags, there are tens of thousands along the coast and they come in like marauders once the winter gales boom in from the west.

I hobbled up through the snowy wood using a couple of sticks and Marie Christine at my elbow to steady me. At the Blue House we dined on shag casserole. The Scaup, as it's known in the Hebrides, is eaten regularly in the southernmost of those islands. Buried for a couple of days in the moss, to take some of the sting from the flavour, it makes a good dish on a cold night.

The freeze lasted until mid-February. Weeks when little or no progress could be made outdoors allowed me, dreadful patient that I am, to fret and gloom the more at not making instant recovery. I made my first tentative run to the road-end at Portle-vorchy a week after the thaw and then I knew it was just a question of keeping going.

At this time I was enormously lucky to have Murdo McEwan as my chief instructor, and Jamie Young was back again, with his wife, Mary. Their honeymoon had been spent sailing the famous twenty-five-foot junk-rigged *Jester* to America, and latterly Jamie had skippered the huge American maxi-rating yacht, *Ondine*. Another powerful addition to the team was Colin Ladd from the Round the World crew. He had a yachtmaster's certificate and an engineering degree, and was the ideal choice to skipper the yacht on cruising courses out to places like St Kilda, and maybe even the Faroes. Marie Christine soon found that places on these cruises went like hot cakes.

The new Bunk House was operational for the first time in that spring of 1979. It made life so much easier, both for catering and for communication, and I blessed Marie Christine's inspiration. But she wasn't going to stop there.

"Now Mary and Jamie are here, we'll have to build a house for them. Now is the time to rebuild the old ruin next door!" My wife was full of ideas, but I groaned. Having the idea was one thing; bringing all the materials over the loch and a hundred feet up the hill was quite another.

Rowan trees were growing twenty feet high in the ruins on No.78. When we had had a hack at them five years ago we must have given them encouragement. The sheep walked along the mossy wreck of the back wall, the front wall bowed outwards, and Lance had refused to tackle it nearly ten years before. Each year saw more collapse. One gable was in reasonable condition. A dry-stone drain ran under the middle of the house and an enormous stone wall four feet thick and eight feet high split the inside into two unequal rooms. We still had most of the 2,000 lightweight concrete blocks which had been standing beside the ruin for some eight years. But fifty further tons of material would need to be manhandled to the site if we wanted to make a serious start. Mary and Jamie were all for it and Marie Christine could imagine moving in there one day herself. But Becca and I felt we could never desert No.76. Becca had known no other home and her little *Tierra del Fuego* meant a lot to her.

"You've picked a tough one this time, Johnny boy!" Heckie was leaning on his stick, his raggedy old coat hanging from his gaunt frame, a sardonic smile tugging at his lips, Mona at his heels. I was glad of an excuse to pause in our site clearing, and hear Heckie talk of No.78 as if it was still as he'd remembered it. "I was only ever once in that room where you're standing. An old aunt had it to herself, with that neat little fireplace in the gable. The crow steps there, above you, they were for the thatch. It was always dark and the walls were just the bare stone. There was a picture of Edward VII and Queen Alexandra in their coronation robes. The colours never faded you know – the sun never shone on it.

"This was Simon's room," he went on, pointing with his stick. "There was a big dresser back here and a settle under the window. But the floor was very humpy-bumpy. He used to sit there, spitting on the floor. I remember him pulling the head right off a cockerel once."

Simon Mackenzie was one of Heckie's childhood heroes. At the end of his days he had lived at No.78 with his sister Kate who was also devoted to Ardmore. Kate was reluctant to leave – even after her death – Heckie told us. When her coffin was being taken by sea to Foindle, a mile and a half across Laxford, the boat broke down and had to be rowed most of the way there. Then, no sooner had they got the coffin up on to the lorry for the six-mile journey to the cemetery by Scourie Bay, than the engine failed on it too, right beside the Claw Loch. The mourners ended up taking turns to share the load of the coffin on their shoulders for the last

165

five miles . . . "No, Kate didn't want to leave Ardmore – there was nobody present that day didn't think that," said Heckie with a sad shake of his head.

Three weeks later Heckie himself was dead. A massive coronary on 19 May was followed by several minor attacks, each of which progressively weakened him. "Hello, Johnny boy, I'm getting too old." His frail fluttery voice confirmed the high face colour. Marie Christine brought him some port and lemon juice.

Hughie was in the front room with him when he died. Poor Granny Ross was broken.

The funeral was on a fine clear Saturday morning in May. Mr Tulloch held the service in the house, and then we passed the coffin out through the window and bore it down to the shore. After carefully placing it aboard his old green and yellow boat, Hughie, Willie the Post, Bobby McLeod and I set off with it for Portlevorchy while Marie Christine stayed with Granny Ross. Jamie Young brought most of the mourners across the loch in the fishing boat, but poor Mona was left behind. She ran along the shore howling pitifully. Tears trickled down my face. Heckie, my quiet friend, was dead.

As we slowly crossed the loch I remembered how he and Mona had come out of the evening mist in the boat to welcome us back from the Sahara in the Nicholson, how he'd swung Mona up into his arms on the clifftop as we came in from the voyage round the world. And more than anything else I remembered "There's only one flag for me, Johnny boy! The White Ensign we ran up for Battle Stations, as we turned and headed for those three German destroyers at the head of the Norwegian fiord."

Many hands helped bear the coffin up the hillside from the boat to the hearse waiting at the Portlevorchy road-end. Then Heckie was taken off, to be laid at rest beside his father in the tiny cemetery by Scourie's sandy bay.

For days life ran on in black tracks. I just barely dragged my legs around. Slowly recovering from having the disc out of my spine, I'd had a particularly grim struggle to reach the top of Arkle, still locked in winter, with the businessmen.

With the start of the Young People's Courses in July came news that planning permission for the rebuilding of No.78 had been secured, and we started to order materials. Fourteen tons of sand and thirteen tons of gravel, stacks of timber, plaster board and pine lining boards tongued and grooved, which had to be handled so carefully, and the three and a half tons of cement which must on no account get wet. Plumbing and wiring, basins and baths, acres of roofing, doors and windows. The quantity surveyor's lists ran on and on. Sinclair Mackintosh came up trumps and let us store the fragile stuff in a large stone store at the end of Laxford Pier. Both pier and storehouse stand alone, a mile or more from the nearest house. Built in grander times simply for shipping coal for the estate, they are monuments to an age of building in stone in a massive style.

At Ardmore we unloaded on the grassy shelf at the top of the tide. And over several weeks, the hydraulic lobster-creel hauler on the fishing boat hauled over 400 loads up the hill to the site, pulling a cart built by Lance, on a 700-foot rope running through a pulley anchored to the ruin. The builders worked away through the autumn, sustained by gallons of Marie Christine's home-brewed beer. Morale got a tremendous boost when we learned that we could after all have electricity installed as part of an EEC grant scheme for isolated rural communities. If mains electricity did indeed come, I felt it would be the major achievement of our time at Ardmore. It might seem quaint to use Tilley lamps and candles, but Marie Christine's life would be revolutionised by electricity. The older members of the community too, would welcome the end of slogging up from the sea with Calor gas bottles, and supplies of peat could be cut back as well. There could be electric saws, sanders and grinders for the workshop, as well as clothes and dishwashing machines. We could communicate with the School by VHF radio during the Young People's Courses. A whole new Aladdin's Cave of toys was discovered to improve our efficiency, and to absorb the funds.

As a consequence of Heckie's death the Rosses' sheep were to be sold at Lairg. How would we now keep the grass clipped? Clearly we must take a hand with sheep ourselves, or the crofts would soon over-run with bracken and revert to the wilderness of the outgrazings.

Self-reliance and consolidation had always been part of our grand design for Ardmore. Much of the attraction of the place lies in the realisation that no matter how hard we try, there will always be scope for improvement. I'd heard often enough from almost everyone locally how the sheep stock at Ardmore could be improved. One fact was always mentioned: it couldn't be done overnight. Before enlarging our meagre stock of half a dozen surviving cast ewes, we must first put the fences in order. If we brought in sheep and the fencing was inadequate, they would simply set off back towards their original home. The Rosses' sheep, born on Ardmore, were content to remain on the ground they knew, but we were in no position to buy until we had improved things, and the Rosses' flock was to be sold immediately. We would have to build up a new flock from a small number of fresh stock. The ground would benefit from a rest in any case. Broken fences allowed the sheep to graze the green inbye land at random and this is no good thing. With new fencing we could control grazing and cut down the infestation of worms and other parasites, like ticks.

Ardmore is a difficult place to fence: near vertical hillsides with the minimum of topsoil over rock. It would have to be a professional job. But grants were available for fencing, the building of a new fank, bracken cutting and regeneration, and the Crofters Commission welcomed our new initiative. Alan Macrae won the contract to do the fencing. It was just the sort of job for this pocket battleship of a man, the only native west-coast Highlander ever to win the Ben Nevis Hill Race. He came up from Lochinver and paced out the ground, heedless of obstacle and gradient. "Now, see here, John, you get the materials on the line of the fences, and I'll come up on my own in the spring next year and do the job!" Alan announced, in his sharp, sing-song voice, bouncing up on his toes.

We decided the most important fence was the one cutting the Ardmore peninsula from the mainland, a distance of 290 yards along the bottom of the waterfall. The old fank (sheepfold) and dipper down there needed replacing as well. We decided to site the spanking new one recommended by the Crofters Commission nearer, on our croft on Lower Ardmore.

Then we fenced each croft, paying particular attention to the seaward end of all our fences to make sure the sheep couldn't get round them at low tide. The last piece of fencing was the 115-yard-wide neck of Paddy's Isle, where we could put the breeding ewes in late November for a month, safe in the knowledge that they couldn't walk out on the tup (ram) at low spring tide.

With the fencing in hand, we set about a three-year plan to cut back the bracken and scrub to the line of the projected fences on the croft boundaries. As soon as the land was clear, we planned to regenerate it with twenty-three tons of lime in the autumn of '82, adding basic slag, grass seed, and fertiliser in due season. We intended starting our flock with fewer than twenty ewe lambs from a local stock with comparable ground, preferably from someone who was selling up, rather than sending weak lambs to market. It was an ambitious project to put new heart into the old place.

I got a letter one day from Charles Stuart, who had come on a Businessmen's Course in '74. He was then an executive with British European Airways, badly out of condition and overweight. He was remembered for being so unfit that he was the only member of the course unable to manage the Foinaven Ridge on the last day of the week. Now, in 1979, he wanted to come up for a weekend with his wife Ann, to have another crack at the morning run.

When he arrived off the boat I didn't recognise him. He'd lost three or four stone, and was a different person. He described how his job as the marketing director for the whole of British Airways took him all over the world. Hopping from one airport hotel to another was no recipe for physical fitness. But he'd turned it to his advantage, making a rule never to eat on a flight and always to run each morning whether it was Sydney Bridge or the Golden Gate in San Francisco.

We ran out round the loch and back. A lean, fit, fifty-four-year-old, he looked no more than thirty. Over lunch he suggested I try running a marathon, casually mentioning the New York Marathon was the best he'd ever run personally. I liked the idea. I bought Jim Fixx's book and suggested to Central Television that the Running Ridgways could be their next psychodrama. Marathon running, I said, would be the next craze to hit Britain from the States. Meanwhile I began running further, pushing out to ten and fifteen miles a couple of times each week, though Marie Christine was quite happy just doing the morning run.

Eventually we came to the end of the season. "I suppose this will be the last holiday of this year?" I said to Vim Heinemann, a Dutch architect, at dinner the last evening. He didn't speak very good English, so I was sitting next to him to try and include him in things.

"Not so. My son is the only non-British doctor in the British Nepal Medical Trust. In twenty-one days I go out to see him there and stay with him for a while."

While Vim spoke slowly and deliberately, a glimmer of an idea flashed through my mind. "Really? Where is his hospital?"

"Oh, no, not a hospital, just a mud hut. He is stationed alone in a very remote place in south-east Nepal, far from Kathmandu."

"Look, I'm very interested in this," I said. "Would you mind if I go up to the house and get my atlas? You could show me just where you'll be going?"

Vim blinked in surprise. I think I was a bit ahead of him.

The Times Atlas has a grand map of Nepal. The route was clear. Fly to Delhi and change for Kathmandu. From there it was possibly going to mean another flight for a couple of hundred miles to the south, then a day or two by Land-rover and finally a three-day walk in to the small town of Bhojpur. This was where we would find the tuberculosis clinic run by Vim's son.

"Marie Christine and I will see you there in four weeks from today," I grinned, uncertain if he understood.

I reasoned that if high-altitude training was good for Olympic athletes, it would be just the ticket for us two would-be marathon runners. This time it was Marie Christine's eyes which opened wide. She loved the idea of all the flowers she would see. I smiled.

A few days before we were due to leave for Nepal, we were woken at one in the morning by a loud banging on the front door. It was Molly Ross from next door: her mother had been taken very ill. Marie Christine went in and stayed the rest of the night with her. She had had a stroke. She had never got over Heckie's death in the spring. Now, partially paralysed down one side she was nearly done for. "God be with you, and farewell, I'll not be seeing you again," she said to Marie Christine and me when we went up to her bedroom to say goodbye on the eve of our departure for Nepal.

That night a light shone from the rebuilt house of No.78 for the first time in forty years as Jamie and Mary moved in. I think Granny Ross would have liked that. She died during the night, and was buried in Scourie beside her husband Hector and son Heckie.

Now there was no reason for the Ross family to live any longer at Ardmore. We would miss them sorely.

14

Nuptse, Everest, Lhotse, Kangchenjunga – there was not a cloud in the deep blue sky as the pilot reeled off the names of legendary mountains I had read of since a boy. They were a stunning sight, a dazzling white barrier beyond the sandy Indian plains. The reason we were enjoying them from the flight deck of the Royal Nepal Airlines Boeing was because we had found ourselves sitting next to the pilot's wife on the flight from Delhi to Kathmandu. Marie Christine put it all down to my smart navy blazer and knife-creased grey flannels. She is a stickler for us being presentable when travelling.

In Kathmandu airport our good fortune continued. I found a new monthly light-plane service direct to Bhojpur. The following day was only its second flight. We bought two tickets with our Traveller's Cheques. The official said he would be at the airport himself in the morning and assured us we need not bother with the usual trekking permit required by all visitors to Nepal. He would endorse our passports himself. We took a bus to Kathmandu and spent a pleasant day looking at the ancient city.

Next morning was not quite as successful, however. New rules seemed to apply, and blazer really was needed with the chief of immigration and customs. The flight was like an aerial circus, so violently was the plane thrown about by air currents as we crossed close over mountain ridges and high above deep valleys. At last circling over a steeply rising spur, I realised we were going to land. I couldn't see how or where. Marie Christine closed her eyes, just as she had done in Chile when there was more water coming over the bows of the rubber dinghy than she could bail out.

Quite suddenly we were standing alone on a small brown foreign field. The plane had gone and there was silence. It was very hot indeed. And we had too much luggage. In the distance a few Nepalis were milling about on the edge of the field, rather as if a village cricket match were going to begin in another couple of hours or so. "We can't possibly carry all this gear," said Marie Christine. Heathrow seemed a long way away.

Fortunately at that point the Nepalis stopped admiring only the second aeroplane most of them had seen and came as one man to offer their portering services. Without exception every one of them knew Dr Eric Heinemann personally. After an agonising climb, carrying absolutely nothing at all, we came to a halt before an old mud building which looked just the same as the few others scattered along a narrow footpath twisting for ever upwards.

I knocked on the door, trying my best to look cool and smiling. Vim Heinemann opened the door. His jaw sagged and we all laughed. His son Eric was just finishing the morning clinic, so over a light lunch, we explained our own situation. We were both exhausted from a long season. We hoped to run in the New York Marathon the following autumn and a month's sustained hard walking in Nepal would be good groundwork for our training. Above all, owing to the nature of our work at Ardmore, we wished to walk without other Europeans. At home we had had the idea to approach the Everest Base Camp, but from the south-east rather than the usual trekking route from Kathmandu in the south-west. Could Eric help us with the hiring of a couple of Nepalis to act as guides and porters for the walk up to Namche Bazar?

It was as I had hoped at the dinner table with Vim back in Ardmore only a very few weeks ago. It just needs one person with local knowledge to get you on your way and Vim's son Eric knew a retired Gurkha second lieutenant whose job was to look after the welfare of all the retired Gurkha soldiers in the district. The lieutenant would produce us a shortlist of candidates to interview. We had an appointment for ten o'clock the next morning.

I was most careful that we presented ourselves at 0955 precisely at the Gurkha officer's house. He was a small, erect figure of about fifty-five. Everything was desperately spartan and we sat outside by a plain wooden table, commanding a tremendous view of the surrounding district in the manner of any good forward observation post. The lieutenant delivered a crisp briefing before the interviews. The walk should take no more than twelve days; we needed no fewer than two guides; the rates of pay were fixed and there should be a small advance. The guides would need the rest of the day to prepare themselves and purchase necessary stores. They would carry all our gear and their own, in their own style, wrapped up in a blanket on their backs and supported by a headband.

There was one small technicality, the lieutenant explained. There were only two candidates available.

At a signal the first presented himself in a suitable manner. Introduced by the lieutenant as Lalbahdur Rai, he waited for a further signal before seating himself at the other end of the table. Weighing in at barely nine stone, and distinguished by a bright green flower-pot hat above a face that expressed at once total defeat and immense cunning, Lalbahdur looked about thirty-five, and exhibited a weary enthusiasm for the expedition. The lieutenant explained that Lalbahdur was an untouchable, and as such, he would not be admitted into any dwelling place we might enter along our way. Terms were agreed by the lieutenant, for Lalbahdur possessed not a word of English, and the first member of our team was dismissed pending further orders.

The second, and of course automatically elected member, was Gunga of the swelling muscles. He appeared remarkably saturnine for a sixteen-year-old, and was a chain smoker of dubious roll-ups. Gunga offered no single comment at the interview; he had the air of "a pressed man". As he shuffled off to join Lalbahdur at the edge of the compound, the lieutenant mentioned that while Lalbahdur had been a rifleman with the Nepalese Army, Gunga had never before left Bhojpur and he spoke no English either.

"All we need is a three-legged, one-eyed dog called Nelson, and we've got the set," I said to Marie Christine, as we left the lieutenant after a short discussion on the merits of Field Marshal Lord Slim.

"Isn't Lalbahdur sweet?" She smiled. "But I'm not so sure about Gunga."

Next morning we four set off on the long trek towards Namche Bazar. Two spoke no English, two no Nepali.

It was the season for tangerines, and we bought as many as we could carry from women travelling into Bhojpur market. We were keener than our two guides to stop at the end of each half hour. The heat was terrific and the gradient only upwards. While they lit up their smokes and rested their loads on a walking stick placed behind them, we slumped down on the nearest boulder. By lunchtime we were exhausted, and pleasantly surprised to find Lalbahdur preparing for a major cooking session, but we just couldn't eat all the dhal and spinachy greens he produced. In spite of my fatigue I was not happy at the leisurely way the whole meal stretched into a couple of hours or more. Nothing seemed to worry Lalbahdur however, and Gunga had still to utter a word. He was very clearly the subordinate.

By four o'clock we were stopped for the day, and I began to fret. "These couple of hoods are trying to force us to raise the wages. We'll never get back to Kathmandu at this rate; we'll miss the plane. I'll give them the sack. We'll carry the gear ourselves. Dump the stuff we can't manage."

Marie Christine thought the flowers were wonderful, and said nothing.

We spent the night at what I took to be a friend of Lalbahdur's. Our Karrimats were a comfortable cushion for the sleeping bags on the floor of the neatly swept porch of the mud hut. It had a fresh coat of red brown emulsion, which we discovered was a mixture of mud and manure. I noticed Lalbahdur wasn't allowed into the house, which was always filled with smoke from a fire with no chimney. This did kill the insects, but it caused the coughing which in turn spread the TB Eric Heinemann spent all of his time trying to combat. Nepal suffers the highest incidence of tuberculosis in the world. Next morning we were woken with a cup of tea while it was still dark. It was time to be on our way. There was no breakfast.

"This is more like it. Must have seen we wanted to push on," I muttered in the half-light of six o'clock, slyly pinching another cheap arrowroot biscuit from the packet Marie Christine and I were sharing. I was astonished to find there was no payment for sleeping in the house, just a nominal charge for some fresh food Lalbahdur bought for our lunch.

We really cracked on all morning, up the side of one valley, across the ridge, and right down into another. Always we crossed the same kind of rickety bamboo bridge, often garlanded with what looked like marigolds. Up and down, up and down, we seemed to cover very little distance on the map I'd so carefully Fablonised the very day I bought it in Stanford's map shop in London.

The same set-piece lunch ritual was performed, but this time I was past complaining about the delay. When we stopped at four, once again at a convenient house, I began to get the drift of Nepali travel. Rise at first light and start walking in the early morning cool, at six o'clock. Push on with short breaks until ten or eleven, then a long halt for a two-hour lunch – the first real food of the day. Crack on until four and stop at any convenient house for the night. Travellers seem to have the right of free shelter in anyone's house, but must pay at cost for any fuel and food they may need.

By eleven next morning we were high in damp cloud, on the crest of a mighty ridge. We came upon a traveller's halt in the mist, a sort of ramshackle Nepali transport café, where an old crone served hot sweet tea and offered some shelter from the drizzle. When we arrived, there was already another team supping tea. They were a sharp-looking outfit, seemed like a government survey or something, and they'd come the other way. We got into conversation with the leader, who spoke good English. He was a stocky, competent, retired sergeant of the Gurkha Engineers. His present job was touring remote villages and investigating claims for government funds to lay on a piped water supply in cases of obvious need. Mostly this would be long coils of black alkathene piping, exactly like ours at Ardmore, except that it had to be carried even further to the site.

The sergeant had attended a language course at the Army Education Corps headquarters in Beaconsfield, in whose old village church we had been married. He also was an admirer of Field Marshal Lord Slim, the former Gurkha officer, whose Burma campaign I had studied. We got on famously, and he answered many questions about our two companions. He questioned them severely, and pronounced they should be all right, although they were just as much strangers to the area as we were. They had never been this way before, and were only finding the route by asking whoever they met. They were most apprehensive about going as far as Namche Bazar, because of the cold and because they believed the Sherpas to be very fierce.

However, they liked us, and they would not let us down. This was our first real communication with our companions.

The sergeant told them that in two more days we should reach the village which he had just surveyed for a water supply. He gave Lalbahdur strict instructions to stop at this village for a night, telling him the name of the headman.

"He is an ex-Gurkha corporal. He'll look after you well," smiled the sergeant, heaving the load on to his back and summoning the other two members of his party to make ready to depart.

We arrived at the village at nine o'clock on the morning of the second day. Clearly the sergeant had not thought we would move so fast. I decided we would just make ourselves known to the headman and then push on towards Namche, still many days distant. There had been no real path for much of the past couple of days, and I doubted Lalbahdur's navigation without a definite path to follow, for he had neither map nor compass.

From the beginning, it was clear the ex-corporal headman had not been to the language school at Beaconsfield. However, he listened intently to what Lalbahdur had to say. I glanced across at Marie Christine, thinking our friend was perhaps laying it on a bit thick. The headman was obviously impressed with the information. His face radiated smiles from beneath a scruffy white Pandit Nehru cap. A threadbare black jacket, cut in European fashion, hung raggedly almost to his knees, flapping gently in the breeze.

We were bade sit down cross-legged with him in the small village square. People of all ages began to appear from every corner. Garlands of flowers were hung round our necks, and musicians began to play. The local drink began to flow. The entire village had been given a holiday by the headman to celebrate our arrival.

"You know what's happened, don't you? Lalbahdur's told him we've come to decide whether or not they are to get the water supply laid on. This headman thinks we're senior government officials," I muttered between sips of nearly neat alcohol, the cross-legged position beginning to clutch at my back.

"Never mind, Johnny. I think I'll start a collection for them in my shop, next season," my wife replied, smiling sweetly at the drummer. I thought she looked rather nice with the garland of flowers.

"I feel as if my whole education has been aimed at this moment. WE MUST NOT LET THE SIDE DOWN," she went on, through gritted teeth.

"Who does Lalbahdur think we are?" I said out loud. He and Gunga were drinking prodigiously, enjoying their importance hugely.

The sun beat down. The females formed themselves into a singing group before us, like an annual school photo formation. The aged bearded drummer was beating out a frenzy. Sweat poured off him and he seemed in a trance. The singing grew steadily in volume; everyone seemed to be having a grand time. I thought things were getting out of hand. I desperately wanted

Heckie at the hay.

Cutting the peats beside Loch Laxford in the spring.

'The electric' comes to Ardmore, 1981.

Winter running with Rebecca.

Willie the Post coming up the waterfall onto Ardmore.

Floating voters. Lance, Marie Christine, author and Ada rowing to the polling booth at a general election.

to spend a penny, but hadn't the nerve to ask and doubted if I could stand up, my legs hurt so much. My head was swimming but I let eager hands fill my mug yet again.

Around one o'clock I was beginning to realise that unless I had something to eat, I wasn't going to finish the course, even though I had almost stopped drinking anything at all. I was conscious of the headman holding a sort of meeting with what looked like the village elders. Marie Christine still looked delighted with things, but wasn't saying much anymore. I was beginning to think I'd heard some of the songs at least once already.

Suddenly the music stopped, and then everyone stood up and began moving off to the right. Marie Christine helped me to my feet and I tried to make this movement look nonchalant. We made our excuses and lurched off in search of some secluded corner of a foreign field. Luckily, with all the villagers concentrated in one place, this didn't present too much of a problem. Then weaving our way back to the square, we reassured each other it was all for the best. A spot of relaxation never harmed anyone, and anyway now we could soon be on our way.

The beaming headman greeted our return with open arms, and ushered us towards a small dry paddy field. I noticed the entire population was ranged round the steep sides, as if it were an amphitheatre.

"Oh, look! They're going to kill that for us." Marie Christine's voice sounded distant but uncertain. A huge beast like a water buffalo was stood in the centre of the tiny field, its head jammed between two iron stakes driven into the ground.

A man came out of the crowd and gave the headman an enormous curved kukri.

"Blimey! It's *Camp on Blood Island* – I saw that film in Staines," I muttered.

We were conducted into the middle of the field. The villagers were hushed, like for Sports Day Prizegiving. I struggled to walk tall. We tottered to a halt beside the buffalo. The headman handed me the scimitar.

Sweat trickled cold down my face. It was just like finding you've too many clothes on when you're feeling seasick. The crowd looked on expectantly. I summoned myself up to my greatest height. With a sickly smile I made an extravagant gesture as if to return the honour to the headman. I forced Excalibur into his hands. There could be absolutely no doubt that I did not want that sword back. The headman was most charming. There wasn't a flicker of contempt. He handed the kukri on to an aide, and it disappeared from sight.

Suddenly a very small man, who had been standing at the beast's head all the while, uttered a wild cry, and struck the buffalo between the eyes with a sledgehammer.

"That's what pole-axed means," I sniffed at my wife, suddenly an expert again.

The beast fell to the ground, and the little man pounced on it with a dagger and began cutting it up. Within fifteen minutes it was spread out in small portions on a mat while the killer weighed out the rations on a set of brass scales.

We retired to the square once more. Singing, dancing, garland presentations and drinking began again. Marie Christine and I were still the centre of attention, in spite of my loss of face over the guillotine job. The crossed legs hurt as before.

Scarcely five minutes elapsed, then steaming dishes were thrust into our hands. From the few hairs floating on top of the greasy water, I recognised our friend the buffalo. I wasn't certain what organs lay beneath the surface, so I let my spoon dig them out and put them in my mouth, while I locked the dancers in a fixed stare and thought of England.

It wasn't nice.

All good things must come to an end, I thought to myself. "We really must be getting on our way. Busy schedule, you know. Demanding job and all that." I was cringing as we left. I felt so guilty. I often wonder if they got their water supply.

We walked on for several more days. It was a magical land. Passing ancient prayer monuments of stone, I wondered if Europeans had ever passed this way before. Slowly we were approaching the snow-covered giants. Just occasionally we crossed a ridge as the cloud lifted like a veil from a priceless work of art. Although it was clear from the place names on our rough map that we were nearing the dazzling peaks, they just didn't seem to be getting any closer.

At length we joined an ancient trade route between India and Tibet. The path was worn several feet below the surface of the surrounding ground by centuries of pounding bare feet. The commercial traffic today was mostly small teams of superhumans oiled with sweat, each man carrying close to his own body weight in a swaying walk-run. They overtook us as if in a trance, bulging

178

neck muscles supporting the headband which held the load on their backs. Calf and thigh muscles sculpted, eyes glazed like the Quechua Indians who'd helped carry our gear in the Andes. Perhaps they were drugged too. It was a busy little world of its own; I had the feeling we were in the Middle Ages. People who passed were usually in high spirits, as if pleased to be out and about in the mainstream of life.

Occasionally there were disasters, where the path had been washed away by a flash flood or a bridge broken. Always men would be labouring eagerly, like worker ants, anxious not to delay the heavy traffic bearing the lifeblood of the nation. Now the villages had become self-important trading posts with open-fronted stalls facing the narrow thoroughfare.

As the days and miles passed, we'd developed a warm bond of fellowship with Lalbahdur. He was always at great pains to see we were well looked after. Even Gunga began to come out of his shell, and the sullen exterior fell away. Suddenly he could play the harmonica, and he would sing to himself as we went along. I don't think Marie Christine and I have ever been happier.

On the tenth day we joined with the Kathmandu trail on the banks of a fast-flowing milky river, then we came to the little airstrip at Lukla. Great crowds of people of all nationalities were gathered there. We were told of delays in flights out to Kathmandu owing to bad visibility in the valleys, and suddenly I was painfully aware that as we had not got a flight booked, we'd be right at the back of the queue. Clearly we wouldn't be flying back to Kathmandu. I would have to find some other way back on foot.

The climb is steep from Lukla to Namche Bazar. It takes two days and lifts the traveller into a different world. As we approached the small Tibetan-looking town our two companions grew visibly apprehensive at entering the land of the Sherpas. They complained bitterly of the cold and any suggestion from me that they might come on further with us was met with a sad shaking of their heads. As we said goodbye, they were both in tears, and with Lalbahdur we felt we were saying farewell to a real friend.

We settled into a rest-house and searched the map until we found a track leading away up to the north-west, over a pass called the Tasi Lapcha La at 18,745 feet and then down into the Rolwaling Valley to the village of Beding. From there, there appeared to be a reasonable walk of several days, similar to what we had already done, leading in the direction of Kathmandu.

"I'm not keen to cross any passes at that height. This isn't a climbing holiday," Marie Christine said rather sharply.

A sort of fuzzy argument developed. We were already feeling the effects of the climb up to Namche at 12,000 feet that morning.

We decided to have a look round the ancient town and see if there was any chance of hiring a guide to take us over Tasi Lapcha Pass. This time there was no Eric to turn to. We began asking any Sherpas who looked as if they might be guides, and also in all the little stores we visited for provisions. But we made no progress, and morale began to sag, so we had something to eat and a hot drink and tried again.

Almost immediately we met a fit-looking young fellow of about twenty-three, dressed in smart modern climbing gear. He answered our questions in good English and told us his name was Tashi, that he had been to the university in Kathmandu, and that he believed his father, Angpusan, was thinking of going over into the Rolwaling Valley to collect money for a herd of yaks he had sold to the people of Beding the previous year. Tashi suggested we called at his house a couple of hours later to discuss the possibility of joining his father on the journey which would have to be soon as the snows were coming and would close the pass for the winter. He warned us it would be a hard trip and wondered if we had the right gear.

Basketball boots had turned out to be the thing for the foothills. They lasted only about a fortnight, but they were much lighter and cooler than the heavy leather climbing boots we'd brought from Ardmore. But now it looked as if we were going to need the boots and the duvet jackets and tent as well.

Tashi's home was one of the most imposing dwellings in Namche. His family had occupied a prominent position in that key outpost on the Tibet–India trade route for the past 500 years. His mother was even now on a secret caravan to Tibet to buy antiquities. We were entertained to Tibetan tea by his father, a tall, dignified man in high boots and cloak. He showed us the family prayer wheel, large and ornate, in an adjoining building, turning it as he did so and uttering a prayer for our safe deliverance on the journey over the Pass. He smiled his sad smile and said something to Tashi.

"Father says he will be pleased to have you with him on the journey. I am to come as well, and we will take prayer flags to fly on the Pass. We shall leave in three days' time and will arrange

180

porters for the four of us." Tashi's youthful modernity contrasted strongly with his father's timeless grace. He seemed as out of place as we did in that spacious dark house with its silent family retainers.

Marie Christine and I went on a two-day walk up to the fabled monastery at Thyangboche to acclimatise. I would never forget the atmosphere, so close to Everest. On the first day after leaving Namche for the Tasi Lapcha Pass, we walked to Thami, and stayed there in the house of a relative of Angpusan. There was considerable celebration of our arrival and we had too much to eat in a place of small grey dusty fields which looked devoid of all agriculture.

There was yak's milk and cheese and great quantities of delicious potatoes little bigger than marbles. The lady of the house had two husbands, one for winter and one for summer. This is apparently a common Sherpa practice, and Tashi told us we should be meeting his Great-Uncle, the winter husband, on the following day, when we arrived at the most upland pastures below the Tasi Lapcha Pass. The old fellow was living alone up there and tending the herd of yaks while the good weather lasted. But with the coming of winter he would soon return and take over his wife again, then the other husband would move out until the spring.

Next day the walking went well. We were with real professionals, who took good care to manage the pace so that it didn't bring on altitude sickness. We made a stop at a small but beautiful monastery. Tashi's family were involved here too, and he was related to some of the saffron-clad monks. The continuous cycle of prayer and the worn timbers of this tiny refuge, built into the mountainside, were so different to the world I knew outside. Lifting one of the big conch-like shells to my ear, I could hear the distant call of the ocean while around us the serene figures continued their endless, timeless chanting. Sadly I felt sure this would not continue for another hundred years, such was the change I saw coming in Nepal.

We walked on up the valley towards the Pass, spending the night at a small stone byre, where Great-Uncle/part-time husband lived alone. We slept in the hay. It was cold and nearly 14,000 feet above the sea which I'd heard in the shell that morning.

I was now suffering from the altitude. Marie Christine and I had gone for a walk soon after arriving at Great-Uncle's little shelter. I'd felt surprisingly fresh, considering we had only to climb a further four to five thousand feet and we should be over the Pass. The sky was a perfect blue. Looking back down the valley towards Namche, I felt a great surge of spiritual uplift. We were above a sea of white cloud, and on the further shore soared the magnificent peak of Ama Dablam, the one the Nepal government has chosen to print on its bank notes.

"I'll just try a little run, see how the lungs go," I'd laughed delightedly at my wife, who was clearly going to try no such thing. At first I found little difficulty traversing along the mountainside. But as soon as I turned up the steep slope, my breathing became strained. Very soon a sharp pain stabbed into my brain. As we walked back to Great-Uncle's, Marie Christine was full of chat, and I was rather quiet. After supper I was sick.

Next morning dawned grey and damp, like the Foinaven valley in winter. There were seven of us in the party; Tashi was carrying his own gear and a couple of young Sherpas from Namche were carrying what Tashi's father and I couldn't manage between us. We'd been joined by a top-flight Sherpa climber-porter who was returning to his home village of Beding at the end of a season on the highest peaks.

My headache remained and I bitterly regretted that trial run. We climbed steadily upwards. Snow swirled all around us and there was one enormous avalanche which roared down into the valley to our left, leaving a great white cloud of powder snow in its wake. I could well understand a death by asphyxiation, if caught by something like that cloud.

We were roped together now, and heading for a cave known to the man from Beding.

We were already at 17,000 feet when we found it, and then there wasn't room for us all. Marie Christine and I put up our tent. She was feeling fine, but Tashi's father, Angpusan, and I were both sick on arrival at the cave, which turned out to be not so much a cave as the overhang of a huge boulder, and it was a pretty miserable party which gathered there for a supper of chicken-noodle soup, which Angpusan promised was an infallible cure for altitude sickness. He was a particularly sorrowful figure, clad still in his long boots but wrapped now in a heavy black overcoat which was apparently a relic from a Polish visitor to Namche. Sadly, the chicken-noodle soup did nothing for either of us.

182

We reached the summit just before noon the following day. Briefly, the sun came out, although it was too local to give us anything more than a glimpse of an enormous glacier flowing down the valley which now lay ahead of us.

Angpusan cheered up as he pulled strings of small flags from the deep pockets of his black overcoat. These were left fluttering bravely between two rocks, and I had the impression this act meant a great deal to him. He posed for a photograph with the flags strung out in the background and his arms round my wife and me, a broad smile lighting his usually sad face.

We hurried thankfully down the smooth snow field towards the glacier. I was desperately keen to descend and be rid of my headache. As is usual in these affairs, our progress became ragged after the main objective of crossing the Pass had been achieved. Word was passed down that we were trying to reach another cave for the night. Conditions had been pretty bad by any standards, and we were all tired as we trudged along the side of the glacier and far too strung out when darkness came. Although Marie Christine had suffered no altitude sickness, she was beginning to mutter about this being "the last holiday I'm ever going on with you".

It was absolutely dark by the time we reached the icefall. The Sherpa with the rope was far ahead with the man from Beding, looking for the cave. I had vivid memories of the icefall in Chile, and I was glad the darkness hid the void beyond the shelves of ice we had to crawl across on our way down. It was just the right situation for an accident. I was frightened, so was Marie Christine. We didn't say much to each other.

The stragglers eventually all met up at the cave, guided in by weak flashes from a torch. It was a grim, cold night in our tent and I was sick several times. We left first thing in the morning. I was pleased for the early start, as it meant release from my headache was in view at last. Tashi explained it was essential we reach the next obstacle before the sun: the glacier flowed into a narrow lake, on which floated numerous small bergs. The lake was narrow because of the steep sides of the valley in which it lay, and we had to pass down the length of the lake on the sunny side. Frozen at night, the sun thawed rocks loose from the side of the valley wall during the forenoon – then it was rather like Russian roulette.

The bare outline of a path was soft, crumbling mud and rock

loosely mixed, and rocks came down fast from far above on this particularly sunny morning. A cry would go up, and we'd all duck behind the nearest shelter we could find. It was not a day for such a walk.

I was vastly relieved when we eventually reached flatter ground at the end of the lake, where a natural dam of rock blocked the end of the valley. The risks of the past two days had caught Marie Christine and myself unawares. The cat had used up more lives. Neither the scattered night descent of the icefall, nor the walk along the exposed face of the valley in hot sunlight were justifiable risks. But we were caught up for once in a situation beyond my control. I hadn't known what lay ahead, and when I found out, we were too scattered for me to call a halt. That we survived with no injury, other than a cut hand suffered by one of the Sherpas who was just too slow avoiding a falling rock, seemed to me to be more by luck than judgment. And for all of these things, crossing the Pass was the more unforgettable. We had unwittingly found ourselves in the daily duel fought out between the young Sherpa braves and the compelling mountains.

"It 'ees a rightt!" exclaimed Angpusan as we sat eating our meagre lunch in the warm sun below the rock dam. A little field mouse had crept out from among the rocks to investigate a bar of fudge I'd laid down beside me, when I tried some of the berries Tashi'd told me were so good for the health. It was the first wild mammal I'd seen since before we'd reached Namche. We must be descending steadily; my headache had quite gone.

All that afternoon we pushed on through the snow beside the river flowing from the foot of the tumbled rock dam, until at last we arrived at the village of Beding. Bathed in the silver light of a full moon, and lying strangely quiet on a bend in the river, Beding was an apparition of safety after the events of the past several days, an ancient refuge locked in the mountain vastness. It looked perfect yet deserted. Had the villagers all fled from some unknown danger? We rested by the edge of the fast-flowing river, while the Sherpa who came from the village went to investigate. The snow muffled all sound, save the burbling waters.

"They have all gone," said the Sherpa, when he returned. We were cold, tired and hungry. This was not good news.

He explained that this was the village of Upper Beding, but the villagers had all gone down to Lower Beding for the winter, within the past few days, from what he could make out. Although his main home was in Lower Beding, we should be most welcome to stay the night in this upper house before proceeding to the lower village in the morning. The house, indeed the entire village, was fully equipped. The people had simply walked out and left their summer grazing homes all ready for their return in the spring. Pretty soon we had the fire lit and a quantity of the inevitable potatoes bubbling cheerfully away in a big black pot. Tired faces shone with content in the glow from the fire. It had been a battle, and that's the way the Sherpas seem to like it. I searched through my rucksack and fished out the solitary half bottle of whisky I'd brought halfway round the world for this precious moment. The crack climber-porter, whose house it was, explained his season's campaign, just like any soldier home from the wars. For him the high mountains were the front line of a battlefield, and he rejoiced in the chance for active service. At different times of the year he assaulted the giants with the best teams of climbers the nations of the world could muster. European, American, Japanese, Australian, he'd seen active service with them all.

For him, the Japanese were the best to be with, because he felt they understood the Sherpa mentality best. Or perhaps he meant the Asian mind. It was no time to quibble. At last we rolled over and slept beside the fire, warm and dry; the front line thankfully some distance away.

I woke up to a mug of hot sweet tea. It was just getting light, and the embers of the fire had been fanned into a cheerful blaze. The snow now lay a foot deep outside the door, and this meant at least five feet on the Pass. We had been luckier than we'd realised, no one else would cross the Pass until the spring.

Snow was still falling as we made our way down beside the river for about an hour to the village of Lower Beding. The silence and the smoke curling straight up from the cluster of houses reminded me of the Alps and Christmas.

Everyone was pleased to see the return of the climber-porter: he was a very popular person in the village with his sunny personality and tireless energy. We took his advice to stay with him until the weather improved and he could find us a couple of guides for the next stage of our journey. Tashi and his father expected to be in Beding for several days before following us down to Kathmandu, where they had a house, but we would have to be on our way well before them.

We all laid our sleeping bags out on the floor of the main room where the fire was. The smoke choked the air and it was vital to stay near floor level if you wanted to breathe anything like fresh air. Everyone lived in the same room: grand-parents, parents, children, even unborn children and the livestock shared the warmth. It was all most interesting, certainly not cold, and there was much celebration of the climber-porter's safe return from the season's climbing. Towards evening things began to get a bit hazy.

By next morning the snow had stopped, two guides were found, we said a sad goodbye to our friends and were on our way down. By lunchtime we were in the tropics. The vertical climate of Nepal allows you to be in the snow one minute, and by rapid descent, among luxurious vegetation only a short while later.

Our walk out was shorter, but no less interesting than our walk in from Bhojpur. Eventually we reached the small provincial town of Charikot, from where the giants around Namche were just a dim blue line on the furthest horizon. This distant view gave us a warm feeling of achievement. Primitive road transport on rough new mud roads brought us out to Lamosangu and thence on to Kathmandu.

It had been great training for the New York Marathon which lay ahead in the coming year.

186

15

We got home to Ardmore just before Christmas, feeling full of go. It was just as well.

It was Christmas Eve when we discovered the disaster. Lance had mentioned an oily smell around the salmon cages, and a white scum floating on the surface inside the cages themselves. We lifted the nets between us that afternoon. Half the big second-year fish, our pride and joy, were dead, and a great many more had been cruelly damaged by some unknown predator. Was it shags, cormorants, otters, or seals? We killed hundreds of damaged fish, took them by boat to the Landrover, and drove round the district giving them to everyone we knew.

Christmas came and went under a cloud. Each morning we removed large numbers of freshly killed fish. People were winding up for the New Year celebrations: there was no access to government advice from Aberdeen or elsewhere. We were simply bleeding to death.

"That's the seal," said Danny Mackenzie flatly, when I took over a couple of typical casualties along with the whisky bottle at New Year. "We've had them at Badcall. That bite is no shag." Danny isn't a man to waste words. "You'll have to shoot them. Once they've learned the trick of getting them, they can't give up."

In the fifteen years we'd been at Ardmore I had steadfastly refused to shoot duck and other game birds on the loch. I preferred to see them often, rather than eat them once. Now we must take some action if we were to survive. "But how can they possibly do it?" I pleaded. The idea of shooting seals with their funny whiskers and melting brown eyes appalled me. "The cages have been there four years now. They've never bothered the fish before – why would they suddenly start now?" It seemed illogical.

"It's the full moon now. You go down to the cages tonight.

187

Give me a ring in the morning, and let me know if you heard the seals or not."

Numbly, we drove home, Becca, Marie Christine and I, united in the hope that it wouldn't be the seals. "Well, at least it's not an otter," said Becca as we tramped along the path through the snow.

Picking our way down the near vertical slope through the trees in the moonlight, we heard them before we'd even left the path high above. It was like Saturday morning at the swimming baths. Peering through the trees on the shoreline, there was no doubt it was seals.

"You'll have to shoot them," someone said.

"Not now. I couldn't see them in the sights." We made our way miserably up to the house, leaving the seals to their sport.

Next morning there were ninety-one dead fish, averaging four pounds. There were also many freshly damaged fish which would die later, unless we killed them and gave them away. It was my fault really. We'd talked long enough about double cages, but my back injury had made me indecisive. Now we were paying the penalty.

I shot the seals in a one-sided battle too painful to describe, and we came to the conclusion that they had perfected a way of working in pairs. One would swim up from below, lifting the weights and the bottom centre of both the predator net and cage net within. The fish would then dive for safety in a panic, crowding into the bottom corners of the cage net, just where the second seal wanted them. Swimming up at its leisure, it simply sunk its dog-like teeth into the juicy fish through the net. The net was never torn, and the great majority of fish were taken just behind and below the gills, the seals preferring to suck out the liver and leave the fish, rather as we might peel an orange.

New predator nets were ordered, but with the bottom a full ten feet below the bottom of the cage net. Lance made forty-eight new weights from four-inch alkathene pipe filled with concrete, twelve to each net. Any seal trying to come up from the sea bed now would have to lift the bottom of the predator net and its extra, heavier weights ten foot before it could begin lifting the cage net containing the salmon.

Jamie and Mary were back from Ireland where they had been prospecting for a place to start up their own adventure school, and we got ready to run the Instructors' Course. Colin Ladd fitted a smart new teak floor he'd made for the saloon of the yacht.

When Jim Archer-Burton arrived with the tenth annual party of boys from Westerleigh School near Hastings that Easter, he brought with him a cutting from the *Daily Telegraph*. It told of a disastrous end to a combined Australian–New Zealand attempt on Annapurna. Staff Morse was one of those who'd died in an avalanche. I remembered the powder snow which came thundering down on our own climb to the Tasi Lapcha Pass. Staff had been on his way back to Ardmore to help with the instructing for another season. He was not somebody we would ever easily replace. Enormously reassuring and patient, Becca would always remember how he read Paddington Bear stories to her on that long-gone winter sailing trip to the Spanish Sahara.

I decided the Atlantic dory had had her last season on the loch. Lance had put up a custom-made building to house her, and I spent the best part of a month painting her in her original colours, right down to the green anti-fouling. This took all my spare time, but I found the job curiously satisfying. She'd looked after Chay and me, fourteen years before, and it felt good that I should still be looking after her.

At the end of April, Alan Macrae came and did the fencing just as he'd promised, astonishing us all with his prodigious strength and stamina. I was pretty fit myself, and by mid-May I was at the end of a twenty-one-day period during which I'd run not less than ten miles each day. I'd managed eighty-six runs already for the year, and my weight was under thirteen stone for the first time in five years. The New York Marathon was not due until 26 October, but already Marie Christine was sick of hearing me urge her training along with "Twenty-six miles is a VERY long way, you know."

We approached the event quite differently, both getting up each morning at five thirty and running from the house, through the wood, past the sleeping Blue House and No.79, and then scrambling down the waterfall to the gate in the fence. From there we timed the run out to the main road, turned right along to the mailbox, and then down to our fuel tanks at the top of the hill above Skerricha. Then it was all the way back to the gate at the bottom of the waterfall. I'd start first, timing myself at several points along the way. Marie Christine was content to be well back. She'd be round about the mailbox as I met her on my way back from the fuel tanks, at which point I'd be about half a mile ahead in a total gate-to-gate distance of just about nine miles. I seemed unable to resist pushing myself every day, striving to improve the times. My wife ran in a much more economical manner, never seeming tired at the finish and always noticing anything of interest along the way. I think hers was the better method. When she ran twenty-two miles on her own, she had a quick bath and then cooked supper for five. My own effort over the same distance – along the hilly course from the waterfall, down to Laxford junction, along the coast road to the Foindle junction and back – resulted in a much faster time. But I barely crawled up to the waterfall. Marie Christine looked the more likely to finish when we got to New York.

They were glorious times. There was much to see. Week by week the sun would be higher and further north over the mountains as we ran along the open last mile or so to the main road. We called that section the "yellow brick road", for although it gives us a good view of the mountains all along, it never seems to end. An old buzzard would flap heavily from one telephone pole to the next just ahead of me, sometimes letting out a harsh cry of annoyance, as if to say, "Watch out you don't collapse on the road, boyo, or I'll have your eyes for breakfast." High above a pair of divers squawked to one another, veering in the sky, uncertain which of the myriad silver moorland pools to land on. Roadside shadows cast by rushes ran like jagged mountains along the thin strip of tarmac ahead of me.

On the return journey I'd usually meet the maker of our private running track: rumbling along in his yellow truck, the county roadman would give me a cheery wave, the only vehicle on the road at such an hour.

I was hungry to run every day, and as the physical effort continued I seemed to soar into a new kind of tirelessness. It was something I hadn't known for twenty years, something wonderful, which I'd all but forgotten and never dreamed would return. It was like the Evelyn Wood march and shoot competition with the Parachute Regiment in my early twenties: if someone dropped back, I could take his rifle and keep up with the best of them; or earlier, at Sandhurst, box each of the fifteen members of my platoon one three-minute round, and then for a five-bob bet march from London to the Academy overnight, to be back in time for the morning parade at seven thirty. It was all coming back. That dreamy, slightly tight feeling down the outside of my legs, right to the ankles as they effortlessly brought me up the grade from No.79 to the level past the Blue House after a run. Quick recovery after physical effort. A deep contentment. A dangerous time to make decisions.

I drew great strength from Borg beating McEnroe at Wimbledon, and even more inspiration from Coe coming back to win the 1,500 metres at the Moscow Olympics a week after losing the 800 metres to Ovett. I took my text from Lillian Hellman: "Go hard, take chances, be very bold."

One fine day in early autumn Donald and Angie Corbett travelled with us in the Land-rover to the Lairg lamb sales. We sat together in the auction building on the hard wooden terraced boards around the ring. Small flocks of lambs were brought in and inspected by a couple of hundred pairs of shrewd eyes. I thought of Heckie: there would be none of his poetry this year. Angie led us round the holding pens outside the ring. Marie Christine, Becca, and Gran up from Brighton, had no more idea what to look for than I. Anyway Gran's concentration was diverted a little by the attentions of an elderly and ever so slightly inebriated tweedy admirer, but the rest of us tried to take in everything Angie was telling us. The most important thing seemed to be to buy lambs from ground as similar as possible to Ardmore.

"They look bonny," Angie grunted, chewing on his pipe and pointing with his crook at a nicely dressed group of lambs. "Billy Calder's, I think. He's selling up, they say," and he shook his head rather sadly, before adding his usual "That's the way it is, you see, boy." I pricked up my ears. Selling up meant both good and poor-quality lambs, not simply weak animals.

"Aye aye," Angie concluded, "ye'll no see better the day."

I found Billy by the entrance to the ring. I hadn't seen much of him since the early days, when we used to run the launch down to Handa together. A cheery fellow, always with a twinkle in his eye, we'd been sorry to lose him when we sold the launch. I'd heard he'd had an artificial hip fitted, and he confirmed this was the reason why he was cutting down his flock – though he wouldn't be selling everything, he assured me. Billy reckoned they were good ewe lambs, and that his ground at Achriesgill would be much the same as Ardmore. I gathered one or two other locals were interested in buying the fourteen lambs as well. That would mean they were good, but it would also raise the price.

"It's a good thing you put up your new fence on Ardmore,"

old Donald said, when we joined the two brothers on the boards up near the roof back from the ring. "If not, they'd be away back to Billy first thing." He chuckled at the thought. I recalled the concentration Rod Liddon and I had given to the purchase of the main School building at the Dingwall auction twelve years before.

Now the day was wearing on and it had been a good sale for the crofters, heads were already a little fuzzy among those who'd already concluded their business. The sharp-eyed dealers from the south weren't missing a trick, hoping to pick up a good bargain late in the day to fill that last bit of space in the big cattle floats waiting outside for the journey home. I'd already missed buying ten of Hughie Ross's ewe lambs from Ardmore, through mis-reading the programme, and I'd been unable to understand the auctioneer. There must be no mistaking Billy Calder's Lot.

They looked fine in the ring and Donald, Angie and the Gaffer kept nodding their approval. But I noticed other bidders straightaway, including Ross McLeod who I was hoping would drive them back to Skerricha for me. Well, there was nothing for it but to keep bidding and hope for the best. My advisers were nearly as excited as I, but I was really thrilled when the hammer went down to me at £21.60 for each of the fourteen. These were the first breeding stock we'd ever bought.

Ross McLeod laughed away his disappointment as I helped him wash out the lorry for the lambs' trip to their new home. And Billy was the first to come across and say how pleased he was we'd got them and that if we needed any advice he'd be only too happy to help.

The Land-rover got a puncture at the bottom of Kinloch Brae and a nagging pain in my back reminded me that keeping sheep would mean hard work for it when it came to shearing. When Ross McLeod's lorry caught us up, Donald and Angie insisted they drive the little flock down the couple of miles from the main road to the safety of their own park at Portlevorchy for the night. So the two old men and their dog went on ahead in the lorry.

Next morning I took a boat over from Ardmore and helped the brothers inoculate and drench the lambs. Then they stamped them with the blue "R" iron Lance had made for the purpose. At the end of this performance Donald, now eighty-one years old, drove the flock with his dog Wily round to Ardmore by the footpath. As Granny Ross had said on our return from the Round

March 1984, return to Ardmore after 203 days non-stop round the world.

Winner takes all.

Ladies at the oars of the Atlantic dory, *English Rose III*.

English Rose VI loading stores from *Ardmore Rose*.

Lizbet arrives at Ardmore, October 1986.

the World Race, "A good neighbour close at hand is better than a brother far away."

The season was drawing to a close. We were sad to think that Jamie was coming to the end of all his years with the School: we'd sorely miss his quiet determination and solid support on the "epic trips" in the future. Jamie was always at his best when the going was rough. And we'd miss Mary too, for her effectiveness and her infectious laughter which could make light of the grimmest disaster. Colin was getting married. His four years had taken us right round the world and through all manner of experiences, but at least we would see him and his Anna, whenever they came up to their house in Balchrick.

Suddenly the New York Marathon was only six weeks away. I had been experiencing the odd sciatic twinge in my left leg through the summer, and just before the close of the season one of the businessmen had slipped off the back of the yacht at Handa and landed on my bad leg in the dinghy below. It hadn't helped. Now my aspirin dosage was replaced by some larger, stronger, yellow capsules which Dr Murphy left for me in the mailbox.

Chris Brasher, soon to mastermind the first London Marathon, came up for a fishing holiday on Loch Dionard. We ran together and, dazzled by the aura of running with an Olympic steeplechase gold medallist, I managed to run my best time ever for the nine miles from the waterfall round to the diesel fuel tanks above Skerricha and back. One hour and three minutes was pretty good on such a hilly course. Marie Christine, running alone on that day, did one hour and fifteen minutes. That was the measure of the difference between us at that stage. She was running as effortlessly as ever, looking on an hour and half spent out on her own as a simple act of pure selfishness. Most of her day is spent doing things for others; running is just for herself. Chris had jotted down a training programme for the last couple of months before the race and I managed the distance running well enough, but his interval running on the tarmac aggravated my sciatic problem considerably. So during an anxious phone call to his Richmond home late one evening we agreed to abandon that side. But looking back now I realise the damage was incurable in the time left before the race. The only real solution was complete rest until the inflamed nerve healed itself. At the time that was unacceptable.

"I'm sending the Iron Man down to you. He's bothered with

rust." This was the phone message which went ahead of me as I
drove down to the Kylesku ferry and along the tortuous road to
the little crofting settlement of Drumbeg. Dr Murphy knew I was
determined to run in New York after the hundreds of miles of
training we'd put in. He thought the only hope was for some
manipulation of my back, and the only osteopath in the area was
the remarkable Squadron Leader Ian Macaulay. I had never met
him before. South of the ferry is like a foreign land to those of us
on the north side.

Captured by the Japanese while serving with the RAF in World
War II, Ian Macaulay had seen two thousand of his comrades die
of malnutrition and disease. His own weight had dropped from
twelve to five stone, and finding himself going blind with malnutrition, he wondered, with his customary optimism, what occupation would be open to a blind man after the War. He'd heard
physiotherapy could be practised by the sightless, and so he set
about learning the trade there and then. After the War he did
great work in the famous Hedley Court Rehabilitation Centre
near Guildford, a place where I'd often visited friends injured in
parachuting accidents. After retiring from the RAF, with his sight
long since recovered, Ian bought a hill farm to the east of Drumbeg.
Together with his dynamic wife Nina he'd spent years struggling
with many of the problems so familiar to us at Ardmore.

"Ha! I've been expecting you," cried the burly figure, clad as
always in kilt and battered Balmoral head-dress. "Dr Murphy
phoned."

I'd been awake all night with the pain, and the jolting drive in
the Land-rover had reduced me to a pretty low state. Nina's hot
tea and cakes helped the inner man, while one click of my sacro-
ileac joint, a few minutes of heat treatment and some reassuring
words from Ian, and the world seemed a much brighter place. He
told me to take it easy for ten days, so the damaged tissue round
the replaced joint would have time to take up the re-adjustment.
We agreed to meet the following day at the Gaffer's house at
Skerricha: it was the nearest point to Ardmore with electricity for
the heat machine, until the EEC and the Hydro Electricity Board
put in their poles to Ardmore.

Central Television were beginning to think there might be
something to my idea of a marathon craze coming to Britain after
all, and they became increasingly keen that their running film
should be first on the screens in the UK. At the end of the filming

at Ardmore, they made arrangements for covering us in New York; this included the use of nine separate film crews along the route. Somewhere I read the sciatic nerve is the longest river of pain in the body. The pressure was building.

Worryingly regular sessions with the ever helpful Ian Macaulay and the heat machine at the Gaffer's was not making much headway. So Central TV arranged further expert back advice for me in the south. Short-wave diothermy, microwave, epidural injections, osteopathic manipulation under a general anaesthetic – they were all tried on me in turn without success. Everyone knew that the only sensible advice was to pull out of the race and give damaged tissue time to heal. But I was grateful to all the specialists between whom I limped, for not discouraging me from keeping going against all medical wisdom.

Marie Christine and I had our own suite on the forty-second floor of the Sheraton Centre, New York. Jimmy Carter was giving an election speech down at ground level. It was a long way from the Tilley lamps of Ardmore. Much was expected of us. I'd lost so much confidence in myself I couldn't even be sure where I'd put the toothpaste.

We ran for four or five miles in Central Park each morning, following part of the long blue line which marks the whole of the Marathon course. The section we practised on covered some of the last few miles, and we knew each gentle hill would seem like a mountain after twenty miles.

That afternoon, at the very last minute, I had a stroke of luck. Out of the milling crowds strode one Noel Pugh, a masseur who'd worked on the *QE II*. He spent three hours on my back and legs and this was like a magic balm at the eleventh hour: a miracle.

Sixteen thousand competitors from all over the world massed at the Verrazano Bridge for the start of the race on the morning of Sunday 26 October 1980.

I don't remember much of the race. Marie Christine held back to run by my side for every step. Heavy overnight rain had made way for the cool clear sun of the American fall which lit our path along that endless blue ribbon. They say more than a million people lined the route.

At the thirteenth mile I took a strong pain killer. At the twenty-first a glucose tablet carried me through the grim streets of Harlem and on in among the twisting lanes and mellow falling leaves of Central Park.

My colours were fast running dry. Marie Christine was strong as ever, and she kept me going. The slim grey figure of Ambrose Salmini slipped out of the crowds, and running backwards, filmed the final stages of the race. I couldn't stop now. Crowded grandstands lined the road, but I heard nothing. I was running to the close of my 193rd and, little did I realise, my last run of the year. I was going to make it. The old diesel machine wouldn't let me down. There was a beautiful, triumphant tranquillity only I could appreciate: it was a high-point in my life.

Then it was over, and Marie Christine and I were among thousands of others, in various stages of exhaustion, clad in silver sheets of insulating foil.

Later in the long hot bath my body seized up as if gripped in a vice. But I felt like a million.

With the filming over, we were free to spend the last few days as we wished. Becca and Gran had flown over for the race over Becca's half term. Now we all took the shuttle up to Boston, hired a car and drove out to Cape Cod, from where Chay Blyth and I had set out to row across the Atlantic in 1966. We met old friends like Skip Norgeot, Fred Powell and Johnny Stello, and discovered Chay had been back just the previous year, while waiting to begin an attempt on the Atlantic sailing record.

Looking for the first time at the plaque on the only rock among the sands of Nauset Inlet, I read that this was the exact point of our departure. The deserted beach had been crowded then, with people standing shoulder to shoulder in the cold waters of the Labrador current, eager to be the last to shake our hands.

Good old Chay! I thought.

16

The euphoria of Central Park didn't last. My left leg has been numb from that day to this. Over the turn of the year my back continued to let me down at unsuspected moments, when I was sawing wood with Becca, or even just when I sneezed.

Morale was low. Black clouds swirled round in my head. Whichever way I looked at things, Ardmore was no place for a man with a broken back. I'd rather die than leave. Ahead lay old age and dwindling powers. Can "THEY" drag you away to an old people's home? Loch a'Chadh-fi seemed surrounded by old people asking themselves that question.

I had only very slowly been recovering from the emotional bruising of the Round the World Race; now the recurring back injury aggravated my self-doubt. I would lie awake at night magnifying my problems. Then through the summer of 1981 my oldest and loyalest friend from Parachute Regiment days died slowly of spinal cancer. Many people I know have been killed over the years, mostly while pursuing some activity of their own choice. A death like Colin Thomson's stunned me with its awful pointlessness. But it also made me stop and think at a time which was pretty much stick or go for me. Memories of Johnstone and Hoare, who died on their Atlantic row when Chay and I survived, came back to admonish me that I was alive and still had much to be thankful for. Perhaps this mid-life crisis business I was experiencing was accentuated in my case because of a particularly physical lifestyle. Colin's death enabled me to put things into a better sense of proportion.

"I think the time has come for us to move into the new house next door," Marie Christine exclaimed one wet night. "This one needs a new roof, and we can't live in it while it's being done." Marie Christine's insistence that we move into the now rebuilt No.78 introduced a sense of purpose and order I badly needed at the time to restore my peace of mind.

No.78 is not now laid out like a conventional croft house: the likelihood of mains electricity coming to Ardmore was allowed for from the start. The kitchen occupies a third of the ground space and is very much the focal point of the house. There are two windows set in the slope of the roof, but the original tiny front window, which once kept the sun off the old lady's picture of Edward VII and Queen Alexandra, still brightens the kitchen with morning light; its sill is three foot deep and littered with things which always need dusting. Spotlights on tracks on the ceiling can be varied in number and direction, and there is a small lamp on a corner cupboard which is often the only light in use. Marie Christine likes to alter the lighting to suit her mood. It is very much Marie Christine's room; indeed it's her house. It is she who brings light to our home.

The sitting room is now split level, taking advantage of the demolition of the old front wall which bulged too badly to repair, and we have large double-glazed windows on two sides. The side view stretches from the edge of the wood down to the salmon cages below, while the front windows command the length of the northern Highlands from Beinn Spionnaidh in the north down to Ben Stack and Quinaig in the south. Loch a'Chadh-fi and everything going on between the Wooden House and the Bunk House is open to my enquiring gaze and anyone walking out along the path from the road-end above Portlevorchy can be seen over a mile away through RSPB binoculars in the summer and Zeiss 7 x 50 night glasses in the winter.

One freezing winter evening shortly after we'd moved in, and while I was still doubtful about whether we'd done the right thing, Marie Christine was playing some Sibelius with power supplied by the little generator out in the shed. We drew back the curtains and immediately had the impression of sitting out in the snow. The huge full moon shone silver from a clear starlit sky, stilling in the wind and freezing the loch at the foot of the crofts. In the north over the low hills around Cape Wrath pale beams of aurora borealis danced as if to Sibelius. All was still; a mantle of snow stretched from the window clear away to the Foinaven Ridge. One solitary yellow light, like a grounded star, shone steadily from all that vast landscape: it was the old brass Tilley lamp across the loch in Portlevorchy. I realised Marie Christine had been right about the move.

Helicopters lifted the tall fir poles for the mains electricity cables, carrying them like exclamation marks across the loch, and placing them exactly into their holes along the hillsides and through the wood. My influence in the house has been with the choice of electrical appliances. After seventeen years, I felt sad at the passing of the paraffin lamps, but the solid-fuel Rayburn would still be on stand-by to do the cooking, as well as heating the house and the water. And now I was determined to turn the inevitable change to our advantage. Indeed I looked on the EEC's decision to support our small community, by bringing the electricity four miles to Ardmore, as a real milestone in our progress. After all the years of washing by hand, I knew Marie Christine deserved the very best available labour-saving equipment. Progressing from a grinding world of peat, Calor Gas, paraffin and carbon paper, we must be allowed to take a delight in the computer age with its fresh sense of speed and efficiency. But a link with the near past shows in the handsome Castelmonte wood-burning stove. In the big autumn gales, wind blasts horizontal rain into vapour where the stove pipe passes through the north-facing wall of the sitting room; and leaves, whirled from the wood, plaster the windows.

That winter, and in the absence of a resident dog at Ardmore, a fox had taken up nightly board under our porch. This was not an encouraging sign for the lambing, nor Ada's chickens. Lance put his mind to outwitting that fox.

He built a false entrance to the chicken coop, and to his surprise he caught the creature on the very first night. It gave him such a shock that before he knew it, the wily thing had jumped clear out of the box and dashed away across the croft. The fox was shocked too, and decided it was time to leave Ardmore. Which was just as well, because Lance's next lure was designed to be rather more permanent: he wired up a piece of meat to his generator and waited in vain for the fox to meet its doom.

The gorse and bracken clearing was in hand, the grass was coming on well, and the small flock of ewes was settling down nicely. We were catching up to 800 mackerel a day with the fishing boat and even selling them at Kinlochbervie fish market, while the salmon farm was slowly recovering from the financial effects of the seal attacks. In lots of little ways we were making things easier to manage. The place, as Lance would say, was becoming "something like". But there were changes too. The most important one involved Lance. He spent New Year 1982 under intensive care in Inverness Hospital and on his return the doctor advised he should be fitted with a heart pacemaker. It was time for him to retire. He and Ada would continue to live on their croft at the Blue House and at long last he would be able to start on all the jobs Ada wanted him to do around the house and gardens.

Marie Christine and I faced the daunting task of replacing them. Lance had virtually built the place, and Ada had helped educate our daughter and stemmed many a crisis in the office. Finding another couple seemed an impossible job but we placed our ads in half a dozen provincial newspapers, mainly in areas of high unemployment among engineers, and were so swamped with telephone calls that for several days it was difficult to get on with anything else. Malcolm Sandals was forty-five and about to be jobless when the Glossop factory where he worked was closed down. He read our advertisement in the *Manchester Evening News*. As well as being an experienced engineer in a firm making carbon fibre fan blades for aircraft, he was also an accomplished fell-runner. Malcolm's wife, Jenny, had accountancy experience and could type. The two elder children were off their hands and ten-year-old Jill could attend Kinlochbervie school.

So by the time spring came to Ardmore in 1983, there were four permanently resident families. On Upper Ardmore: Lance and Ada Bell lived in No.80, and Gordon and Barbara Monshall, who had arrived in 1979, were in No.79, while on Lower Ardmore: Malcolm, Jenny and Jill Sandals were in No.76, and John and Marie Christine Ridgway in No.78. Rebecca came home for her holidays. And Hughie and Elizabeth Ross came up from Inverness to No.77 to work with the sheep and improve their own croft house as often as possible.

We had had to advertise for a new yacht skipper as well, in early 1982. Andrew Briggs was a Quaker Yorkshireman who came with a recommendation from Arun. Tall, gaunt, ginger bearded and professorially bespectacled, he was also the sort of chap who only requires a basic understanding of the workings of a problem to be able to go ahead and sort it out by himself. Andy's arrival coincided with renewed feelings of restlessness within me. At forty-five I rather desperately wanted to recapture my sensitivity to events and feelings once more through the unbroken rhythms of the oceans and seasons. It was to be with Andy that I set out in September 1983 to sail round the world non-stop. As Miss Armatrading's bewitching voice was soon to sing through head-phones in the long watches of many a bad night, "If you're gonna do it, do it right; don't leave it overnight." That really was the essence of the trip and Andy was exactly the right man to take along. I knew from rowing the North Atlantic with Chay that two men can get on fine. Interdependence is a good thing for compatibility. For myself, I felt like the man who has made a heap of all his winnings in life and wants to risk it "on one throw of pitch and toss". The boat was not insured.

The Round the World Race had achieved what its title claimed. We had gone round the world, but it had done nothing for my own self-esteem and little to make up for having to abandon that previous single-handed attempt in 1968 which for me had ended in Brazil. Neither Andy nor I were eager for ports of call. On the previous expedition they had been unsettling digressions. I took my wristwatch off as we sailed out of Loch a'Chadh-fi on September 1 1983: I would not be needing it until the following spring. This was going to be my long-dreamed-of Ardmore to Ardmore direct on the "magic carpet" which stretches from the moorings at the foot of the croft clear round the planet.

Our aim was simple: the fastest non-stop circumnavigation Europe to Europe of any vessel ever.

For Andy the record was the thing that mattered, but he knew as well as I that 27,000 miles non-stop is a different exercise from the Whitbread Race, where there is a stop to refit every 7,000 miles. It was going to be a case of "softly, softly, catchee monkey". In Andy I could not have had a better man husbanding our resources. It seemed he looked forward to leaks and breakages so he could dream up some way of repairing them.

Rolling down the Atlantic this time, I felt as if I was walking down the tunnel from the dressing room to the ring in my boxing days at Sandhurst. I think I understood what Damodara meant when he said, "There are none happy in the world but beings who enjoy freely a vast horizon." The Southern Ocean was waiting for us, with its springtime storms just two months ahead. A misty glimpse of Gran Canaria sixteen days out of Ardmore was our only sight of land before Cape Horn. The first albatrosses appeared 6,000 miles south of home. How I wish we had them in the northern hemisphere. When I leave them behind I wonder, will I ever see them again? Fifty-foot finback whales kept us company and clouds of delicate grey icebirds whirled round us as we roared along due east towards the southern tip of South America. In mid-November we were knocked down by a big sea which came rumbling over the port quarter, tossing me out of my bunk and across the cabin. But we kept up a good average and our best run was 213 miles noon to noon.

Disconnecting the Aries self-steering gear, it was grand to be alone at the wheel in high seas in this lonely place, brilliant flashes of grandeur making up for all the immense monotony and claustrophobia. Nearing Cape Horn, black hail squalls battered in. Great wintry black clouds with ragged hazy tops – like winter at home. This is the finest sailing in the world. Patches of blue sky, racing clouds, wild blue seas and lots of foam. Alone on deck, with this super machine driving for the Horn, I felt fulfilled – there could be nothing more to life than this. I found myself humming the "Marseillaise" – over and over again.

Forty to seventy-knot squalls brought snow, which drifted in the angle of the cockpit seats as the dim outline of Diego Ramirez Islands rose abeam to the south. It was Thursday 12 January and we were keen to round the Horn before it turned into Friday 13. We were 19,000 miles out from Ardmore and the little patches of vivid green grass on Hermite Island were the first we'd seen since leaving home. We edged inshore to feast our eyes on them and the brown rock and dazzling snow peaks beyond. I sailed the boat right in under the cliffs of the Horn with a force 10 snow squall over my right shoulder, and thought of the dramas played out there over the centuries. Then it was gone. We turned downwind heading north-east for home. The Horn is 56 S, Ardmore 58 N. Only another 8,000 miles.

We picked up the mooring below Ardmore wood under sail after 202 days, two hours and fifteen minutes at sea. We had our record. Ninety days faster than any boat in history. It had been a grand way to spend the winter.

But even grander was being home with Marie Christine and Becca in time for the lambing again. Home to No.78 where Pussy Ridgway and Fat Oliver still meet the returning boat on the shoreline and then dispute for flat surfaces in the sitting-room sun with each other and an outnumbering army of Marie Christine's green-leafed pot plants.

I took a boat across the loch to call on Donald and Angie Corbett at Portlevorchy. The two old boys were deep in their chairs before the fire, and plainly delighted with the circumnavigation. I asked them how they'd survived the winter. "Och, ye can't take the whip out of an old stick without breaking it!" chortled Angie, sucking noisily as he struggled to light his pipe. Glancing through the window it was hard to believe I'd ever been away. The great grey widow-maker seas of the Southern Ocean were half a world away from the cheerful ripples now dancing round the big white yacht in the spring sunshine. She just lay there, motionless at her mooring again – waiting – beyond the lambs playing together on the green foreshore.

But the trip had left its mark on me. For 200 of the 202 days there had been no land to see, but for all that the planet seemed a smaller place now. The sea really is a "magic carpet". The whales and albatrosses, winds and currents, rain and shine – everything fits into place. For the first time, I had really come to terms with my own mortality. There is no point in looking back with regret: there is only the future. At forty-five I'd had some valuable breathing space to consider my position. Since rowing the Atlantic with Chay, I had tried to look on life as bonus time. It seems to me that time is somehow falsely imprisoned by clock measurement. It is altogether more precious: it is all we have. Being is more important than having.

The most satisfying tangible result of all that thinking on the long night watches was my decision to try and become re-united with my adoptive parents, with whom I'd had no contact for many years.

Going to meet them again for the first time so many thoughts raced through my head: those long happy childhood days fishing beside the Thames seemed so long ago now. Cherry blossom on the young trees brightened the late afternoon as I walked through a modern Wimbledon estate before knocking on the door of a house I'd never seen before.

My father opened the door. At seventy-six, he looked older, but still strong and steady. I suppose most children admire their fathers. He took my elbow and walked me to the post box at the end of the avenue, explaining the situation before we returned to the house. I was thinking how much I'd tried to model myself on him.

My mother was very ill, upstairs in bed. She fell asleep frequently, but the famous sense of humour was undiminished. I gave her a framed photograph of the yacht rounding Cape Horn, and she asked me to hang it on the wall at the foot of her bed. She died just a few months later, and I was grateful for those long night watches in the Southern Ocean which had brought us together again.

FLOOD TIDE

My father visited Ardmore for the first time before the year was
out, and within days he was supporting Marie Christine's plans
for an office extension to the northern end of No.78. "It's no good.
We can't go on running the school office – and now the salmon
farm – from this kitchen!" She waved at the typewriter, sitting
silently in its place on the end of the table. I just kept on eating
my supper. I knew all about bringing building materials over the
sea from Laxford Pier and up the hill, and I'd promised I'd never
let myself in for it again. But my father hadn't spent decades
running his own civil engineering firm for nothing. His pencils and
paper gave way to the Terms & Conditions for the Appointment of
Architects, and then he was out in his wellies, imploring Becca to
hold the measuring staff steady, while he adjusted the wheels of
his dumpy-level. I bolted four ex-Army assault boats together and
towed all the materials behind the fishing boat like a floating
island. An eight-wheeled Argocat made short work of the hill,
while Norman Mcleod showed the way on clearing the site and
making a hole for a doorway through the stone gable. My father
measured out the complicated settings for the floor pillars in a
giant cobweb of strings and posts. And before we knew it, we
were holding the 1985 end-of-season party in the smart new
pine-lined office.

Next morning we left for Peru.

When Becca was a little girl we had taken her off on a holiday
to remember before she went away to boarding school. Now the
long-promised expedition to celebrate the end of her schooling
was suddenly upon us. I had known for a long time what I
wanted to do. I wanted Becca to see Osambre, an inaccessible
hacienda-cum-jungle fortress, tucked away on the eyebrow of the
Amazon rain forest. This would be my fifth visit to South America.
I wasn't worried about Becca's fitness, as she had been girls'
cross-country champion at Gordonstoun, and Marie Christine and
I were reasonably fit, but to strengthen the team, I asked a couple
of instructors, Ed Ley-Wilson and Justin Matterson, along as well.

The aim was to find my old friend of fifteen years before, Elvin
Berg, in the most remote place I had ever been. But when I started
making enquiries from the UK, I discovered Abel and his wife had
died some years before, but I found no one had heard from Elvin
for five years, and his family in Oslo were anxious. I phoned
Father Bede Hill at Worth Abbey in Sussex. In 1970 he'd been
head of the Benedictine Mission, just four days downstream of

204

Elvin's home at Osambre. "Haven't you heard? The Mission is closed. The Apurimac valley is the centre of a Maoist guerrilla war in Peru. The *Sendero Luminoso* or Shining Path are like Pol Pot's *Khmer Rouge* in Kampuchea. They want to eliminate all established authority and begin history again at Year 1."

I explained the situation to Ed and Justin on the plane, passing round cuttings sent overnight by the Catholic Institute for International Relations in London. They told of mass graves containing corpses without index fingers and faces smashed by sledgehammers to prevent identification. Military and guerrillas appeared equally savage and, as usual, the poor *campesinos* were caught in the middle.

A chargé d'affaires at the British Embassy in Lima told us some 500 people had been murdered in fifteen incidents over the past seven weeks. "The *Senderos* attack villages by night, killing everyone. If you happened to be in a village at the time of an attack – you would be unlikely to survive." He concluded by telling us that the Apurimac Valley, where Elvin lived at Osambre, was a dangerous place, and the Embassy could only advise us not to go.

Next day we flew across the snow-covered Andes. From the plane, the mountains and valleys looked hostile enough, without people trying to kill us as well. We landed at Cuzco, the old Inca capital, at 11,500 feet. That night, on returning to the hostel after a meal, I was surprised to find a note from an English woman doctor who had heard we were in the city. She had just left to continue her journey with an international expedition which was attempting to canoe our 1970 route from the furthest source of the Apurimac/Amazon to the mouth of the river in Brazil. The note ended "Many people remember you up on the *Altiplano* – particularly Adam at San Juan."

"Well, that's nice, after all these years," I said, a plan hatching in my head. "Look, why don't we go up on to the *Altiplano* ourselves – back to Cailloma – where we started in 1970? We could spend a month walking down along the river, at about 12 to 15,000 feet. We could use it as training: Phase One, in fact. There aren't supposed to be any terrorists up there." This suggestion was agreed, mainly because any plan was better than no plan at all. Phase Two would be trying to reach Osambre and find Elvin.

Next morning we started on ways and means. The Secret

Police headquarters was in a nondescript house, but anyone looks sinister once you know they are in the Secret Police. The man in a grey suit and dark glasses told me that two of old Abel Berg's four sons had been killed, one in November 1984 and another in March 1985. Instinctively I felt Elvin, now thirty-eight, must be one of the two survivors: he was that sort of person.

Owing to a lull in the fighting in the Apurimac Valley, and the clearance of the Secret Police, we were able to get a letter of permission to enter the Emergency Zone from the *prefecto* of the Department of Cuzco, dated 14 October 1985.

After three days by train and bus we set up camp beside a mountain torrent, off a dirt road at 12,000 feet. To save weight we had no tents, and we were just about to crawl into our peculiarly vulnerable bivvy bags when Ed noticed a fire in the brush between us and the road. The ensuing moonlit chase proved without doubt that someone was trying to burn us out. It was an unhappy start. The following night found us far away in Cailloma, and my sortie to the old silver mine at 13,000 feet revived the awful memories of altitude sickness on the 1970 expedition. The difference now was the Army garrison, brought in after a *Sendero* raid on the mine.

Heavy-laden, the long first day's walk down the Apurimac river ended at the bleak little settlement of Tarucamarca. In my diary I scrawled: "Pains: legs, heart, head. Self-doubt." With the rest of us away attending to our ablutions, the village headman, assuming every *gringa* to be a trained nurse, called on Becca to give first aid to a bloodstained young *alpacero* named Jesus, who had just tottered in from the empty plains where he had been tending his flock of alpacas. He'd escaped after three *bandidos* had robbed and tried to kill him by pounding his head with rocks. Choking back her nausea, Becca noticed a red bubble among the black hairs, as she dabbed TCP on the concave wounds in his skull. Marie Christine and I were called in during the three-hour treatment, which concluded with a majority decision to slice the red bubble with a razor blade.

Next day, we carried our knives at the front of our emergency-belt order. And we kept on going at 12 to 14,000 feet for another sixteen days, gradually building up fitness on a simple diet of potatoes and rice to walk all day without guides or mules, carrying everything we needed on our backs. We gained confidence in our ability to navigate and survive as a small team in harsh conditions.

Complete self-reliance was essential for Phase Two: the march in to Osambre. Elvin was very much in our thoughts as we strode on through the mountains. The crystal-clear air enabled us to see vast distances until the horizons were barred with great white peaks. It was truly a land of giant skyscapes. We spent the nights mostly in little *pueblos*, and when we awoke we often found the mud and stone huts had been dusted with snow while we slept. In one place it hadn't rained for three years. The people spoke the unwritten Inca language of Quechua. They were desperately poor, but the further they were from civilisation the friendlier we found them.

Phase One came to an end when Becca contracted *Otitis Media*, an excruciating ear infection linked to sudden changes in barometric pressure. It frightened us all while it lasted. We gave her a course of antibiotics, rested for a couple of days, and walked slowly down from the *Altiplano*. On the way back to Cuzco we had an extraordinary stroke of luck, meeting a young woman schoolteacher who had news of Elvin. Although the *Senderos* had burned Osambre to the ground, he was, she claimed, alive and well in the neighbouring village of Lucmahuayco.

A month had passed since the *prefecto* had signed our letter of permission to enter the Emergency Zone in search of Elvin at Osambre, and now we heard fighting had begun again in the Apurimac Valley. So, to avoid cancellation of our permit, we stayed at a different hostel and kept clear of anyone we'd met previously in the city. I had lost two stone in weight, and the others looked painfully thin, but we were a strong little team, now well able to move across country without local assistance, and after four days' rest in Cuzco we boarded the coach for a few hours of the two-day journey to Lima.

I knew we'd be halted by the police if we took the old Inca mule-train route up the Vilcabamba River from the north, so I decided we'd use the old back-door trick, and make our own way in from the south, following the route we'd taken fifteen years previously.

Nobody on the coach had ever heard of Huanipaca, and as we clambered down on to the rutted dirt track and into a bleak mountainside world of potato patches and yellow grassland, it began to snow. The other passengers, pressing their noses to the misted windows as the coach lumbered forward once more, clearly thought we'd made an awful mistake.

During the night *bandidos* stole the bull from the *campesino* who let us sleep outside his hut, and in the heavy rain of morning we met a man who told us he'd seen two dead men brought down the track from Huanipaca in the past week, both killed by *bandidos*. At nine o'clock that moonless night, four hours from the dirt road across the Andes, a decrepit truck brought us into Huanipaca village square, lit by the luminous white of glaciers slithering down from the 20,000 foot peaks across the Apurimac Valley. And after a can of pilchards by candlelight, to lift morale, we settled down for the night on the puddled floor of a semi-built house. As the one nearest the gaping hole where the door might one day go, my sleep was broken by the snuffling of marauding pigs in the darkness, and whenever I became sufficiently frightened, I threw stones to keep them at bay.

Three days of tropical rain kept us bogged down in Huanipaca, which had decayed considerably since I was last there. It seemed the agrarian reforms had not increased production for export, but the reverse, and now, individual *campesino* families were growing only enough to feed themselves. At last we managed to hire a couple of mules, and head off into the mountains.

Despite its grandiose name, Cachicunga (Cut-throat) Salt Mine was still just a small hole in the red rock. We reached it two days later, at the end of a desiccated rocky spur 3,000 feet above the brown ribbon of the Apurimac River. With the mules and guide gone, we still outnumbered the gaunt Indian miner and his son, hacking out one fifty-kilo block an hour. He knew the raging river was effectively the boundary of the Red Zone of the Emergency, and he gave us the answer most likely to send us on our way – "Yes, the balsa raft is operating."

Thirty hours later we reached the river, exhausted by dehydration, the path long since overgrown by the jungle. After a bad night we stumbled downstream.

"There's the raft – over there – behind the rocks!" Marie Christine shouted above the roar of the river. And I could just make out the ends of some balsa logs. But she was right: I checked the place against the photo in my book *Amazon Journey* from fifteen years before – the rocks matched up, crack for crack.

Justin almost drowned, swept downstream as he swam the river, but he found Indians in the jungle above, and next morning they rebuilt the raft and ferried us across. Realising their lives were at risk for having strangers in their village, we were marched

208

under guard through the night and for two days, to *El Comandante*. Now prisoners, we were filled with despair when we heard rumours that Elvin had been burned alive.

Coming down the 2,000-foot wall of the Mapito River Valley, we heard shooting and the clatter of helicopters coming from the little *pueblo* of Amaybamba halfway up the other side. A couple of hours passed before we finally emerged from the trees at the edge of the village itself, and were taken before a hostile crowd in a sort of district headquarters.

This was the front line. The Army, under *El Comandante*, had just left by helicopter. Eleven days previously, thirty-eight buildings, including the new school, had been burned in an overnight rampage by *Senderos*. But although death lists were frequently pinned to village doors by terrorists under cover of darkness, this particular attack was by way of a final warning, and only two villagers had been killed. A *Sendero* squadron had been seen crossing the Apurimac from the west, and the air force had destroyed their boats, but only after the guerrillas were successfully ashore, and on their way up the Mapito Valley towards Amaybamba. The *Senderos* had let it be known they intended to control the whole Mapito Valley by 1 December – in just seven days' time.

A crowd of some four hundred people, mostly visiting leaders from other villages, thronged the entrance to the building as we were led in like prize prisoners. I wondered how we might be treated. An elderly clerk, sitting behind an ancient typewriter, responded to my poor Spanish and seemed impressed by my copy of *Amazon Journey* and the Norwegian newspaper cutting about our search for Elvin. He claimed to know the Berg family personally, and re-affirmed Elvin's brutal murder. He spoke with a simple finality which extinguished my last flickering hope. I had so set my heart on renewing that long-gone friendship. Perhaps it is a mistake to try and recreate the past. But there was little time now to mourn Elvin. This quixotic quest had led my wife and daughter, not to mention Ed and Justin, into an extremely tight corner. "We are alone now," the clerk told us. "The *terroristas* are watching us from the forest above. They have seen *El Comandante* and the military leave. Soon they will attack again. This is a dangerous place."

Protected only by the *ronda*, a patrol of half a dozen Indians carrying pointed sticks and a couple of ancient rifles, we slept uneasily on the mud floor of the unfinished HQ building. There was no way forward from here. The clerk had told us the *Senderos* would kill us just for our equipment, if nothing else.

An Army patrol came in next morning. Clothed in black, they were a sinister sight, and we worried lest the young lieutenant might have us shot. He was injured, and Marie Christine suggested I give him a tot from our half bottle of whisky.

"You must leave here. It's not safe for your wife and daughter. Believe me, you must go," he urged. I could see his logic. It was desperately hot in the village, and we spent the day trying to arrange for mules. But we were in a land of refugees now. Everything was in short supply, particularly food, and the guerrillas stole mules to eat.

Next day, with heavy hearts, we began the long plod towards the two snow-covered mountain passes, which Elvin had told me about in Osambre in 1970. A day's walk beyond the passes lay the end of a dirt track, where we might expect to find a truck to take us on a six-hour drive to the little jungle town of Quillabamba.

In the late afternoon, we arrived at a cluster of rough huts called Accobamba, unmarked on the sketchmap I'd made in Amaybamba. At 9,000 feet it was much cooler, almost at the source of the Mapito River, and directly overlooked by the glittering white 17,000 foot summit of Choquesapra, which Elvin had so enthused about fifteen years before. He'd told me a legend of Inca gold to be found in the "beard of Choquesapra", and how, one day, he would find that gold, in the very glacier which now lay across the valley from us. But we wouldn't be looking for gold. The Indians told us the *Senderos* controlled the forest on the other side of the narrow river now, forbidding them to cross over and work the *chacras*, their little plots of land. They were expecting an attack from across the stream at any time.

We were exhausted after the long, hot climb, and agreed to stay for the night, but slept in our clothes, packed and ready to flee into the jungle if the *ronda* fired a warning shot in the darkness.

Next morning, continuous tropical rain fell from a leaden sky, and a dense mist shrouded the surrounding forest. A streaming cold seemed to reinforce my despair at not finding Elvin. Unwilling to risk *Otitis Media* on the high passes, I suggested we stay a further day in the village. Everyone would benefit from a rest in the cool at 9,000 feet, away from the biting black fly which had so troubled us down in Amaybamba.

Deprived of its scenic grandeur by the rain, Accobamba looked its pathetic self: a tiny *campesino* community shattered by a war it wanted no part in. The *Senderos* were no better than robbers, and the Army useless, because soldiers had never come this far up the valley. Never more than a halt on the old Inca trail, half the villagers of Accobamba had already fled, their huts eagerly taken by refugees passing through from the jungle below.

Over a cup of home-grown coffee in one of the huts, we were astonished to learn that Elvin's six-year-old daughter was living nearby. Eagerly, Marie Christine, Becca and I followed friendly Simeona along the path through the rain. The bushes seemed to be smoking with mist. We stopped by a handful of tiny graves on a bend, scrambled over a broken wall, and emerged into an unkempt meadow, across which we could see woodsmoke filtering through the back of an old stone hut. "Go quietly," whispered Simeona. "This family has suffered terribly. They are very nervous."

I could just make out two women and three children, sitting in the dark smoky recess. Immediately I focussed on one small girl. "That's Elvin!" I said instinctively. "I can see him in her face." A second later, without thinking, I added, "How would she look at Ardmore?"

It was done on impulse. In that moment of setting eyes on her, I knew I must see Elvin right and do what I could for the child.

The small figure was sitting cross legged on a sheepskin, slightly apart from the others, drinking soup from a chipped enamel bowl. Her skin was unusually pale and her hair a deep, wavy brown, not black, under a grimy, crocheted yellow and white hat. Her pink knitted dress looked as if it had seen many owners. She stared at us unblinking, with a solemn, rather sad look.

Simeona spoke to the older woman, who said Lizbet was her grandchild, and asked us to come in and bade us sit down on a bench. Simeona began a long conversation in Quechua with the family, while we sat looking at the little girl and she stared back at us.

Marie Christine took her Irish grandmother's ring from her finger, threaded it on Becca's confirmation chain, and kneeling down, put it round the child's neck. I could see Becca fighting back her tears.

Simeona then told us what the granny had been saying. After killing Elvin and destroying Osambre, eighteen months before, the *Senderos* had advanced up the valley to her own home village of Lucmahuayco, where her husband was the headman. The terrorists had burned the village to the ground and her husband had fled for his life, into the mountains. In revenge for his escape, the *Senderos* had murdered his old mother and then dismembered his only son, throwing his bloodied trousers at the granny's feet as a warning. Since that day, the family had been refugees. Her sixty-four-year-old husband, Lizbet's grandfather, had rejoined them after three months alone in the mountains. Although they were not officially residents of Accobamba and couldn't own land, they had been sold the house as an act of compassion after it had been abandoned by the previous occupant, who had fled before the advancing *Senderos*. But it was just a bare shelter, not a home.

Lizbet's mother, her mind unhinged by these terrible events, now worked for her keep in the home of relatives across the high passes. Lizbet was pining away, and Granny kept repeating that she and her husband were old and poor, and just couldn't afford to look after the child.

The atmosphere was becoming so highly charged that we felt we must leave, at any rate for the time being. Granny took Marie Christine's hands and embraced her. Lizbet followed us out, as if not wanting us to go, and called to me, *"Ciao, Pappi."* The little salutation took my breath away.

Walking back up the meadow, I felt I'd abandoned the child. Rods of rain slanted down through an all-embracing greyness, and Becca was walking ahead to avoid conversation. As we came up to the wall, Simeona turned to Marie Christine and me, saying, *"Lizbet esta triste. No tiene mamá, no tiene papá. Pobre niña."* Then she told us that Granny hoped we would adopt Lizbet and take her back to Europe with us.

"What do you think, Flower?" I said quietly.

"Oh, I don't know, Johnny," Marie Christine was crying. "I'll have to think about it."

I could see that she wanted to do it, but was astonished that I did: it was completely unlike me. For the moment I left it at that, embarrassed by the presence of Simeona.

I thought of my 202 days' sailing non-stop round the world and how, during that period, I'd made one or two decisions about the rest of my life. If Marie Christine and Becca both agreed, we would adopt Elvin's daughter.

We were on the path to the village now, walking down the

212

slope through the scattered huts, towards the school building where we were staying. Curtains of pale grey rain obscured the other side of the valley. I caught up with my daughter, and put my arm round her shoulders. "Do you want Lizbet for a sister?" I felt I must find this out before we reached the school and had to share any news with Justin and Ed.

"Of course I do!" she sobbed.

Simeona left us at the archway into the school. Justin and Ed were astonished at the change of events, and wondered if we'd thought out the consequences of adoption.

We had the afternoon to think it out. But by the time Lizbet's grandfather returned from the fields we needed to have our minds made up. It seemed miraculous that we were all three together in this remote place at this particular time in our lives. Rebecca was just about to leave home and step off into the outside world, and her agreement was essential. Marie Christine was one of four children from a good, secure home, and she would have liked to have had a large family.

My own views are different: since my early twenties I have felt strongly, that if each couple had only one child, then world population would soon be halved – and at least some of the problems facing mankind would be solved. Simplistic perhaps, but better than drifting into catastrophe. Becca was our one child. Lizbet was already alive, however, and she was in need.

We told Grandfather we would adopt Lizbet, and take her home to Scotland, but only if her mother agreed. He asked us to wait for three days, and then he would take us to see his daughter – Lizbet's mother – across the passes. The old man was clearly delighted, saying he knew the terrorists were just about to attack Accombamba, and that he would be bringing Lizbet with him, as well as his other daughter and her two small children.

In the event, Lizbet was left behind: the weather was very bad and Granny insisted the child was in such poor health she might die on the snow-covered passes. Following Grandfather up through the trees towards the distant snows that rainy morning, waving back to the little figure with ring and chain firmly round her neck, I think we all felt we would never see her again. It all seemed to me one long chain of coincidences, and fate would have to continue playing a strong hand in things if Lizbet were to become a Ridgway living at Ardmore.

A month later we arrived home on one of those precious still

213

days of bright sun and blue sky. The snow was too deep for the Land-rover on the side-road to Portlevorchy, so Becca, Marie Christine and I set off on foot along the familiar three-mile trek into Ardmore. As we tramped along, with our packs on our backs, we could have been still in the Andes, and we continued our endless discussion on the ways and means of bringing Lizbet to join us. At the Blue House, Lance said Lizbet would be the best thing to happen at Ardmore in years.

We'd heard Accobamba had been attacked by the terrorists at night, less than twenty-four hours after we'd left. They were ambushed by the *ronda*, losing two dead and a prized automatic rifle. Granny and Lizbet had spent the night, unharmed, in the forest.

Once New Year was over, we began the long business of seeking adoption in Peru and Britain. Forms were filled out and letters of reference concerning our physical, mental, moral, religious, financial and legal fitness to adopt were translated into Spanish and sent to Peru. A red book entitled *Phone Calls to Peru* began to run out of pages. We were impressed by the thoroughness and humanity of the Social Works Department of the Sutherland District Council.

Avalanches and floods close the Inca trail up the Vilcabamba River towards Accobamba for the first three months each year. But Nick Asheshov, a friend from the 1970 Amazon expedition who had been living in Lima for twenty years, used this time to organise a search for Lizbet once the weather improved. On our way back to Cuzco we had found Padre Santiago, a Dominican priest based in the jungle town of Quillabamba, who had baptised Lizbet on one of his biannual visits to the Emergency Zone. The entry in his Register of Baptism was the only document proving the existence of little Elizabeth Berg Huaman. Padre Santiago had overseen his vast parish for many years, and within a few weeks he was able to inform Nick that Lizbet's mother, grandparents and indeed all the family, were united in their support of our plans for the adoption.

With the rains over and an entry permit in his pocket, Nick and his son Igor flew over the Andes to Cuzco, to bring Lizbet out of the jungle. After a couple of days by train and truck, they hired horses and a guide, and rode back up the Inca trail we had come down the previous year. During the rainy season, the *Senderos* had tightened their grip on the area, and Nick was risking his life by going to Accobamba. Once in the village things moved fast. Lizbet's mother and grandparents had the child ready to travel, and quickly signed the adoption papers before a district Justice of the Peace, and then, within the hour, they were on their way back. Bringing only her ragged clothing, and speaking only the Inca language of Quechua, Lizbet had come out, over the snow-covered passes and into a new world. She sat so silently on the front of Nick's saddle, that women in the villages where they rested believed she was struck dumb.

When they reached Quillabamba by night, the blaze of street lighting was the first electric light the child had seen. At the hostel she encountered her first stairs. On the train next morning she cowered back, unbelieving that a material called glass would protect her from the oncoming branches of jungle trees. Strangely, the jet from Cuzco to Lima seemed to affect her less.

The doctor found she had lice in her hair, and a big tapeworm in her stomach. He wrote "chronic malnutrition" on the medical certificate. At the dentist she just wouldn't open her mouth, and under general anaesthetic the remains of many of her teeth were removed.

Nick's wife, Consuelo, took her in with her own seven children. And for a while the little Quechua girl attended a private school in a smart quarter of Lima, where she gradually began to participate and learn Spanish.

We had a busy summer at Ardmore. Marie Christine had been perfecting her salmon smoking over several years, and now she began a little mail-order business of her own. We started special hill walking courses during the weeks the yacht took RYA cruises out to St Kilda, and companies were beginning to use the remoteness of a week at Ardmore to build management teams.

Over on the Skerricha side of the loch we used the buildings to house forty young people at a time for the residential week of government Youth Training Scheme Courses, during May and June. Then we moved into the International Summer School Courses during the school holidays of July and August.

But eventually the eighteenth season came to a close, and Ardmore assumed its winter silence once more.

In the gathering dusk on a fine early October evening, I took the red fishing boat across the empty loch to Portlevorchy. Marie Christine and Becca went ashore in the dinghy and ran up towards

215

the road to meet the party from Peru. Nervously I held the boat just clear of the rocks, wondering what I should think when I saw Lizbet, and what we should both feel.

I caught my first glimpse through the wheelhouse window: a tiny, dark-haired figure in a vivid red skirt, white blouse and black waistcoat, her Peruvian dress brightened Portlevorchy. It was as if the sun had come from behind a cloud. Tears were filling my eyes. I found myself thinking of Elvin, as he had been all those years before: a proud, dashing young fellow of twenty-two, straining forward from the bows of the dugout canoe as we shot through the rapids on the Apurimac. I felt I had done something right.

At supper, Lizbet sat silently beside me at the end of the kitchen table. She tore the chicken into small pieces with her little fingers, to make it last, then she set about crunching up the bones. I could feel her staring, as if she'd been told I was very important to her. She called me Danny. Marie Christine was Mummy and Becca, Rebeeka. Putting her to bed, they found the necklace with the ring still round her neck.

The four of us were alone at Lower Ardmore for the winter. Becca had completed her secretarial course in London and took over the office so she could be with Lizbet, and two mornings a week, she took her new sister to the little school in Kinlochbervie, where she had been ten years before, staying with her until she felt happy on her own.

On Christmas Eve Lizbet tried to sleep in Becca's bed. She was frightened at the idea of Santa Claus coming in the night. But looking at the small figure at the other end of the table from me as we ate our Christmas dinner, our first meeting in that stone hut in the Inca Kingdom of the Clouds, the previous December, was already long ago.

The shortest day was past. They say we gain half an hour of daylight each week after 21 December, and we began to prepare for the new season. Before too long, Lizbet would discover that Ardmore was not always cold, though she didn't seem to mind in the least.

One stormy night, I was saying goodnight to her, and the hailstones were battering on the window in the roof over her bed. She pulled me down and whispered, "Danny, *casa gusta*!" (House good.)

17

One of the best things about living at Ardmore is the trout fishing on the lochs on the Ardmore peninsula. At the end of a long summer day on the courses it is still light enough for me to take a favourite rod up the hill behind the croft.

A few years ago much of Sir Francis Chichester's tackle was passed on to me by his son, Giles. Solid reels stamped with the address of the shop where he bought them in New Zealand in the 1920s. Yellowish tweedy wet-flies from Ireland, painstakingly packed away in a makeshift case made from a cut-away navigation book he'd written at a later period. The gear showed little use in recent years. I determined to get it going myself.

Dour Loch is out towards Ardmore Point, and aptly named. In twenty years of watching it, I've concluded that on just a few evenings in May and June, in certain years only, the loch is right for fishing.

Walking along the path through the wood, I notice all fatigue has vanished from the legs. Spring and rhythm tell me I'll reach the Dour Loch in twenty-five minutes. All those runs are paying off.

The wood is in shade now, the birds are growing quiet, preparing for the short night. Away to the east the Foinaven Ridge glows molten pink in the last of the sun. Although it's the end of May, the stunted trees still give off a fresh smell of spring, a reminder we are on the same latitude as Moscow and real summer is yet a month or two away.

Emerging from the wood, on to Upper Ardmore, there are signs of recent activity where Lance's aerial wire ropeway ends by the side of the path. He's getting set up to send the hessian sacks of peat down from his various cuttings out of sight further up the hill. Ada's restraining rope, which halts the whizzing bags, hangs among the bushes at the side of the path. I notice the seedlings are coming on under the cold frame at the end of the byre – that red telephone kiosk, demolished nearly twenty years ago, was put to good use. Still no sign of a leak in the experimental patch of brown paper and pitch on a corner of the byre roof, but I think pitch-soaked hessian would be stronger. The chickens are safely in the coop; foxes often prowl around the crofts at the end of lambing. I wave to Lance and Ada through the honeysuckle on the garden wall, and call out to Gordon Monshall who's busy with the wheelbarrow in front of No.79 below.

Leaving the footpath close to the Blue House, I cut away to the west. The going is smooth here and I'm moving easily with the butt of the rod held forward, just in case I trip in one of Lance's grass-covered drains. A short path leads me to a ruined byre, and then through a couple of tiny squares of grass and rushes. In the middle of one of these ancient gardens Lance's plum tree is showing signs of establishing itself at last. The withered brown twig at its side is a reminder of one that failed. The final outpost of civilisation is the top garden, all black acidy soil, and hard to drain. It's used for potatoes and not much else. A broken-down wall of grey stones marks the end of the inbye land, then a vague sheep path meanders through low heather and rock along the side of a shallow but steep-sided valley, ending in a narrow neck of wet bog which I must skip across if my short running boots aren't to be swamped.

It's wonderful to be alone. My mind races with plans. What a pity I never got round to planting that shelter belt of sitka spruce and lodgepole pine by the top garden. I can still see the two fellows from the Forestry Commission standing there nodding wisely; that was back in sixty-six but it seems like yesterday. Lance and Ada would appreciate the shelter now. The climatic difference between the top and lower gardens is so marked.

The scrapes in the ground are signs of worked-out peat cuttings along the valley. The spring Heckie used to talk of is still running, in spite of the drought we've had this past month or so. On my right, on the other side of the ridge, the ground falls in a wild cliff down through a tumble of rocks into Loch Dughaill. Hughie maintains the cairns right by the edge of the sea are a sanctuary for foxes, but it's so steep I've never been down there, nor has anyone else that I know of. But I have seen a buzzard homing on to a nest there, when I've been over on the north side of the loch. I must go down there soon.

Loch Dughaill slumbers gently with the last traces of the westerly swell. No sign of otters in the pale green waters over the

218

sands at its inner end. The Ceathramh Garbh lies a jumble of bare rock and narrow green valleys along the north shore – the Rough Quarter indeed. It is all part of the Ardmore outgrazings, shared with Achlyness up on Loch Inchard, but it's hardly been used for many a year. For us it would mean a mile of fencing to join all the lochans and prevent the sheep from wandering off towards Foinaven, or back to Billy Calder. The Dour Loch glimmers into view. It's half a mile long, beginning in a narrow neck and broadening like a wedge towards its western end. The southern shore is one long cliff, too steep to cover on foot. The north side is shallow with pretty little bays. I like to fish from a couple of points which jut like fingers from the broad end of the wedge. As usual a pair of red-throated divers are swimming on the loch. They don't care for me, and begin their long splashy take-off run with harsh cries into the remains of the easterly breeze.

It's still too windy for me. I need a warm flat calm to bring on a hatch of fly, then the shoals of cruising fish will appear like magic from the deep water for their brief annual visit to the surface. I'll take a turn over to Consolation Loch, a couple of minutes walk beyond. An oval pool, hardly two hundred yards long, shallow and littered with weed, Consolation Loch is what its name implies. It has lived up to its reputation many times, I can always catch fish there – the windier the better. Small and game, the best fish I ever had was a couple of ounces short of a pound. Still, it's a grand place to get my hand in for the Dour Loch.

I'm in no hurry. The lochan is so small I can fish the whole length of its steep north side in under half an hour. Anyway after the brisk climb from home I'm perfectly happy to sit on a rock and bask in the pleasure of being alone at the end of a hard day. As the sun sinks into the Minch, surely I can see the curve of the earth round which I have sailed. No trace of civilisation up here. Boulders scattered along the spine of the peninsula haven't moved since their stranding at the end of the Ice Age. The slab I am sitting on displays its ice-gouged grooves. I could be in a time warp. But a flicker of movement on the rough ground away to my right reveals one of our sheep to remind me it was not just like this a thousand years ago. The ground would have been covered with tangled bushes, small trees and tall heather, as it is on the islands of Loch Eileannach below me. The sheep, and the heather-burning for their benefit, have stripped the land of much of the natural growth. Even as I watch, the sun dips below the horizon. Now "the sun is off the water", as fishing pundits would have it, and it's a good time to get started from the burn end of the lochan.

My tackle is designed for the long-casting needed on the Dour Loch: a Hardy 9'3" carbon fibre rod with a forward taper white floating line and three flies on a slow-sinking cast. I could easily cast right across the lochan. At first there is no movement near me, but then I hear the far-off "suck" of a rising fish in the shadows further up. Catching nothing immediately, I wish Marie Christine and Becca were with me. The fun we've had, all three fishing here at once, with Becca dashing around the end of the loch with the landing net, eager to have a good one for her breakfast.

"Bang!" As usual the fish comes when I'm thinking of something else, and I miss it. This is good practice for the Dour Loch. I can't afford to miss a rise there. Concentration brings me a couple of half-pounders as I move steadily along the side of the lochan. Carefully wetting my hands before unhooking them, I slide them back into the water. Maybe they'll be bigger next time. Then the wind dies away completely, and I know it's time for the main event. I find I'm almost running towards Ada's Point on the Dour Loch, but drawing close, I force myself to slow to a stealthy walk. Thank goodness the divers haven't returned, though now and then the silence is broken by a pair honking on their way down the coast.

Confidence floods warm through my veins. I'm a fisherman. I know what I'm about. I know this is exactly the right time. I must calm down and stop this childish trembling in my hands and legs.

The water's absolutely flat now. A great silence grips the air. The fish really are cruising on the surface. Their lazy rises make fat plopping noises in the dusk, in the bays and out by the weed beds under cliffs. Now and then there's a rise right close in, in the fingers of water on either side of Ada's Point. She'd be thrilled to see it now. It's never like this when she's up with her tin of worms during the day, but she catches the biggest fish with her porcupine quill float off the end of her point. Still, it's not the same, I sniff to myself.

Stripping line off the reel I drop it carefully on a green otter slide, right on the end of the point. No good snagging the heather now. I begin to work the flies further and further out over the

220

water, letting the stiff action of the carbon fibre do the work for me. When the heavier shooting head is free of the rod tip, I shoot the line towards a good fish thirty yards off the point, and the pool of line swirls up from the otter-slide at my feet.

The flies unravel at the end of the cast and fall lightly on to the water. I let them sink for just a moment, before beginning the retrieve with a twisting motion of my left hand. Now, now, any moment now.

"Bang!" He hits my fly at full speed. Up he comes, straight out of the water, trailing a belly of sunken line behind him. The few inches of slack line I've taken in hiss through the rings, then he's dragging the backing off the reel. The whipped join between the fly line and the backing, so lovingly smoothed and varnished one winter's night, causes no obstruction. I play him carefully. There may not be another evening like this again this year. At last he slides gently over the sunken ring of the landing net, a plump and brightly speckled fish of a bit under two pounds, in prime condition. I dot him on the head and string him through the gills with the rough cord I keep in one of the waistcoat pockets. Tomorrow's breakfast.

After that first cast the magic is broken. I only take one more, smaller fish in half an hour's work and put it back. It's that first cast, when the fish think I'm the first person in history to send them a fly. That's when I have the initiative.

Just across from Ada's Point, on the northern shore, another smaller point encloses a reedy bay, and a tiny, overgrown island further constricts its entrance. A good fish is gently gulping insects in there. His head and tail rises remind me of the finback whales off the Kerguelen Islands, down in the Southern Ocean. The thing for him would be one of Walter Hafner's little black cork-bodied flies from Switzerland. I'll put it right in the path of the fish and it'll float until it's swallowed.

I move with extreme care now. It's going on for eleven. The chill will soon stop the hatch and then the fish will go off the feed. Any movement seems to make a noise like a roll of drums in the dusk.

Just let me catch this last fish and I'll be satisfied. Motionless on the point I wait, giving the fish all the time in the world to settle. Another movement catches my eye; is it another, even bigger fish in the dark channel between the island and the shore? It's only twenty yards. I could reach it. I don't know, should I just be satisfied with the nearer fish? I postpone the cast and wait for a moment. A "V" comes steadily out of the shadows, making straight for the point. I'll have him and no mistake. Ten feet away we recognise each other. The flat head and whiskery face of an otter sink below the surface, followed by the round bulge of his back and long thin tail. The fishing is over for the night.

Walking home in the gloaming, the single fish dangles from my side. It was grand. Beyond the waterfall I can just make out the dull yellow ribbon of Gentle's Brae. The five-mile run is seven hours away. Beyond the gloomy ridge of Foinaven lie the wild lochs of my dream. I'll live that dream. I fall into Lance's drain, dreaming of this and that as usual. Coming through the wood, the light from our bedroom window beckons warmly. Marie Christine, Becca and Lizbet will be asleep already.

Appendix of Gaelic and Norse Place Names

Acarsaid Mhic Mhurchaidh Oig	Anchorage of the son of young Murdoch
Achadh Loineas	Achlyness, achadh (G), field; lin-nes (N), flax, flax headland
Achadh Reisgeill	Achriesgill, achadh (G), field; hris-gil, (N), brushwood ravine
Aird Bheag	Small heights or drumlins
Allt Horn	Hell river
Am Balg	The bag
Am Buachaille	Cowherd
An Cadha	Pass, ravine
An Cosan	Little hollow, crevice
An Grianan	Sunny spot
Annait	A mother church
Arcall	Arkle, ark-shaped mountain (N)
Ardmor	Ardmore, great height, high sea point
Bagh an Aoil	Bay of lime
Bagh Geodh' nan Daoine	Bay of the inlet of the men
Bagh Glac Cul a' Gheodha	Bay of the hollow at the back of the inlet
Bagh nan Cleathan	Bay of ribs, i.e. reefs
Baile a' chnuic	Farmstead of the hillock Balchrick
Baile na cill	Balnakiel, church farm
Beinn Spionnaidh	Hill of strength
Ceann an t-Saile	Kintail, head of the salt water
Ceann Loch Beirbhe	Kinlochbervie, head of the loch of the fort
Ceathramh Garbh	Rough quarter
Claise Carnaich	Hollow of the place of cairns
Cnoc a' Mhuilinn	Hill of the mill
Cnoc an Daimh	Hill of the stag
Cnoc an Loin Bhain	Hill of the fair meadow
Cnoc Carn a' Bhodaich	Hill of the old man's cairn
Cnoc Corr	Hill of an odd shape
Cnoc Fhir Bhreige	Hill of the false man
Cnoc Garbh	Rough hill
Cnoc Glac na Stairne	Hill of the hollow of thundering, i.e. of hooves
Cnoc Gorm Mor	Big green hill
Cnoc na Suil Chruthaiche	Hill of the quaking bog

Creag a' Fhraoich	Heather crag
Creag an Iolaire	Eagle rock
Creag Riabhach	Brindled, grey rock
Creagan Meall Horn	Rocky hill of hell
Druim Beag	Drumbeg, little ridge
Druim Lochan Iomhair	Ridge of Ivor's little loch
Durness	Deer promontory (N)
Eadar a' Chaolais	Eddrachillis, between two narrows
Eilean an Eireannaich	Irishman's Island
Eilean an t-Saile	Island of the salt water
Eilean an t-Sithein	Island of the fairy knoll
Eilean Meall a' Chaorainn	Island of the rowan-covered hill
Eileannan Dubha	Black isles
Gainneamh Mor	Ganu Mor, big sand
Geodh' Creag nan Sgarbh	Inlet of the skarts' rock
Geodh' Criom an Duain	Inlet of the morsel on the hook
Glas Leac	White-grey slab of stone
Handa	Sandy island (N)
Kearvaig	Brushwood bay (N)
Kylestrome	Narrows of the tide-race (N)
Leum a' Choin Dheirg	Leap of the red dog
Loch a' Chathaidh	Loch a' Chadh-fi, loch of the sea spray
Loch a' Phreasain Challtuinn	Loch of the hazel bush
Loch an Roin	Loch of the seal
Loch Crocach	Loch of the antlers, i.e. branching inlets
Loch Laxford	Loch of the salmon fiord (N)
Loch Poll a' Bhacain	Loch of the little bank
Lochan a' Mhullaich	Lochan on the height
Lochan Bad 'ic Iomhair	Lochan of MacIver's clump
Lochan na Buaile	Lochan of the cattle fold
Lochan na Cloiche	Lochan of the stone
Lochan nam Ban	Lochan of the women
Lochan nan Cnamh	Lochan of the bones
Lochan Saile	Lochan of brackish water
Lochan Thuill	Lochan of holes
Poll an Innein	Pool of the anvil
Port Leamharcaidh	Harbour of the elm trees
Rubha Sgeir a' Bhathaidh	Point of the skerry of drowning
Sgeir Earna	Skerry of the invocation
Sgeir Iosal	Low skerry
Sgeirean Cruaidhe	Steel-hard skerries
Strath Dionard	High sheltered valley